SCOTTISH
PLACE NAMES

WAVERLEY
BOOKS

Published 2016 by Waverley Books, an imprint of
The Gresham Publishing Company Ltd, Academy Park, Building 4000,
Gower Street, Glasgow, G51 1PR, Scotland

www.waverley-books.co.uk
info@waverley-books.co.uk

First published 2009. Reprinted 2011, 2016

ISBN 978-1-902407-87-6

Printed and bound in Poland

Introduction

The place names of Scotland reveal the historical presence of the three main groups of peoples who occupied the country and whose descendants still form the vast bulk of the population. These are the Celtic, Nordic and Anglo-Saxon groups. They came at different times and over a period of almost two thousand years that stretches, from before the beginning of the Common or Christian era to the 11th century. The earliest and most numerous of these groups were speakers of a Celtic language or languages, of the same group that modern Breton and Welsh belong to, and referred to in this Dictionary as Brythonic. The first of the many generations of incoming Celts did not find an empty land; the country was already inhabited but we know virtually nothing of the languages of the people who lived in Scotland between the Ice Age and the coming of the Celts. A few of the place names we still use, especially river names, may be theirs. A number of place names have been ascribed to the Picts, a people who may have preserved elements of a Pre-Celtic language just as they may have formed or absorbed a Pre-Celtic population. The likelihood of this is still a subject of research and debate.

It is clear, however, that the present toponymy (landscape-naming) began with the Celts. The earliest recorded Celtic names from the 1st century are from Brythonic. From the 6th century, with the arrival of the Scots in Argyll, Gaelic names begin to appear. Gaelic became the dominant language and the majority of Scottish place names are Gaelic (referred to as Scottish Gaelic to distinguish it from the similar Irish Gaelic). From the 7th century onwards, in the Borders areas and Lothian, Anglian names appear, given by the Old English speakers moving in from the south. Their language, with many contributions from Gaelic, French and Dutch, went on to become the Scots tongue of the Middle Ages and later. The advent of the Norsemen in the 9th century, and their political control of the North, the Northern and the Western Isles, produced many Norse names in those parts of the country and indeed elsewhere, notably the south-west.

The study of place names, apart from its own interest, provides valuable support to others areas of scholarship, particularly certain aspects of history. Investigation of the history of a place name can sometimes show the sequence of people who lived there and when they came. The form of the name can establish the period at which it was given.

Many names thought of as typically, and quaintly, Scots are in fact Gaelic names, meaningless in the Scots language and only yielding up their identity when the original Gaelic form is established. Thus Auchenshuggle, long thought of as an appropriate-sounding destination for Glasgow's tramcars, is simply a Scots version of the Gaelic for 'rye-field'. Names of Gaelic and Pre-Gaelic origin are found in areas where Scots or English has been the standard speech for hundreds of years. They show us how far the tide of Gaelic has receded. It should be emphasised that this was a linguistic, not a population, change. Over successive generations, political, economic and cultural changes, hardly noticeable except over the course of a lifetime, established Scots as the majority language, just as Gaelic had once been. Place names, however, were not (on the whole) renewed or translated; they were merely scotticised and their meanings gradually forgotten except in areas where Gaelic remained a living language.

The Gaels, as with most earlier peoples, were both precise and prosaic when it came to applying names to places, hence the many 'red hills', and 'boggy places' that are found. In a country whose population was mostly illiterate, precision in place-naming was important: the name was the chief means of identifying and describing a locality. Many names show their significance in land-use, of which Arrochar, Pittendreich and Pennyghael are three examples. But clear as all names must once have been, they are by no means all clear in their meaning today. Gaelic in Scotland formed a number of dialects and the same word did not always have the same meaning in all of them. Words fell out of use or acquired new or additional meanings but the place name incorporating the old or forgotten form did not change. The etymology of place names is not a straightforward business and the serious student of Scottish toponymy, apart from Gaelic and Scots, needs to have an acquaintance with the Norwegian and Danish forms of Old Norse, with the Anglian form of Old English, with Medieval Latin, Norman French, Middle Low German and Frisian, as well as a knowledge of the structures and hypothetical sounds of the extinct Indo-European languages that predate the Celtic and the Germanic languages. There are still many Scottish place names whose origin and meaning have not been established or on which scholars disagree. The pioneering 20th-century researchers, like Alexander MacBain and William Watson, had the advantage of being brought up as Gaelic speakers and of being able to consult native Gaelic speakers in areas like Perthshire and mainland Argyll, where few now remain. Theirs is the foundation on which the School of Scottish Studies builds in its work of compiling a record of all known Scottish place names and their meanings.

This Dictionary presents the names of virtually all of Scotland's settlements from villages upwards, as well as the names of its topographical features such as rivers, mountains, lochs and islands.

A

Aberbrothock *see* **Arbroath.**

Abercairney (Perth & Kinross) 'Confluence by the thicket' or 'cairns'. *Aber* (Brythonic-Pictish) 'confluence' or 'river mouth'; *cardden* (Brythonic) 'thicket'; with *-ach* (Scottish Gaelic suffix) indicating 'place'; or alternatively *càirneach* (Scottish Gaelic) 'place of cairns or rough rocks'.

Aberchirder (Aberdeenshire) 'Mouth of the dark water'. *Aber* (Brythonic-Pictish) 'confluence' or 'river mouth'; *chiar* (Scottish Gaelic) 'dark'; *dobhar* (Brythonic-Gaelic) 'waters'.

Aberdeen 'Mouth of the River Don'. *Aber* (Brythonic-Pictish) 'confluence' or 'river mouth'; the second element seems to suggest the River Dee, which flows into the North Sea at the centre of modern Aberdeen, but the name was recorded as Aberdon in the early 12th century and at that time referred to the original settlement now known as Old Aberdeen, situated immediately to the north at the mouth of the River Don, close to the Cathedral of St Machar. By the 13th century, the current name form, probably a conflation of the two, was emerging as Aberdoen in 1178 and Aberden in 1214. *See also* **Rivers Dee** and **Don.**

Aberdour (Fife) 'Mouth of the River Dour'. *Aber* (Brythonic-Pictish) 'confluence' or 'river mouth'; *dobhar* (Brythonic-Gaelic) 'waters'.

Aberfeldy (Perth & Kinross) 'The confluence of Pallidius or Paldoc'. *Aber* (Brythonic-Pictish) 'confluence' or 'river mouth'; *phellaidh* (Old Gaelic) refers to St Paldoc, Christian missionary to the Picts in the 5th century, or alternatively, a water sprite, or urrisk, believed to live where the local Urlar (Scottish Gaelic 'land floor') Burn meets the River Tay.

Aberfoyle (Stirling) 'The confluence of the pool'. *Aber* (Brythonic-Pictish) 'confluence' or 'river mouth'; *phuill* (Scottish Gaelic) 'of a pool'.

Abergeldie (Aberdeenshire) 'Confluence of the white water'. The Geldie Burn here flows into the River Dee. *Aber* (Brythonic-Pictish) 'confluence' or 'river mouth'; *geall* (Scottish Gaelic) 'white'. The *-die* suffix is, from an Old Gaelic ending used to form adjectives, from nouns.

Aberlady (East Lothian) Possibly 'river mouth of the lady', as in the Virgin Mary. *Aber* (Brythonic-Pictish) 'confluence' or 'river mouth'; *hlaedig* (Old English) 'lady' or 'loaf-kneader'.

Aberlemno (Perth & Kinross) 'Confluence of the elm wood'. *Aber* (Brythonic-Pictish) 'confluence' or 'river mouth'; *leamhanaich* (Scottish Gaelic) 'of the elm wood'.

Aberlour (Moray) 'Loud confluence'. *Aber* (Brythonic-Pictish) 'confluence' or 'river mouth'; *labhar* (Gaelic) 'loud'.

Abernethy (Perth & Kinross, Highland) 'Mouth of the River Nethy'. *Aber* (Brythonic-Pictish) 'confluence' or 'river mouth'; the second part is possibly derived from *an eitighich* (Scottish Gaelic) 'gullet', indicating water rushing through a gorge. The Tayside place was a stronghold of Nechtan, King of the Picts around AD 700. His name has been identified with that of the river but a more likely derivation is the old Celtic river name *Nedd*, which stems from a root-word indicating 'gleaming'.

Abington (South Lanarkshire) 'Albin's village'. *Ael-wine* (Old English) 'noble friend'; *tun* (Old English) 'enclosure' or 'settlement', giving the Scots place termination '-ton'.

Aboyne (Aberdeenshire) 'White cow ford'. *Ath* (Scottish Gaelic) 'river ford'; *bó* (Scottish Gaelic) 'cow'; *fhionn* (Scottish Gaelic) 'white'.

Abriachan (Highland) 'Mouth of the steep burn'. *Aber* (Brythonic-Pictish) 'confluence' or 'river mouth'; *bhritheachán* (Scottish Gaelic) 'of the steep hillside'.

Achallader (Stirling) 'Field of the stream'. *Achadh* (Scottish Gaelic) 'field'; *Chaladair* (Scottish Gaelic stream name) anglicised as 'Calder', perhaps, from Brythonic *caleto-dubron*, 'hard water'.

Achanalt (Highland) 'Field by the river'. *Achadh* (Scottish Gaelic) 'field'; *an* (Scottish Gaelic) 'by the'; *allt* (Scottish Gaelic) 'stream' or 'river'.

Acharacle (Argyll & Bute) 'Torquil's ford'. *Ath* (Scottish Gaelic) 'ford';

Torcuil (Gaelic-Norse proper name) 'Torquil', from Thor-ketil, meaning 'vessel of Thor'. Thor was the Norse god of thunder and warfare.

Achiltibuie (Highland) Possibly 'field of the yellow stream'. *Achadh* (Scottish Gaelic) 'field'; *allt* (Scottish Gaelic) 'stream'; *buidhe* (Scottish Gaelic) 'yellow'. An alternative is 'field of the yellow (-haired) lad', derived, from *achadh-a- gille-buidhe*; with *gille* (Scottish Gaelic) denoting a lad or a young man.

Achmelvich (Highland) 'Field of the place of sea-bent'. *Achadh* (Scottish Gaelic) 'field'; *mealbhain* (Scottish Gaelic) 'bent grass', from Old Norse *melr*, 'bent grass' or 'grassy dunes'.

Achmore (Highland) 'Big field'. *Achadh* (Scottish Gaelic) 'field'; *mór* (Scottish Gaelic) 'big'.

Achnacarry (Highland) 'Field of the wrestlers'. *Achadh* (Scottish Gaelic) 'field'; *na* (Scottish Gaelic) 'of'; *caraiche* (Scottish Gaelic) 'wrestlers' or 'tumblers'. 'Field of the fish-weir', from *coraidh* (Scottish Gaelic) 'fish-weir', has also been suggested.

Achnacloich (Highland, Strathclyde) 'Field of stones'. *Achadh* (Scottish Gaelic) 'field'; *na* (Scottish Gaelic) 'of'; *cloich* (Scottish Gaelic) 'stones'.

Achnahannet (Highland) 'Field of the patron saint's church'. *Achadh* (Scottish Gaelic) 'field'; *na h-* (Scottish Gaelic) 'of the'; *annait* (Scottish Gaelic) 'church of a patron saint' or 'church with relics'.

Achnasheen (Highland) 'Field of the storms'. *Achadh* (Scottish Gaelic) 'field'; *na* (Scottish Gaelic) 'of the'; *sian* (Scottish Gaelic) 'storm'. This mid-Ross-shire village is in quite an exposed situation.

Achnashellach (Highland) 'Field of willows'. *Achadh* (Scottish Gaelic) 'field'; *na* (Scottish Gaelic) 'of'; *seileach* (Scottish Gaelic) 'willow trees'.

Achray, River and **Loch** (Stirling) Possibly 'ford of shaking'. *Ath* (Scottish Gaelic) 'ford'; *chrathaidh* (Scottish Gaelic) 'shaking'. *See also* **Crathie**.

Adder, River (Borders) 'Water'. *Adder* is one of the numerous river words that go back to the language of the European Celts. Cognate with the German *Oder*. Its original form is conjectured as *adara* indicating 'flowing water'.

Addiewell (West Lothian) 'Adam's well'. *Addie* (Scots) diminutive form of 'Adam'.

Ae, River and **Forest** (Dumfries & Galloway) 'Water'. The river name, from *aa* (Old Norse) 'water', has given its name to the modern forest and to the new village housing the foresters and their families.

Affleck (Aberdeenshire) 'Place of flagstones'. *Achadh* (Scottish Gaelic) 'field'; *na* (Scottish Gaelic) 'of the'; *leac* (Scottish Gaelic) 'flagstones'. A compressed form of **Auchinleck**.

Affric, River, Glen, Loch (Highland) Possibly 'speckled ford' or 'ford of the trout' or 'of the boar'. *Ath* (Scottish Gaelic) 'ford'; *breac* (Scottish Gaelic) 'speckled trout' or *bhraich* (Scottish Gaelic) 'boar'.

Afton (East Ayrshire) 'Brown stream'. *Abh* (Scottish Gaelic) 'stream'; *donn* (Scottish Gaelic) 'brown'.

Aigas (Highland) 'Place of the abyss'. *Aigeann* (Scottish Gaelic) 'chasm'. The Beauly river flows here in a deep gorge, divided by *eilean* (Scottish Gaelic) 'island', Aigas.

Ailort, Loch (Highland) Perhaps, from *él* (Old Norse) 'snow shower' and *fjordr* (Old Norse) 'sea inlet' or 'fiord', with *loch* (Scottish Gaelic) 'lake', 'loch'.

Ailsa Craig (South Ayrshire) 'Fairy rock' has been suggested, from *aillse* (Scottish Gaelic) 'fairy'; *creag* (Scottish Gaelic) 'rock'; also *ail* (Old Gaelic) 'steep rock'. Perhaps more likely is an Old Norse origin, Ael's Isle, from *Ael* (Old Norse proper name) and *ey* (Old Norse) 'island', with the Scots *Craig* added after the significance of the *-ey* had been lost. This prominent island landmark on the Firth of Clyde is also known popularly as 'Paddy's Milestone'.

Aird (Highland) 'The high ground'. *Airde* (Scottish Gaelic) 'high'. The name comes from the hilly district around Kirkhill and Kiltarlity in Inverness-shire.

Airdrie (North Lanarkshire) 'High hill pasture'. *Airde* (Scottish Gaelic) 'high'; *ruighe* (Scottish Gaelic) 'slope' or 'shieling'.

Airth (Stirling) 'Level green place', from *àiridh* (Scottish Gaelic), which apart from 'summer pasture' has the meaning 'level green place', with the sense of being among hills.

Airthrey (Stirling) Derived in the same way as **Airdrie**.

Aith (Shetland) 'Isthmus' or 'neck of land'. *Eidh* (Old Norse) 'isthmus'.

Alder, Ben (Highland) 'Mountain of falling water'. *Beinn* (Scottish Gaelic) 'mountain'; *all dobhar* (Old Gaelic) respectively 'rock' and 'water'. The Alder Burn would thus appear to have given its name to the mountain (3,765 feet/980 metres).

Ale, Water of, *see* **Ancrum.**

Alexandria (West Dunbartonshire) Named after the local member of parliament, Alexander Smollett, a relative of the town's developer, around 1760.

Alford (Aberdeenshire) 'High ford'. The most probable derivation is from *ath* (Scottish Gaelic) 'ford'; *aird* (Scottish Gaelic) 'high'.

Aline, Loch (Highland) 'The beautiful one'. *Aluinn* (Scottish Gaelic) 'beautiful'; *loch* (Scottish Gaelic) 'lake' or 'loch'.

Allan (Perth & Kinross, Borders, Stirling) **Allan Water** and the **River Allan** have a Pre-Celtic root, *alauna*, meaning 'flowing'; cognate probably with Welsh Alun.

Alligin, River and **Ben** (Highland) The original name is that of the river, associated with other *al-* river names with a Pre-Celtic root indicating 'flowing water'.

Alloa (Clackmannanshire) 'Rocky plain'. Derived from a compound word *ail-mhagh* (Scottish Gaelic) 'rocky plain', most apposite to the town's location on a flood plain on the north bank of the River Forth.

Alloway (South Ayrshire) 'Rocky plain'. This village, the birthplace of Robert Burns, lies on the flat land of the Ayr Basin. Its name has the same derivation as that of Alloa.

Almond, River (Midlothian, Perth & Kinross) The river name is from Pre-Celtic *Ambona*, deriving from an Indo-European root-word meaning 'water'. The Gaelic name is *Abhainn Aman*.

Alness (Highland) 'Stream place'. Recorded as *Alenes* and *Alune* in the 13th century, it probably has the same Pre-Celtic river name origin, *alauna,* as Allan, the River Alun in Wales and Rivers Aln and Lune in England. The *-ais* suffix is found as an indication of 'place' in many locations in the former Pictland. The emphasis is on the first syllable, which rules out *nes* (Norse) 'headland' as an element.

Alsh, Loch (Highland) 'Fairy loch'. *Aillse* (Scottish Gaelic) 'fairy' or 'spectre'; *loch* (Scottish Gaelic) 'lake' or 'firth'.

Altnabreac (Highland) 'Stream of the trout'. *Allt* (Scottish Gaelic) 'river'; *na* (Scottish Gaelic) 'of'; *breac* (Scottish Gaelic) 'trout', from the adjective *breac*, 'speckled'.

Altnaharra (Highland) 'Walled or embanked stream'. *Allt* (Scottish Gaelic) 'stream'; *na* (Scottish Gaelic) 'of'; *earbhe* (Scottish Gaelic) 'wall'.

Alva (Clackmannanshire) 'Rocky plain'. The derivation of this town's name is the same as that of its neighbour, Alloa.

Alvie (Highland) 'Rocky place'., from the root-word *al* - (Brythonic-Pictish) 'rock' or 'rocky', giving *aillbhe* (Gaelic) 'rock', as the prefix of Alloa.

Alyth (Angus) 'Steep bank or rugged place'. This descriptive name comes from the Hill of Alyth that rises steeply on the town's northern edge. *Aileach* (Scottish Gaelic) 'mound' or 'bank'; or alternatively *aill* (Old Gaelic) 'steep rock'.

Amisfield (Dumfries & Galloway) 'Amyas's field'. One Amyas de Charteris was a medieval lord of the local manor. His name, Amyas, deriving from *amatus* (Latin) 'beloved'.

Amulree (Perth & Kinross) 'Ford of Maelrubha'. *Ath* (Scottish Gaelic) 'ford'; the second element refers to the 7th-century missionary saint who, though chiefly associated with Wester Ross, became the local patron saint here.

Ancrum (Borders) 'Bend on the River Ale'. Older forms include Alnecrumba (12th-century). 'Ale' stems from the Pre-Celtic form *alaua*, 'water'; *crum* from *crwm* (Old Welsh) 'bend'.

Angus One of the old counties (also known as Forfarshire), now one of Scotland's unitary authorities. The name is generally taken as commemorating the 8th-century King of the Picts, *Aonghus* or *Oengus* (Pictish and Scottish Gaelic proper name) 'unique choice', a highly successful warrior king, who died in 761. Together with the Mearns it formed one of the major divisions of Pictland, recorded in the 12th century as Enegus.

Annan (Dumfries & Galloway) On the basis of the earlier latinised form *Anava*, it has been construed as deriving from Anu, the Gaelic goddess of prosperity; *an* is also an obsolete Gaelic term for 'water'. Medieval forms of the name have a final *t* or *d*, as in Stratanant (Strath Annan) in 1152.

Annat (Highland, and other areas) In Irish Gaelic, *andóit* indicates 'church holding relics of its founder'. The numerous Annats in Scotland mostly have evidence of an ancient church or burial ground and, in Scotland, the name may simply indicate the latter rather than any special church. Often the Annats are by a clear stream and this has also been suggested as the source of the name.

Anstruther [Current local pronunciation is Ainster] (Fife) 'The little stream'. *An* (Scottish Gaelic) 'the'; *sruthair* (Scottish Gaelic) 'little stream'. Recorded as Anestrothir in 1205 and Anstrother in 1231.

Aonach Eagach (Highland) 'Airy notched ridge'. *Aonach* (Scottish Gaelic) 'steep hill', normally applied to ridged mountains; *eagach* (Scottish Gaelic) 'notched'. An aptly descriptive name for this exposed mountain ridge (3,173 feet/951 metres) of rock spires and pinnacles rising above Glencoe.

Aonach Mór (Highland) 'Great steep ridge'. *Aonach* (Scottish Gaelic) 'steep hill', normally applied to ridged mountains; *mór* (Scottish Gaelic) 'big'. This mountain near Ben Nevis, where a ski centre has recently been developed, forms the peak of a two-mile open ridge that ends to the south with the slightly higher, and thus curiously named, Aonach Beag, 'little ridge' (4,060 feet/1,218 metres).

Appin (Argyll & Bute) 'Abbey lands'. *Apuinn* (Scottish Gaelic) 'abbey lands'. The name probably refers to the land that was owned here in medieval times by St Moluag's foundation on the nearby Isle of Lismore, across the Lynn of Lorn.

Applecross (Highland) 'Mouth of the Crosan River'. *Aber* (Brythonic-Pictish) 'mouth of a river'; *Crosan* (Brythonic-Pictish river name of uncertain derivation). The 11th-century *Annals of Tighernach* refer to it as Aporcrosan. Some writers have suggested that the second element may be the Gaelic *crossain*, 'crosses', associated with the monastery founded here in Wester Ross in AD 673 by St Maelrubha.

Arbirlot (Angus) 'Confluence of the Elliot Water'. *Aber* (Brythonic-Pictish) 'confluence' or 'river mouth').

Arbroath (Angus) 'Mouth of the Brothock Water'. *Aber* (Brythonic-Pictish) 'confluence' or 'river mouth'; the second element refers to the name of the local burn, the root of which is *brothach* (Scottish

Gaelic) 'filthy', but perhaps here 'boiling' or 'turbulent', from the related Gaelic *bruth*, 'hot', referring to its waters.

Ardbeg (Argyll & Bute) 'Small height'. *Ard* (Scottish Gaelic) 'high'; *beag* (Scottish Gaelic) 'small'.

Ardchattan (Argyll & Bute) 'The high place of Catán'. *Ard* (Scottish Gaelic) 'high'; *Chatáin* (Old Gaelic personal name) 'Catán', a Celtic saint associated with Bute and the coast of Argyll.

Ardeer (North Ayrshire) 'Western headland'. *Ard* (Scottish Gaelic) 'high', 'height' or 'headland'; *iar* (Scottish Gaelic) 'west'.

Ardelve (Highland) 'Height of the fallow land'. *Ard* (Scottish Gaelic) 'high' or 'height'; *eilghidh* (Scottish Gaelic) 'fallow ground'. Recorded in the mid-16th century as Ardillie.

Ardentinny (Argyll & Bute) Although suggested as 'heights of the fox', with *àrd* (Scottish Gaelic) 'high' and *an t-sionnaigh* (Scottish Gaelic) 'of the fox', the latter part is more likely to be *teine* (Scottish Gaelic) 'fire' or 'beacon.

Ardersier (Highland) Possibly 'high western promontory'. *Aird* (Scottish Gaelic) 'high'; *ros* (Scottish Gaelic) 'promontory'; *iar* (Scottish Gaelic) 'west'. Since 1623, it has had the alternative name of Campbelltown, after the Campbells of Cawdor, who were local proprietors.

Ardgay (Highland) 'Height of the wind'. *Ard* (Scottish Gaelic) 'high' or 'height'; *gaoithe* (Scottish Gaelic) 'wind'.

Ardgour (Highland) Possibly 'promontory of Gabran'. *Ard* (Scottish Gaelic) 'promontory'; the second element referring to Gabran, son of King Fergus of Ulster, in ancient times. More plausible alternatives include promontory of the 'goat', from *gobhar* (Scottish Gaelic) or 'sloping' or 'crooked' promontory (fitting the local topography) derived from *gwyr* (Brythonic).

Ardkinglas (Argyll & Bute) 'Height of the dog-stream'. *Ard* (Scottish Gaelic) 'high'; *con* (Scottish Gaelic) 'dog' or 'wolf'; *glas* (Scottish Gaelic) 'water'.

Ardlamont (Argyll & Bute) 'Height of Lamont'. *Ard* (Scottish Gaelic) 'high' or 'height'; *mhicLaomuinn* (Scottish Gaelic personal name) 'Lamont', the man of law. This is in the territory historically occupied by the Clan Lamont.

Ardle, River and **Strath** (Perth & Kinross) Perhaps 'river dale'. *Aar* (Old Norse) 'water'; *dalr* (Old Norse) 'valley', gaelicised into Srath Ardail.

Ardlui (Argyll & Bute) 'Height of the calves'. *Ard* (Scottish Gaelic) 'high' or 'height'; *laoigh* (Scottish Gaelic) 'calves'. An area where cows were brought to calve.

Ardmeanach (Highland; Strathclyde) 'Middle height'. *Ard* (Scottish Gaelic) 'high' or 'height'; *meadhonach* (Scottish Gaelic) 'middle' or 'central', referring to the main ridge of the Black Isle. The same name is given to an area of West Mull.

Ardmore (Highland, Strathclyde) 'Big height'. *Ard* (Scottish Gaelic) 'high' or 'height'; *mór* (Scottish Gaelic) 'big'.

Ardnamurchan (Highland) Probably 'promontory of the otters'. *Ard* (Scottish Gaelic) 'promontory'; *na* (Scottish Gaelic) 'of the'; *muir-chon* (Scottish Gaelic) 'sea dogs'. A less likely derivation of the last two parts of this name, *muir-chol* (Scottish Gaelic) 'sea villainy', suggests piracy, which may have been associated with this remote peninsula. The point marks the westernmost edge of the Scottish mainland.

Ardoch (Dumfries & Galloway, Perth & Kinross, Highland) 'High place'. *Ard* (Scottish Gaelic) 'high'; *-ach* (Old Gaelic suffix) 'place'.

Ardrishaig (Argyll & Bute) 'Promontory of thorny brambles by the bay'. *Ard* (Scottish Gaelic) 'promontory'; *dris* (Scottish Gaelic) 'thorns' or 'brambles'; *aig* (Gaelic form of Old Norse *vik*) 'bay'.

Ardross (Highland) 'Height of the promontory'. *Ard* (Scottish Gaelic) 'high' or 'height'; *rois* (Scottish Gaelic) 'of the promontory'. The name refers to the highest ground between the Cromarty and Dornoch Firths.

Ardrossan (North Ayrshire) Perhaps 'Height of the little cape'. *Ard* (Scottish Gaelic) 'promontory' or 'height'; *rois* (Scottish Gaelic) 'cape' or 'headland'; *-an* (Scottish Gaelic suffix) 'little'.

Ardtornish (Highland) 'Promontory of the hill'. *Ard* (Scottish Gaelic) 'promontory'; *torr* (Scottish Gaelic) 'hill'; *ness* (form of old Norse *nes*) 'point'. The Gaelic *ard* having been prefixed when the sense of *ness* was lost. This Morvern castle close to Loch Aline was a stronghold of the Lords of the Isles.

Argyll (Argyll & Bute) 'District or land of the Gaels'. *Airer* (Scottish Gaelic) 'coastland'; *Gaidheal* (Scottish Gaelic) 'of the Gaels'. The Gaelic-speaking Scots, originating in Ireland, colonised much of the western seaboard of Scotland during the 6th, 7th, 8th and 9th centuries. The name was first recorded as Arregaithein in a 10th-century manuscript.

Arinagour (Argyll & Bute) 'Summer pasture of the goats'. *Airidh* (Scottish Gaelic) 'summer pasture' or 'shieling'; *nan* (Scottish Gaelic) 'of'; *gobhair* (Scottish Gaelic) 'goats'.

Arisaig (Highland) 'River mouth bay'. *Ar-óss* (Old Norse) 'river mouth'; *aig* (from Old Norse *vik*) 'bay'.

Arkaig, Loch (Highland) 'Dark water'. Loch *Airceig* (Gaelic), from *arc* (Celtic root-form) 'dusky' and also from *airc* (Gaelic) 'strait'. The *-aig* ending here is of uncertain origin.

Arkle (Highland) 'Ark mountain'. *Arkfjall* (Old Norse) 'ark-like hill'. A mountain in the Reay Forest, rising to 2,580 feet/774 metres.

Arklet, Loch (Stirling) Perhaps 'dark water', of similar derivation to Arkaig, or 'steep-sloped', from *airc* (Scottish Gaelic) 'difficult' and *leathad* (Scottish Gaelic) 'slope'.

Armadale (West Lothian, Highland) Perhaps 'arm-shaped dale'. The Lothian town is named after a local landowner, Lord Armadale, who took his title from the village of Armadale on the north coast of Sutherland. The name's likely meaning, 'arm-shaped valley', is Scandinavian in origin and also applies to Armadale on the Isle of Skye. *Arm- r* (Old Norse) 'arm' or 'arm-shaped'; *dalr* (Old Norse) 'dale' or 'valley'. The Old Norse personal name, *Eorm*, has also been suggested for the first part.

Arngask (Stirling) Perhaps 'Place or height of the crossings'. *Ard* (Scottish Gaelic) 'height' or 'promontory'; *na* (Scottish Gaelic) 'of'; *chroisg* (Scottish Gaelic) 'crossings'. But *gasg* (Scottish Gaelic) 'tail' (of land) may be more likely.

Arnisdale (Shetland) 'Orn's valley'. *Orn* (Old Norse proper name) 'eagle-like'; *dalr* (Old Norse) 'valley'.

Arnprior (Stirling) 'The Prior's land'. *Earann* (Scottish Gaelic) 'portion' or 'share of land'; *na* (Scottish Gaelic) 'of' with 'prior'. A hybrid Gaelic-English combination; the priory is that of Inchmahome in the Lake of Menteith.

Aros (Argyll & Bute) 'River mouth'. *á* (Norse) 'water'; *óss* (Norse) 'river mouth' or 'oyce'. As *óss* on its own implies the river, the reason for the prefix is unclear. There is also the possibility of *àros* (Scottish Gaelic) 'house' or 'palace'.

Arran (North Ayrshire) The name may indicate 'place of peaked hills'. *Aran* (Brythonic) 'height' or 'peaked hill'. Alternatively, the derivation may be related to that of the Irish Aran Islands where *arainn* (Irish Gaelic) 'kidney' implies an arched ridge. However, this is only true of Arran when viewed, from the mainland to the north, from where it assumes the commonplace description of the 'sleeping warrior'.

Arrochar (Argyll & Bute) 'Ploughgate'. The 'aratrum' – an ancient Scottish square land measure of 104 acres, 'ploughgate' in Scots – was the area of land eight oxen could plough in a year at 13 acres each. Derived as a Gaelic form of *aratrum* (Latin) 'plough', early medieval recordings include Arathor in 1248 and Arachor in 1350. In the 19th century, it was often spelt Arroquhar. Alternatively, a local hill spelt as Ben Arrochar on an early map is derived from *Beinn Airigh-chiarr* (Scottish Gaelic) 'mount sheiling-dark'.

Arthur, Ben (Argyll & Bute) 'Arthur's Mountain', in Gaelic *Beinn Artair*. Arthur was the legendary hero of the Britons during their resistance to the invading Saxons and it is not surprising to find this prominent mountain (2,891 feet/867 metres) in the old Strathclyde kingdom, named after him. The modern alternative name, 'The Cobbler', known from around 1800, originally referred to the central peak and is said to be a translation of *an greasaiche crom* (Gaelic) 'the crooked shoemaker'.

Artney, Glen (Perth & Kinross) 'Pebbled'. *Artein* (Scottish Gaelic) 'pebble', presumably with reference to the valley sides or floor.

Askaig, River and **Loch** (Highland, Argyll & Bute) Perhaps 'river strip'., from *á* (Old Norse) 'river' and *skiki* (Old Norse) 'strip of land'.

Assynt (Highland) Perhaps '(land) seen from afar'. *Asynt* (Old Norse) 'visible', referring to the sight of the area's many isolated and distinctive peaks as seen from out at sea in The Minch. This is a conjectural derivation. *Ass* (Old Norse) 'ridge' has also been put forward for the first part of the name.

Athelstaneford (East Lothian) 'Athelstan's ford'. King Athelstan of Mercia and Wessex, took Northumbria and invaded Lothian in the early 10th century. In AD 934 his troops were defeated near this village, which possibly commemorates his name, which means 'noble stone' (Old English). Legend has it that during another battle near here in 761, the Picts, under their king, Aengus, and facing a Northumbrian army, saw a St Andrew's cross in the sky. Inspired by it to victory, they took Andrew as their patron saint and the saltire as their national flag. It has also been suggested that the origin of this place name has no connection at all with the Anglo-Saxon name Athelstan(e) but represents a tautology of *ath-ail -stane* (Gaelic, Scots) 'stone ford'.

Atholl *see* **Blair Atholl.**

Attadale (Highland) 'Ata's valley'. *Dalr* (Old Norse) 'valley', prefixed by the Old Norse personal name *Ata*.

Attow, Ben (Highland) 'Long mountain'. *Beinn* (Scottish Gaelic) 'mountain'; *fhada* (Scottish Gaelic) 'long'. This mountain (3,385 feet/1,015 metres) rises in the Kintail Forest of Wester Ross, behind the 'Five Sisters'.

Auchendinny (Midlothian) 'Field of the height or fortress'. *Achadh* (Scottish Gaelic) 'field'; *denna* (Old Irish, genitive of *dind*) 'of the height'.

Auchenshuggle (Glasgow) 'Rye field'. The name derives from *achadh* (Scottish Gaelic) 'field'; *na* (Scottish Gaelic) 'of the'; *seagal* (Scottish Gaelic) 'rye'.

Auchinleck (East Ayrshire, Dumfries & Galloway) 'Field of the flat stones'. *Achadh* (Scottish Gaelic) 'field'; *na* (Scottish Gaelic) 'of the'; *leac* (Scottish Gaelic) 'flat stones'.

Auchmithie (Angus) 'Field of the herd'. *Achadh* (Scottish Gaelic) 'field'; *muthaidh* (Scottish Gaelic) 'herd'.

Auchnagatt (Aberdeenshire) 'Field of the wild cats'. *Achadh* (Scottish Gaelic) 'field'; *na* (Scottish Gaelic) 'of the'; *cat* (Scottish Gaelic) 'cat'. *See* **Cadboll, Lynchat.**

Auchterarder (Perth & Kinross) 'Upland of high water'. *Uachdar* (Scottish Gaelic) 'upper' (land); *ard* (Scottish Gaelic) 'high'; *dobhar* (Brythonic) 'water'.

Auchtermuchty (Fife) 'Upper pig enclosure'. *Uachdar* (Scottish Gaelic) 'upper'; *muc* (Scottish Gaelic) 'pig'; *garadh* (Scottish Gaelic) 'enclosure'. Early records show Huedirdmukedi in 1250, Utermokerdy in 1293 and Utremukerty in 1294.

Auchtertool (Fife) 'Athwart-lying upland'. *Uachdar* (Scottish Gaelic) 'upper' (land); *tuathal* (Scottish Gaelic) 'crosswise-set' or 'leftwards'.

Auchtertyre (Highland) 'Upper section of land'. *Uachdar* (Scottish Gaelic) 'upper' (land); *tir* (Scottish Gaelic) 'land'.

Auldearn (Moray) 'River'. *Allt* (Scottish Gaelic) 'river'; *Earn* is likely to be one of Scotland's many ancient river names derived from a Pre-Celtic root-form, perhaps *Ar-* or *Er-*, indicating 'flowing water'. The traditional derivation, 'river of Erin', *Eireann* (Irish Gaelic) 'of Erin', is thought to be unlikely.

Auldhouse (South Lanarkshire) 'Stream of the ghost'. *Allt* (Scottish Gaelic) 'stream'; *fhuathais* (Scottish Gaelic) 'spectre' or 'apparition'.

Aultbea (Highland) 'Stream of the birches'. *Allt* (Scottish Gaelic) 'stream'; *beithe* (Scottish Gaelic) 'birches'.

Averon, River (Highland) An alternative name for the Alness river. It may stem from the Celtic prefix *ab-*, *av-*, indicative of a stream; while the latter part seems cognate with that of Deveron.

Aviemore (Highland) 'Big pass'. *Agaidh* (Scottish Gaelic) 'pass'; *mór* (Scottish Gaelic) 'big'. This popular mountain and ski resort lies at the centre of the wide Strathspey and at a strategic entry point into the Cairngorms.

Avoch (Highland) 'Place of the stream'. *Abh* (Old Gaelic, obsolete) 'water', related to *abhainn*, 'river', and stemming from the same continental Celtic root, *ab* or *av*, as **Averon**; *-ach* (Scottish Gaelic) a variant on *achadh*, 'field'.

Avon, River and **Loch**, (Highland, Moray, West Lothian) 'Stream'. *Abhainn* (Scottish Gaelic) 'stream' or 'river'. It is cognate with Welsh *afon* and the numerous Avons of England, and stems originally from an Indo-European root-form, *-ab* or *-aub*, seen in Danube and Punjab.

Avon, Ben (Moray) This mountain (3,843 feet/1,171 metres), a lofty eastern outlier of the Cairngorms, takes its name from the river above which it rises.

Awe, River and **Loch** (Argyll & Bute, Highland), from *àbh* (Old Gaelic, obsolete) 'water'. *See* **Averon, Avoch**.

Ayr (South Ayrshire) The former county town of Ayrshire, still an important administrative centre, market and resort town, takes its name from the river at whose mouth it stands on the Firth of Clyde. Ayr is a Pre-Celtic river name that possibly means 'smooth-running'. It has many variants in England (Aire, Oare) and elsewhere in Europe (Aar, Ahr, Ahre, Ara, Ohre, Ore).

Ayton (Borders) 'Place on the River Eye'. The river name is *éa* (Old English) 'running stream' with *-tun* (Old English) 'farmstead'.

B

Badachro (Highland) 'Place of saffron'. *Bad* (Scottish Gaelic) 'particular place'; *chròch* (Scottish Gaelic) 'saffron'. *Chro-chorcur* is the saffron crocus.

Badcall (Highland) 'Hazel clump'. *Bad* (Scottish Gaelic) 'particular place' or 'clump'; *call* (Scottish Gaelic) 'hazel tree'.

Badenoch (Highland) 'Drowned or marshy land'. *Bàithte* (Old Gaelic) 'liable to flooding'; and the suffix *-ach* (Old Gaelic) 'land'. The name was given to the area of Strathspey between Kingussie and Grantown.

Badentarbet (Highland) 'Place of the isthmus'. *Bad* (Scottish Gaelic) 'particular place'; *an* (Scottish Gaelic) 'of the'; *tairbeart* (Scottish Gaelic) 'isthmus' or 'portage place'.

Baldragon (Dundee) 'Place of the hero'. *Baile* (Scottish Gaelic) 'place'; *dreagan* (Scottish Gaelic) 'dragon', used figuratively to describe a great warrior. His identity has been lost.

Balerno (Edinburgh) 'Village of the sloe tree'. *Baile* (Scottish Gaelic) 'place', 'homestead' or 'hamlet'; *airneach* (Scottish Gaelic) 'sloe tree'. The name of this western suburb of Edinburgh was first recorded in the 13th century as Balhernoch and has since been further anglicised to its present form.

Balfour (Angus) 'Pasture place'. *Baile* (Scottish Gaelic) 'place' or 'homestead'; *pór* (Scottish Gaelic) 'pasture'.

Balfron (Stirling) Perhaps from a personal name, prefixed by *baile* (Scottish Gaelic) 'place' or 'homestead'. The 'fron' part may be related to the same uncertain root as 'fruin' in Glen Fruin.

Balgie (Highland, Perth & Kinross) 'Bubbly stream'. *Balg* (Scottish Gaelic) 'bag' or 'swelling' has been suggested; also *baile* (Scottish Gaelic) 'homestead'; *gaoth* (Scottish Gaelic) 'marsh' or 'bogland'.

Balintore (Highland) 'Place of the bleaching ground'. *Baile* (Scottish Gaelic) 'place', 'homestead' or 'hamlet'; *an* (Scottish Gaelic) 'of the'; *todhair* (Scottish Gaelic) 'bleaching green'.

Ballachulish (Highland) 'Village of the narrows'. *Baile* (Scottish Gaelic) 'homestead' or 'hamlet'; *caolas* (Scottish Gaelic) 'narrows' or 'straits'. This name is descriptive of this West Highland village's location on Loch Leven at the typical narrow fiord entrance by which it stands and over which the main Glasgow–Fort William road now crosses by bridge.

Ballantrae (South Ayrshire) 'Village on the shore'. *Baile* (Scottish Gaelic) 'homestead' or 'hamlet'; *an* (Scottish Gaelic) 'of the' or 'on the'; *traighe* (Scottish Gaelic) 'tidal beach'. A long stretch of open sandy shore is found here.

Ballater (Aberdeenshire) Possibly 'broom land'. *Bealaidh* (Scottish Gaelic) 'broom'; *tir* (Scottish Gaelic) 'land'. Alternatively, it could be 'pass of the water', which describes well the situation of this Royal Deeside village. *Bealach* (Scottish Gaelic) 'mountain pass'; *dobhar* (Brythonic) 'water'. Certainly, 18th-century records (Balader in 1704 and Ballader in 1716) would suggest the latter derivation:

Ballingry (Fife) 'Village of the cave or den'. *Baile* (Scottish Gaelic) 'homestead'; *an* (Scottish Gaelic) 'of the'; *garaidh* (Scottish Gaelic) 'cave'.

Ballinluig (Perth & Kinross) 'Township by the hollow'. *Baile* (Scottish Gaelic) 'hamlet' or 'homestead'; *an luig* (Scottish Gaelic) 'towards the hollow', from *lag*, 'hollow'. The village is located in the gap where the Rivers Tummel and Tay converge.

Balloch (West Dunbartonshire) 'Pass' or 'gap'. *Bealach* (Scottish Gaelic) 'mountain pass', a reference to its location in the river-gap linking Loch Lomond to the Clyde. 'Balloch' is often found as an element in other place names.

Ballochmyle (East Ayrshire) Perhaps 'Pass of the rocky brow'. *Bealach* (Scottish Gaelic) 'mountain pass'; *maol* (Scottish Gaelic) 'brow of a rock'.

Balmacaan (Highland) 'Steading of the sons of Cathan'. *Baile* (Scottish Gaelic) 'homestead'; *mac Cathain* (Scottish Gaelic proper name) 'of the sons of Cathan'.

Balmacara (Highland) 'Place of the MacAras'. *Baile* (Scottish Gaelic) 'homestead'; *mac Ara* (Scottish Gaelic proper name) 'of the MacAras'. MacAra is not a name of the Lochalsh region. An older form from the 16th century is Ballimaccroy, which may be a form of Macrae, a much more common name in the locality.

Balnagown (Highland) 'Place of the smith'. *Baile* (Scottish Gaelic) 'place', 'homestead' or 'hamlet'; *na* (Scottish Gaelic) 'of the'; *ghob-hain* (Scottish Gaelic) 'smith'.

Balmaha (Stirling) 'St Maha's place'. *Baile* (Scottish Gaelic) 'place' or 'homestead'; *Mo-Thatha* (Scottish Gaelic form of Irish *Tua*, 'the silent one', perhaps indicating a hermit-saint). St Maha's well is nearby.

Balmerino (Fife) 'St Merinac's place'. *Baile* (Scottish Gaelic) 'place' or 'homestead'. St Merinac was one of the associates of St Regulus, who is said to have brought the bones of St Andrew to Scotland.

Balmoral (Aberdeenshire) Perhaps 'homestead in the big clearing'. *Baile* (Scottish Gaelic) 'homestead' or 'settlement'; *mór* (Scottish Gaelic) 'big'; *ial* (Brythonic-Pictish) 'clearing'. *Mòrail* (Scottish Gaelic) 'majestic' or 'splendid' has also been suggested, perhaps influenced by the castle's royal ownership.

Balornock (Glasgow) 'Louernoc's place'. *Bod* (Old Welsh) 'place'; *Louernoc* (an Old Welsh proper name) 'little fox'. The earliest form (12th-century) is Budlornac.

Balquhidder (Stirling) Apparently 'settlement of fodder'. *Baile* (Scottish Gaelic) 'homestead' or 'settlement'; *foidir* (corrupt Gaelic form of Old Norse *fothr*) 'fodder'. This typically long, straggling

Highland township has long been associated with cattle rearing.

Balta (Shetland) This has been derived as 'belt island', from *balti* (Old Norse) 'belt' and *ey* (Old Norse) 'island'.

Banavie (Highland) A stream name originally, perhaps 'Pig's burn', from *banbh* (Scottish Gaelic) 'pig'.

Banchory (Aberdeenshire) 'Horns'. *Beannach* (Scottish Gaelic) 'horned' or 'forked'. The *-y* ending has been explained as the dative form of *beannchraigh*, 'by the bends'. The bends are on the River Dee, both at Banchory Devenick and Banchory Ternan (names applied to churches dedicated to the Celtic saints, Devinicus and Ternan). The meaning has also been sought in *beinn* (Scottish Gaelic) 'mountain', as 'place among mountains'. The terms are related, since *beinn's* original sense was 'horn'.

Banff (Aberdeenshire) The origin of this name is uncertain. Some authorities have suggested *banbh* (Scottish Gaelic) 'land left fallow for a year'; others have made a connection with a traditional Gaelic name for Ireland, *Banba*.; *banbh* (Scottish Gaelic) 'young pig' has also been suggested (*see* **Banavie**). Medieval documents record the development of the name form, from Banb in 1150, Banef in 1160 and Bamph in 1290 to Banffe in 1291.

Bangour (West Lothian) 'Goats' peak'. *Beinn* (Scottish Gaelic) 'mountain'; *ghobhar* (Scottish Gaelic) 'goats'. Shown as Bengouer in the early 14th century.

Banknock (Stirling) 'Hill place'. *Baile* (Scottish Gaelic) 'place' or 'settlement'; *cnoc* (Scottish Gaelic) 'hill'. The form Ballinknok is found in the early 16th century.

Bannockburn (Stirling) 'Little shining stream'. *Ban* (Brythonic) 'shining', 'fair' or 'white'; *oc* (Brythonic diminutive) 'little'; *burn* (Scots) 'stream'. This village, now a southern suburb of Stirling, stands on the banks of the Bannock Burn, which was the site of the famous battle in 1314, when the Scots, led by Robert the Bruce, routed the English army of Edward II.

Barassie (North Ayrshire) 'Summit of the droving stance'. *Barr* (Scottish Gaelic) 'crest'; *fasadh* (Scottish Gaelic) 'stance' or 'level place'.

Barcaldine (Argyll & Bute) 'Ridge of the hazel trees'. *Barr* (Scottish Gaelic) 'crest' or 'clump'; *calltuin* (Scottish Gaelic) 'hazel trees'.

Barlanark (Glasgow) 'Bare hill or ridge'. *Barr* (Scottish Gaelic) 'crest'; *lanerc* (Brythonic) 'clear space' or 'glade'.

Barlinnie (Glasgow) 'Hilltop by the pool'. *Barr* (Scottish Gaelic) 'summit' or 'top'; *linne* (Scottish Gaelic) 'pool'. A suburb of Glasgow, Barlinnie is well known for its prison, popularly referred to as 'the Bar-L'. The name refers to its location on top of one of the city's many hills and close to Hogganfield Loch, features left after the retreat of the last Ice Age glaciers.

Barnton (East Lothian) 'Barn farm'. *Berne* (Old English) 'barley store'; *tun* (Old English) 'farmstead'. In the Anglian period, barley was the main cereal crop along the Lothian coast

Barra (Western Isles) 'Isle of St Barr'. St Barr or Finnbarr (*circa* 560–615) was bishop of Cork. His name is from the Irish Gaelic *fionn*, 'white' and *barr*, 'crest' and his monastery was a vigorous mission centre. Monks from there evangelised much of the West. There are the ruins of a church dedicated to him on Barra at Cille-bharra.

Barrhead (East Renfrewshire) 'Hilltop'. *Barr* (Scottish Gaelic) 'crest' or 'top'; *head* (Scottish Gaelic) 'summit' or 'top'.

Barskimming (East Ayrshire) 'Simon's heights'. *Barr* (Scottish Gaelic) 'crest'; *Sími* (Scottish Gaelic personal name) 'Simon'. Recorded as Barskinning in 1639.

Barry (Angus) Perhaps 'barrows'. *Beorg* (Old English) has the sense of both 'hill' and 'grave-mound'. There was at least one battle fought here between Picts and Danes, which could have resulted in the raising of grave-mounds.

Bass Rock (East Lothian) 'The brow'. *An* (Scottish Gaelic) 'the'; *bathais* (Scottish Gaelic) 'brow' or 'forehead', referring to the distinctive shape of this famous rock in the Firth of Forth off North Berwick.

Bathgate (West Lothian) 'Boar wood' or 'house in the wood'. *Baedd* (Brythonic) 'boar'; *coed* (Brythonic) 'wood'. Alternatively, the first element could be derived as *bod* (Brythonic) 'house'. Recorded in the 12th century as Batket.

Bearsden (Glasgow) 'Boar's valley'. *Bár* (Old English) 'boar'; *denu* (Old English) 'valley'.

Beattock (Dumfries & Galloway) Probably 'sharp-topped (hills)'.

Biodach (Scottish Gaelic) 'sharp-topped'. The village lies among hills in upper Annandale, a few miles south of Beattock Summit, over which the main Glasgow to London road and rail links pass into Upper Clydesdale.

Beauly (Highland) 'Beautiful place'. *Beau* (French) 'beautiful'; *lieu* (French) 'place'. Compare Beaulieu in Hampshire. Beauly is recorded in 1230 as *Prioratus de Bello Loco* (Latin) 'priory of the lovely spot', with reference to the then newly founded Valliscaulian monastery here.

Beeswing (Dumfries & Galloway) This village name comes from an inn here, named after the 19th-century racehorse, Beeswing.

Beith (North Ayrshire) 'The place of the birch tree'. *Beithe* (Scottish Gaelic) 'birch tree'.

Belladrum (Highland) 'Ridge of the ford mouth'. *Beul* (Scottish Gaelic) 'mouth'; *àtha* (Scottish Gaelic) 'ford'; *druim* (Scottish Gaelic) 'ridge'.

Bellahouston (Glasgow) 'Settlement of the crucifix'. *Baile* (Scottish Gaelic) 'settlement' or 'hamlet'; *cheusadain* (Scottish Gaelic) 'crucifix'. Although now a southside suburb of Glasgow, it is assumed that the original place manifested a holy cross in some form. In later centuries, the name has been confused with Houston.

Ben, from *beinn* (Scottish Gaelic) 'mountain'. The original sense of the word was 'horn' and it was probably first applied to mountains with distinctive peaks. It has become the standard word for a Scottish mountain because of its application to the highest peaks and the fact that it is used more frequently than any other 'mount' term.

Benarty (Fife) 'Stony hill'. *Beinn* (Scottish Gaelic) 'mountain'; *artaich* (Scottish Gaelic) 'stony'. The two parts of the name appear to have been welded togther in common usage.

Benbecula (Western Isles) 'Hill of the salt-water fords'. *Beinn* (Scottish Gaelic) 'hill', 'mountain' or 'peak'; *na* (Scottish Gaelic) 'of the'; *faoghail* (adapted Scottish Gaelic form of *fadhail*) 'salt-water ford'. Alternatively, the last element may have been *faoghlach* (Scottish Gaelic) 'strand' or 'beach'. Both these possible derivations fit this low-lying island which, until the construction of causeways to the north and south, could only be reached on foot by fording the sand banks that divide it from North and South Uist at low tide. The name is recorded in early documents as Beanbeacla in 1495, Benvalgha in 1549 and Benbicula in 1660.

Benderloch (Argyll & Bute) 'Hill between lochs'. *Beinn eadar* (Scottish Gaelic) 'hill between'; *dá* (Scottish Gaelic) 'two'; *loch* (Scottish Gaelic) 'lake' or 'firth'.

Bennachie (Aberdeenshire) 'Mountain of the nipple'. *Beinn* (Scottish Gaelic) 'mountain; *na* (Scottish Gaelic) 'of'; *ciche* (Scottish Gaelic) 'nipple' or 'breast'. Although not lofty (1,733 feet/529 metres), it is a conspicuous peak. The less likely derivation 'blessed place', from *beannaichte* (Scottish Gaelic) 'blessed', has also been suggested. This area has often been suggested as the most likely site for the celebrated Battle of Mons Graupius between Romans and Caledonians in AD 84.

Bernera (Western Isles) *see* **Berneray**.

Berneray (Western Isles) 'Bjorn's isle'. *Bjorn* (Old Norse proper name) 'bear-like'; *ey* (Old Norse) 'island'.

Berriedale (Highland) A possible derivation, from *borgar* (Old Norse) 'fort' has been suggested but the reason for the vowel change is not clear. It may be from *berg* (Old Norse) 'hill', like the Berry on Hoy in Orkney, or perhaps a proper name. The suffix is *dalr* (Old Norse) 'valley'. Noted as Berudal in the *Orkneyinga Saga* (*circa* 1225).

Berwick (Borders) 'Barley farm'. *Bere* (Old English) 'barley' or 'bere'; *wic* (Old English) 'farm'. The name is found as Berwic, from 1095. The town, officially known as Berwick upon Tweed, was Scotland's main trading centre in early medieval times. Since the 14th century, it has been an English possession but the former Scottish county of Berwickshire still bears its name.

Bettyhill (Highland) Named after Elizabeth, Countess of Sutherland. This village was set up about 1820 as an agricultural and fishing centre to provide housing and work for some of those evicted during the Highland Clearances.

Biggar (South Lanarkshire) 'Barley field'. *Bygg* (Old Norse) 'barley'; *gardr* (Old Norse) 'enclosure'. Alternatively, the latter may be the more specific *geiri* (Old Norse) 'triangular plot'. Early records include Bigir and Begart.

Birkhall (Aberdeenshire) 'Birch bank'. *Birk* (Scots) 'birch'; *haugh* (Scots) 'bank' or 'meadow'. Because of the Scots habit of dropping the final *-ll* sound in words like 'hall', a confusion between this and 'haugh' has crept in.

Birnam (Perth & Kinross) 'Village of the warrior'. *Beorn* (Old English) 'warrior'; *ham* (Old English) 'homestead' or 'hamlet'. In Middle English, *beorn* had mutated to *birn*. This is unusually far into the Highlands to find a name with an Old English source.

Birsay (Orkney) 'Hunting ground island'. *Birgis* (Old Norse) 'hunt'; *herath* (Old Norse) 'valley'. The name is found as Birgisherad in the *Orkneyinga Saga*. It was the seat of the Norse Earls of Orkney.

Bishopbriggs (Glasgow) 'Bishop's lands'. The 'bishop' is that of Glasgow; *riggs* (Scots) 'fields'. The *b* has crept in through confusion with the word *brig* (Scots) 'bridge'.

Black Isle, The (Highland) The name of this broad and fertile peninsula between the Beauly and Cromarty Firths may be an English translation of *eilean* (Scottish Gaelic) 'island' and *dubh* (Scottish Gaelic) 'dark', referring either to black soil or dark forest cover. An alternative explanation is that the Gaelic name was *Eilean Duthac*, 'St Duthac's Island', mistakenly rendered into English as the 'Black Isle'.

Blackadder, River (Borders) 'Dark stream'. Adder comes from a Pre-Celtic root-word, AD or *adr*, indicating a stream. The 'Black-' was prefixed to it in medieval times, presumably to distinguish it from the other, nearby Adder, which received the prefix 'White-'. *See* **Adder.**

Blackwater, River (Highland, Central, Tayside) Translation of *Allt* (Scottish Gaelic name) 'stream' and *dubh* (Scottish Gaelic) 'water'. This is a frequently found river name.

Blair Atholl (Perth & Kinross) 'Plain of the New Ireland'. *Blar* (Scottish Gaelic) 'plain' or 'level clearing'; *ath* (Scottish Gaelic) 'next' or 'second'; *Fhodla* (Old Gaelic traditional name for Ireland, linked with the legendary Irish goddess, Fodla).

Blairgowrie (Perth & Kinross) 'Plain of Gabran'. *Blar* (Scottish Gaelic) 'plain' or 'level clearing'. The second element relates to the district of Gowrie, perhaps to distinguish it, from Blair Atholl, which is not far away.

Blantyre (South Lanarkshire) 'Edge-land'. *Blaen* (Brythonic-Gaelic) 'edge'; *tir* (Scottish Gaelic) 'land'. The name of this town south of Glasgow, birthplace of David Livingstone (1813–1873), is descriptive of its situation above the steep-sided valley of the River Clyde.

Blaven (Highland) 'Yellow mountain'. *Blà* (Old Scottish Gaelic) 'yellow'; *bheinn* (Scottish Gaelic) 'mountain'. This Skye mountain rises to 3,034 feet/928 metres.

Boat of Garten (Highland) 'Boat' as an inland name indicates the one-time existence of a ferry across the wide River Spey, close to its confluence with its tributary, the River Garten. The need for the ferry was ended in 1898 when a bridge was built here.

Bochastle (Stirling) 'Hut of the castle'. *Both* (Scottish Gaelic) 'hut' or 'cot'; *chaisteil* (Scottish Gaelic) 'castle'.

Boddam (Aberdeenshire, Shetland) 'Bottom place'. *Botm* (Old English) 'bottom'.

Bogie, River and **Strath** (Aberdeenshire) Perhaps 'stream with the bag-like pools'. *Balg* (Scottish Gaelic) 'bag'. Earlier forms include Strath Bolgy.

Bonar Bridge (Highland) 'Bridge at the lowest ford'. *Bonn* (Scottish Gaelic) 'bottom' or 'base'; *àth* (Scottish Gaelic) 'ford'. A bridge was first built here in the early 19th century to replace the frequently impassable ford.

Bonawe (Argyll & Bute) 'Water-foot'. *Bonn* (Scottish Gaelic) 'bottom' or 'base'; *abh* (Scottish Gaelic, obsolete) 'water'. There is a Bonawe on both banks of Loch Etive, at a point where the loch narrows.

Bo'ness (West Lothian) 'Burgh on the promontory'. This abbreviated place name is a contraction of Borrowstounness, from *borrowstoun* (Scots) 'burgh town' or 'town with a charter' and *naes* (Old English) 'promontory'. It is an apt description for this long-established coastal royal burgh, situated on a headland protruding into the Firth of Forth.

Bonhill (West Dunbartonshire) 'Hut by the stream'. *Both* (Scottish Gaelic) 'hut'; *an* (Scottish Gaelic) 'by'; *uillt* (Scottish Gaelic) 'stream'.

Bonnybridge (Falkirk) 'Swift stream bridge'. *Buan* (Scottish Gaelic) 'swift'. Originally referring to the stream, the name was at some stage transferred to the settlement which grew up round the bridge and the stream found itself reduced by back-formation to being the 'Bonnybridge Burn'.

Borders Although since 1975 the 'Scottish Borders' name has been officially associated with the south-eastern region, the term has long been used to describe the area lying immediately north and south of the border with England.

Boreraig (Highland) 'Fort bay'. *Borgar* (Old Norse) 'fort'; *aig* (Scottish Gaelic from Old Norse *vik*) 'bay'. The piping school of the MacCrimmon family was located here.

Borgue (Western Isles) 'Fort'. *Borgar* (Old Norse) 'fortified site'.

Borrobol (Highland) 'Fort-place'. *Borgar* (Old Norse) 'fort'; *bolr* (Old Norse) 'settlement'.

Borrodale (Highland) 'Dale of the fort'. *Borgar* (Old Norse) 'fortified place'; *dalr* (Old Norse) 'valley'. A superfluous 'Glen' has been added – the *-dalr* ending never having been borrowed into Gaelic.

Borthwick (East Lothian) 'Home farm' or possibly 'wood farm'. *Bord* (Old English) 'table' but as a derivation, from 'plank' or 'wood'; *wic* (Old English) 'farm'.

Borve (Western Isles) 'Fort'. *Borgar* (Old Norse) 'fort'. This name, found in several of the Outer Hebrides, is related to Burgh and Brough in Shetland and Orkney.

Bothwell (South Lanarkshire) 'Buth's well'. *Buth* (Old English proper name). A well was an important possession. Bothwell became a strategic site and the seat of an earldom.

Bowling (West Dunbartonshire) Perhaps 'the place of Bolla's people'. *Bolla* (Old English proper name); *inga* (Old English) 'of the people of'. Such names oftern terminate with *-ham* (Old English) 'village', but not in this case.

Bowmore (Argyll & Bute) Place of the 'big hut'. *Both* (Scottish Gaelic) 'hut' or 'house'; *mór* (Scottish Gaelic) 'big'. The reference is presumably to the house of a local chief. In 1767, the old clachan was laid out as a 'model town'.

Braan, River and **Strath** (Perth & Kinross) The name of this Perthshire strath and its river means 'roaring'. *Freamhainn* (Scottish Gaelic), from an older root, *bremava*, 'noisy' or 'rumbling'.

Bracklinn (Stirling) 'Speckled cataract'. *Breac* (Scottish Gaelic) 'speckled'; *linne* (Scottish Gaelic) 'waterfall'. This waterfall in the hills above Callander is a well-known attraction for visitors.

Braco (Perth & Kinross) 'Grey place'. *Braca* (Scottish Gaelic) 'grey' or greyish'; *-ach* (Scottish Gaelic) affix denoting place.

Braemar (Aberdeenshire) 'The upper part of Mar'. *Bràigh* (Scottish Gaelic) 'upland'. The second element, 'mar', is a personal name of unknown derivation. Early records include Bray of Marre in 1560, Brae of Mar in 1610 and Breamarr in 1682. In the 19th century, it was known as Castleton of Braemar, having grown up around the castle.

Braemore (Highland) 'Big upland'. *Bràigh* (Scottish Gaelic) 'upland'; *mòr* (Scottish Gaelic) 'big'. A descriptive name from several localities.

Braeriach (Highland, Aberdeenshire) 'The brindled or grey hill'. *Am* (Scottish Gaelic) 'the'; *bràigh* (Scottish Gaelic) 'upland' (giving the Scots 'brae'); *riabhach* (Scottish Gaelic) 'brindled' or 'greyish'. This is the second-highest peak of the Cairngorm Mountains (4,248 feet/1,296 metres). The River Dee rises on its stony summit plateau.

Braes (Highland and other regions) 'Uplands'. *Bràigh* (Scottish Gaelic) 'upland'. The name is given to numerous places, the best known of which is on Skye, where a battle was fought between crofters and police in the land disputes of 1880.

Brahan (Highland) Possibly 'place of the quern' (hand-mill). *Brathainn* (Scottish Gaelic) genitive of *bràth*, 'quern'. This is noted as the local tradition for the name.

Brander, Pass of (Argyll & Bute) This narrow pass, carrying road and railway by the side of Loch Awe and along the shoulder of Ben Cruachan, may mean 'the pot'. *Am* (Scottish Gaelic) 'the'; *brannraidh* (Scottish Gaelic) 'pot', though older Gaelic meanings also include 'trap' or 'snare'.

Braid (Edinburgh) 'Upper slopes' or 'gullet'. *Bràghad* (Scottish Gaelic) 'upper part' or 'neck'. It is possible that the reference may be to the deeply indented Braid Hills on the southern edge of Edinburgh.

Breadalbane (Perth & Kinross, Stirling) 'Upper part of Alban'. *Braghad* (Scottish Gaelic) 'higher', 'upper part' or 'hill district'; *Albainn*

(Scottish Gaelic) 'Scotland'. Breadalbane, a former earldom, is an area name applied to a large tract of the central Highlands lying to the west of Atholl.

Breakachy (Highland) 'Speckled field'. *Breac* (Scottish Gaelic) 'speckled'; *achadh* (Scottish Gaelic) 'field'.

Breacleit Bray-cleet] (Western Isles) 'Broad cliff or hill'. *Breidhr* (Old Norse) 'broad'; *klettr* (Old Norse) 'rocky holm' or 'cliff'. Breascleit in Lewis is from *breid-áss-klettr* (Old Norse) 'broad-ridge-cliff'.

Breich (West Lothian) '(Steading on the) bank'. *Bruaich* (Scottish Gaelic) genitive form of *bruach*, 'bank' or 'brink'.

Brechin (Angus) 'Brychan's place'. The personal name of a legendary character, from Celtic legend, the Brythonic hero, Brychan, (as in modern Brecon, Wales) is preserved here. In Scottish Gaelic, *brychan* may mean 'holy' or 'high' and is related to the Celtic goddess named Brigantia.

Bressay (Shetland) Probably 'breast-shaped island'. *Brjost* (Old Norse) 'breast'; *ey* (Old Norse) 'island'. This refers to its main conical shaped hill, the Ward of Bressay.

Bridge of Allan *see* **Allan**.

Bridge of Don *see* **Don**.

Bridge of Dun (Angus) 'Bridge of the brown stream'. *Donn* (Scottish Gaelic) 'brown'. The Gaelic name of the river is *Abhainn Donn* but the name comes from the former railway station on the now-closed railway line through Strathmore.

Bridge of Earn *see* **Earn**.

Bridge of Orchy *see* **Orchy**.

Bridge of Weir (Renfrewshire) 'Bridge of Vere's stream'. *Vere* is a Norman-French proper name, imported to Lanarkshire, from *ver* (Old Norse) 'stance' or 'station'.

Brig o' Balgownie (Aberdeenshire) 'Bridge of the smith's place'. *Brig* (Scots) 'bridge'; *baile* (Scottish Gaelic) 'place' or 'homestead'; *gobhainn* (Scottish Gaelic) 'of the smith'.

Brig o' Turk (Stirling) 'Bridge of the pig'. 'Brig' is the Scots translation of *droichead* (Scottish Gaelic) 'bridge'; *nan* (Scottish Gaelic) 'of'; *tuirc* (Scottish Gaelic) 'hog' or 'boar'. In Gaelic, it was more often known as *Ceann drochaid*, 'bridge at the head'.

Brittle, Glen (Highland) 'Broad bay'. *Breithr* (Old Norse) 'broad'; *vik* (Old Norse) 'bay'. The 'Glen' is a later addition to designate the valley behind the bay.

Broadford (Highland) 'The broad ford'. English translation from *an t-ath* (Scottish Gaelic) 'the ford'; *leathan* (Scottish Gaelic) 'broad'. *An t-ath Leathann* remains the Gaelic name.

Brodick (North Ayrshire) 'Broad bay'. *Breithr* (Old Norse) 'broad'; *vik* (Old Norse) 'bay'. Early records show Brathwik in 1306 and Bradewik in 1488. This main Arran resort stands on what is now tautologously called Brodick Bay.

Brodie (Moray) 'Place by the ditch' or 'muddy place'. *Brothag* (Scottish Gaelic) 'ditch' or 'hollow'.

Brogar (Orkney) 'Place by the bridge'. *Bru* (Old Norse) 'bridge'; *gardr* (Old Norse) 'enclosure' or 'garth'.

Broom, River and **Loch** (Highland) 'Water' or 'falling water'. *Braon* (Scottish Gaelic) 'water' or 'drop'. The upper loch, which still retains its Gaelic name, *Loch a'Bhraoin*, and the sea loch (with the nearby Little Loch Broom) take their name from the river which flows, from the one to the other.

Broomielaw (Glasgow) 'Hill of broom'. *Law* (Middle English and Scots) hill. This highly urbanised Glasgow riverbank site, formerly a busy Clyde steamer terminal, was once in open country.

Brora (Highland) Place of 'the bridge's river'. *Bru'r* (Old Norse) 'bridge'; *aa* (Old Norse) 'river'. Unusually, a river has been named after a bridge here, presumably because for centuries it was Sutherland's only one.

Broughton (Borders) 'Brook place'. *Bróc* (Old English) 'brook'; *tún* (Old English) 'village' or 'farmstead'.

Broughty Ferry (Dundee) This suburb of Dundee lies on the north bank of the Firth of Tay at its entrance narrows, across which there was once a ferry crossing to Fife. *Bruach-taibh* (Scottish Gaelic) 'bank of the Tay' thus provides the first part of the name and 'ferry' (English) the second. Records show Brochty in 1595.

Broxburn (West Lothian) 'Badger's stream'. *Brocc-s* (Old English) 'badger's'; *burna* (Old English) 'stream'.

Bruar (Perth & Kinross) Perhaps 'bridge stream', referring to natural arches formed by the river. *Briva* (Old Gaelic) 'bridge'; *ara-* (Old Gaelic) suffix denoting 'water' or 'stream'. It seems cognate with Brora but the location makes an Old Norse name unlikely.

Buachaille Etive (Argyll & Bute) 'The shepherd of Etive'. *Buachaille* (Scottish Gaelic) 'shepherd'. This Gaelic name for the two mountains looming over the eastern end of Glencoe is relatively recent; the older names are Stob Dearg ('red peak') and Stob Dubh ('black peak'). There are two 'shepherds', *Mór*, 'big' and *Beag*, 'small' (at 3,345 feet/1,022 metres and 3,029 feet/926 metres respectively).

Buchan (Aberdeenshire) Possibly 'place of the cow'. *Buwch* (Brythonic, with the suffix *-an*) 'cow place'. *Baoghan* (Scottish Gaelic) 'calf' provides an alternative derivation that produces the same meaning. The name was recorded as Buchan around AD 1000 in the 'Book of Deer' and as Baugham in 1601. Either way, as a major beef cattle farming area and home of the Aberdeen Angus breed, the description still fits the Buchan of today.

Buchanan (Stirling) This district name may be related to Buchan or may be from *both* (Scottish Gaelic) 'house'; *chanain* (Scottish Gaelic) 'priest'. In the latter case, its adoption as a surname may have led to a wider area of reference.

Buchanty (Angus) 'House of the cow-place'. *See* **Buchan**. The *-ty* suffix is *taigh* (Scottish Gaelic) 'house'.

Buckhaven (Fife) Probably of similar derivation to Buckie, 'harbour of bucks or buckies'. A name dating from the mid-16th century.

Buckie (Moray) Probably 'place of bucks'. *Bocaidh* (Scottish Gaelic) 'whelk'. However, *bucaidh* (Scottish Gaelic) 'pimple' or 'protuberance', has also been suggested. Bucksburn, Aberdeen, would seem to suggest the latter meaning. It is recorded as Buky in 1350.

Bunchrew (Highland) 'Low place of trees'. *Bonn* (Scottish Gaelic) 'bottom'; *chraobh* (Scottish Gaelic) 'trees'. Recorded as Bunchrive in the 16th century.

Bunessan (Argyll & Bute) 'Foot of the waterfall'. *Bonn* (Scottish Gaelic) 'bottom'; *easan* (Scottish Gaelic) 'waterfall'.

Bunnahabhainn (Argyll & Bute) 'Stream-foot'. The name of this Islay distilling village is, from *bonn* (Scottish Gaelic) 'bottom' and *abhainn* (Scottish Gaelic) 'stream' or 'river'.

Burghead (Moray) 'Headland of the fort'. *Borgar* (Old Norse) 'fort'. The fort was established in 880. 'Head' may be an English translation of a lost *nes* (Old Norse) 'headland'.

Burntisland (Fife) Possibly 'Burnet's land'. *Burnet* (a personal name); *land* (Old English) 'estate'. Local legend ascribes the name of this Fife harbour town, specialising in bauxite import and once a ship-building centre, to fisher-huts burnt down on an island close to the present harbour. In 1538, it was noted as Bruntisland.

Burra (Shetland) 'Fortified isle'. *Borgar* (Old Norse) 'fort'; *ey* (Old Norse) 'island'. Burray(Orkney) has the same derivation.

Busby (East Renfrewshire) 'Bushy place'. *Busk* (Old Norse) 'bush'; *by* (Old Norse) 'farm' or 'place'. This town, south of Glasgow, may be the place where the headpiece known as the 'busby' was first made.

Busta (Shetland) 'Farmstead'. *Bolstadr* (Old Norse) 'farmstead', usually found as a suffix but here on its own. Bosta in Lewis has the same origin.

Bute (Argyll & Bute) Possibly 'patch of land'. *Bót* (Old Norse) 'patch' or 'piece of land'. This derivation could tentatively be explained by the situation of Bute, which although an 'Isle' is all but a 'piece of the (main)-land', separated only by the 400-metres-wide Kyles of Bute. A derivation from *bot* (Old Irish Gaelic) 'fire', has also been suggested. Early records show Bot in 1093; Bote in 1204 and Boot in 1292.

Butt of Lewis (Western Isles) The origins of Scotland's only 'butt' are unclear. Old French *buter*, 'to butt out', has been suggested, as has Danish *but*, 'stumpy', as a root, but neither seems very plausible. There may be some connection with the several Buddons/Buttons of eastern promontories.

C

Cabrach (Moray) In Scottish Gaelic, *cabrach* means 'stag', but also 'thicket', and in adjective form, 'antlered'. This remote community on the upper Deveron still has many deer in the vicinity.

Cadboll (Highland) 'Place of wild cats'. *Cat* (Scottish Gaelic) 'cat'; *ból* (Old Norse) 'farm'. Noted as Kattepoll in the 13th century and Katte Pole in the 16th century. The Pictish carved Cadboll Stone, from here, is one of the treasures of the Museum of Scotland in Edinburgh.

Cadder (East Dunbartonshire) 'Circular stone fort'. *Cathair* (Scottish Gaelic) 'round fort of stone'. There is a (square) Roman fort at Cadder, now bounded by the Forth and Clyde Canal, but an earlier fortification may also have been built there, above the haughs of Kelvin.

Caddon Water (Borders) Compound of an original Pre-Celtic river name, *cal*, also found in Calder and other places, with *denu* (Old English) 'valley'.

Cadzow (South Lanarkshire) Perhaps 'battle hollow'. Cadzow, the former name of Hamilton, may commemorate a battle, from *cath* (Scottish Gaelic) 'battle'. The latter part may be cognate with *howe* (Scots) 'hollow'. The name is recorded in 1360 as Cadyow. As in many Scottish place names, the *z* is in fact properly a *y*, as a result of the old-time writing style, which confused these two letters.

Caerlaverock (Dumfries & Galloway) 'Fort in the elm trees'. *Cathair* (Scottish Gaelic) 'fort'; *leamh-reaich* (Scottish Gaelic) 'elm tree'. The ruins of an impressive 14th-century castle, surrounded by trees, are still to be found here today. The Scots form of the name is influenced by the phonic resemblance to *laverock*, 'skylark'.

Cairnbawn, Loch (Highland) 'Loch of the bright hills'. *Càrn* (Scottish Gaelic) 'humped hill'; *bán* (Scottish Gaelic) 'fair' or 'bright'.

Cairndow (Argyll & Bute) 'Dark mount'. *Càrn* (Scottish Gaelic) 'humped hill'; *dubh* (Scottish Gaelic) 'dark'.

Cairn Gorm (Moray, Highland) 'Blue, humped hill'. *Càrn* (Scottish Gaelic) 'humped hill'; *gorm* (Scottish Gaelic) 'blue', although *gorm* can also mean 'green'. This single mountain's name has been adopted for the whole range and though 'blue' seems right for this granite massif that appears from afar as blue, rounded high hills, its Gaelic name is *Monadh Ruadh*, 'Red Mountains', probably because of the reddish granite of which they are formed. Cairn Gorm rises to 4,084 feet/1,245 metres.

Cairnie (Moray) 'Place of thickets'. *Carden* (Brythonic-Pictish) 'thicket'; *ach* (Scottish Gaelic) locative suffix.

Cairnpapple (West Lothian) Probably 'hill of the priest's place'. *Càrn* (Scottish Gaelic) 'humped hill'; *pabail* (Scottish Gaelic) 'priest's place'. There is a prehistoric hill fort on this hill, which just tops 1,000 feet/306 metres.

Cairnryan (Dumfries & Galloway) 'Fort by (Loch) Ryan'. *Caer* (Brythonic-Welsh) 'fort'. *See* **Ryan**.

Cairn Toul (Moray) 'Barn hill'. The Gaelic name of this Cairngorm mountain, which rises to 4,241 feet/1,293 metres, is *Càrn an t-Sabhail*, from *càrn* (Scottish Gaelic) 'humped hill' and *sabhal* (Scottish Gaelic) 'barn'. Perhaps its rounded shape resembled a thatched barn. It has also been suggested that it may signify 'ominous' or 'thwarting' hill, from *tuathal* (Scottish Gaelic) 'athwart-placed' or 'ominous'.

Caithness (Highland) An ancient name, the earlier part perhaps Pre-Celtic, first recorded as *cat* or *cait*; taken as an indication that the cat was a tribal emblem. It was one of the seven provinces of Pictland. The suffix, added much later, is *nes* (Old Norse) 'ness' or 'headland', an obvious feature of the coastal outline as seen by seaborne visitors.

Calder (Highland, West Lothian, North Lanarkshire) Possibly 'hard or rapid water'. *Caled* (Brythonic) 'hard'; *dobhar* (Brythonic) 'water'. Alternatively, the first part may be derived from *callaidh* (Scottish Gaelic) 'rapid' or 'nimble'. *Call* (Old Gaelic) 'hazel' has also been suggested for the first part.

Caldercruix (North Lanarkshire) 'Bends of Calder'. *Crux* (Scots), from *krókr* (Old Norse) 'crooks' or 'bends'.

Calgary (Argyll & Bute) 'Cali's garth'. *Kali* (Old Norse proper name); *gerdhi* (Old Norse diminutive of *gardr*) 'garth', meaning the land between the machair and the moorland, taken into Gaelic as *gearraidh*; appropriate to this Mull township.

Callander (Stirling) Probably, as for Calder, the meaning of this town's name is 'hard or rapid water' (from the River Teith, which is quite turbulent here). The name was recorded as Calentare in 1164 and Callanter in 1350.

Callanish (Western Isles) 'Kali's ness'. *Kali* (Old Norse proper name), *nes* (Old Norse) 'cape' or 'point'. At this Lewis location on East Loch Roag (*ró-vagr* [Old Norse] 'roe-deer bay'), is a large and celebrated complex of standing stones dating back to around 1800 BC.

Callater, River and **Glen** (Angus) *see* **Calder**.

Cally, Bridge of (Perth & Kinross) 'Ferry'. *Caladh* (Scottish Gaelic) 'ferry', which was replaced by the bridge over the River Ardle.

Calton (Edinburgh, Glasgow and other areas) 'Hazel (place)'. *Calltuinn* (Scottish Gaelic) 'hazel'. Some more recent post-Gaelic Caltons might be 'cold place', from Scots *cauld*, 'cold', and *toun*, 'farmstead'. Farm and field names were quite often given to ward off ill luck.

Calvine (Perth & Kinross) Perhaps 'smooth wood'. *Coille* (Scottish Gaelic) 'wood'; *mhìn* (Scottish Gaelic) 'smooth'.

Cambus (Stirling) 'Place of the bay'. *Camus* (Scottish Gaelic) 'bay'. Most *camus* names have some further designation but not here.

Cambuskenneth (Stirling) 'Cinaed's Bay'. *Camus* (Scottish Gaelic) 'bay'; the second part may be an anglicisation of the Old Gaelic proper name, *Cinaed*, or less probably a translation of the Scottish Gaelic name, *Choinnich*, 'Kenneth'.

Cambuslang (Glasgow) 'Bay of the ship'. *Camus* (Scottish Gaelic) 'bay'; *luinge* (Scottish Gaelic) 'ship's'. The name indicates that small, oared vessels could come up the River Clyde at least as far as here.

Cambus o' May (Aberdeenshire) 'Bay on the May Water'. *Camus* (Scottish Gaelic) 'bay'. It has been inferred that 'May' comes from the Old Irish *Miathi*, a form of Maeatae, one of the tribes identified by the Romans. More probable is *magh* (Scottish Gaelic) 'plain'.

Camelon (Falkirk) 'Crooked pool'. *Cam* (Scottish Gaelic) 'bent' or 'crooked'; *linne* (Scottish Gaelic) 'pool'.

Campbeltown (Argyll & Bute) The chief town of Kintyre was named after Archibald Campbell, Earl of Argyll, in 1667. Formerly it had been called Lochhead and even earlier was known as Kilkerran.

Campsie Fells (Stirling, East Dunbartonshire) 'Crooked hills'. *Cam* (Scottish Gaelic) 'crooked'; *sìth* (Scottish Gaelic) 'hill'. As *sìth* also means 'fairy', the name has sometimes been taken as 'fairy hills' but it cannot be both. 'Fells', from *fjall* (Old Norse) 'hill', is a later addition – an unusual but not unknown hill word in Scots. Recorded as Kamsi in 1208, Camsy in 1300 and Campsy in 1522. The *p* would appear to have crept in through a fancied connection with 'camp'.

Camster (Highland) 'Kam's steading'. *Kami* (Old Norse proper name); *bolstadr* (Old Norse) 'small farm'.

Canisbay (Highland) 'Canons' farm'. *Canane* (Scots) 'Canon'; *by* (Old Norse) 'farmstead'. Shown *circa* 1240 as Cananesbi.

Canna (Highland) 'Bucket' island. *Kanna* (Old Norse) 'can' or 'bucket', presumably from the island's shape. This is the northernmost of the 'Small Isles' lying to the south of Skye.

Canonbie (Dumfries & Galloway) 'Canons' village'. *Canon* (Middle English) refers to the Augustinian priory that was here, from 1165 to 1542; *-by* (Old Danish) 'village'.

Canongate (Edinburgh) 'Street of the canons'. *Gata* (Old English) 'street'. This continuation of Edinburgh's high street, for centuries an independent burgh, leads down to Holyrood Abbey.

Cannich, River and **Glen** (Highland) Perhaps 'place where cotton sedge grows'. *Canach* (Scottish Gaelic) 'cotton sedge'.

Caputh (Perth & Kinross) 'Hilltop'. *Ceap* (Scottish Gaelic) 'hilltop'; *-ag* (Scottish Gaelic) diminutive ending. The word is related to *caput* (Latin) 'head', which it closely resembles.

Carbost (Western Isles, Highland) 'Kari's steading'. *Kari* (Old Norse proper name) and *bolstadr* (Old Norse) 'small farm'.

Cardenden (Fife) 'Den or hollow of the thicket'. *Cardain* (Scottish Gaelic from Brythonic *cardden*) 'thicket'; *den* (Scots from Old English *denu*) 'small steep valley'.

Cardrona (Borders) Possibly 'fort of winds or breezes'. *Cathair* (Scottish Gaelic) 'fort'; *drothanach* (Scottish Gaelic) 'breezy'. Noted as Cardronow in 1530.

Cardross (Argyll & Bute) 'Wooded promontory'. *Cardden* (Brythonic) 'wooded'; *ros* (Brythonic) 'promontory'. Recorded in the 13th century as Cardinros.

Carlops (Borders) 'The hag's leap'. *Carline* (Scots) 'old woman'; *loups* (Scots) 'leaps'. In Wyntoun's *Chronicle* (*circa* 1400), it is referred to as Karlinlippis. This curious name was first given to the stream, then to the village founded in 1784.

Carloway (Western Isles) 'Karl's Bay'. *Karla* (Old Norse proper name);

vágr (Old Norse) 'bay', gaelicised into Càrlabagh. There is a well-preserved Pictish broch on this west Lewis site, Dun Carloway.

Carluke (South Lanarkshire) Possibly 'Fort on the marsh'. *Caer* (Brythonic-Celtic) 'fort'; *lwch* (Brythonic) 'marshland'. Alternatively, the first element may be derived from *carn* (Scottish Gaelic) 'cairn' or 'humped hill'; and the latter part could be an obscure personal name. First recorded in 1320 as Carneluke.

Carmyllie (Angus) 'Warrior's fort'. *Caer* (Brythonic) 'fort'; *milidh* (Scottish Gaelic) 'warrior'.

Càrn Mòr Dearg (Highland) 'Great red cairn'. *Càrn* (Scottish Gaelic) 'cairn' or 'heaped stones'; *mòr* (Scottish Gaelic) 'great'; *dearg* (Scottish Gaelic) 'red'. This mountain (4,012 feet/1,223 metres), just east of Ben Nevis, is tallest of a north–south group that includes Càrn Dearg Meadhonach ('middle') and Càrn Beag ('little') Dearg (3,313 feet/1,010 metres).

Carnoustie (Angus) Possibly 'rock of the fir tree'. *Carraig* (Scottish Gaelic) 'rock'; *na* (Scottish Gaelic) 'of the'; *ghiuthais* (Scottish Gaelic) 'fir tree'. A document of the late 15th-century records this place as Donaldus Carnusy. The *t* of the name was interpolated at a later date. The links here have become a championship golf course.

Carnwath (South Lanarkshire) Apparently 'Kaerandi's ford'. *Kaerandi* (Old Scandinavian personal name); *vath* (Old Scandinavian) 'ford'.

Carrbridge (Highland) 'Bridge at the rocky shelf'. *Drochaid* (Scottish Gaelic) translated to English 'bridge'; *charra* (Scottish Gaelic) 'rock shelf'.

Carrick (North Ayrshire) 'Rocky place'. *Carraig* (Scottish Gaelic) 'rock' or 'crag'. This is one of the three districts of the former Ayrshire, formerly an earldom and, since the time of Robert Bruce, an appanage of the heir of the crown

Carron (Falkirk, Highland, Moray, Dumfries & Galloway) 'Rough river'. The names of the river and strath in Wester Ross and the stream near Falkirk, as well as other Carrons, derive from the Pre-Celtic root *kars*, 'harsh' or 'rough', which also gives rise to the place name, Carrick. Carron on the Spey, above Aberlour, may refer to a particularly rough section of this fast river.

Carse This Scots word, derived from *kerss* (Old Norse), means 'low-lying land by a river'. It is often found in local and farm names, sometimes in the suffix form *-kerse, -kersie*.

Carse of Gowrie *see* **Gowrie.**

Carsphairn (Dumfries & Galloway) 'Carseland of the alder trees'. *Carse* (Scots from *kerss* [Old Norse]) 'low-lying land by a river'; *feàrna* (Scottish Gaelic) 'alders'.

Carstairs (South Lanarkshire) 'Castle Tarras'. *Caisteil* (Scottish Gaelic) 'castle'; *Tarras* is of obscure origin, probably a personal name.

Carter Bar (Borders) 'Short-horn head'. This location, on a Border pass, derives, from *kort-r* (Old Norse) 'short-horn' and *barr* (Scottish Gaelic) 'crest'. It has nothing to do with carters. Carter Fell, nearby, has a similar derivation, from *fjall* (Old Norse) 'hill' or 'fell'.

Cassillis (North Ayrshire) 'Castles'. *Caiseal* (Irish Gaelic) 'stone fort'. A number of similar names are also linked to the presence of brochs or forts, including Cashel Point on Loch Lomond, and Glen Cassley in Ross-shire.

Castlebay (Western Isles) The name of the main settlement on Barra, referring to the MacNeil castle of Kisimul, which stands on a rock in the bay and around which this town lies. In Gaelic, the usual name was *Baile MhicNéill*, 'MacNeil's Place'.

Castle Douglas (Dumfries & Galloway) 'Castle of the Douglas family'. This town was acquired and developed in 1789 by Sir William Douglas who had made his fortune trading with Virginia. The settlement here was first known as Causewayend, then Carlingwark.

Castlecary (North Lanarkshire) 'Fort of the fortifications'. 'Castle' is post-medieval; *caerydd* (Brythonic) 'forts'. There is a Roman wall fort here.

Castlemilk (Glasgow) 'Castle on the milky white stream'. *Chaisteil* (Scottish Gaelic) 'castle'; *melg* (Old Irish Gaelic) 'milk'. This is one of the vast outer Glasgow housing development zones, often referred to simply as 'The Milk'.

Catterline (Aberdeenshire) 'Fort by the pool'. *Cathair* (Scottish Gaelic from Brythonic *cader*) 'fort'; *linne* (Scottish Gaelic) 'pool'. An old form is Katerlyn.

Cathcart (Glasgow) 'Wood of Cart'. *Coet* (Brythonic) 'wood'; *Cert*

(Brythonic river name), which has been hazarded as meaning 'cleansing', from a Pre-Celtic root. However, it seems more closely connected with the same Pre-Celtic root-form as Carron – *kar*, 'hard' or 'stony'.

Cathkin (Glasgow) 'Place of common pasture'. *Coitchionn* (Scottish Gaelic) 'common pasture'.

Catrine (East Ayrshire) 'Battle point'. *Cath* (Scottish Gaelic) 'battle'; *roinne* (Scottish Gaelic) 'point'.

Cauldcleuch (Borders) 'Cold hollow'. *Cauld* (Scots) 'cold'; *cleuch* (Scots) 'hollow' or 'cleft'.

Cawdor (Highland) Possibly 'hard or rapid water'. The derivation of this name is probably the same as for Calder. In this case, the river name has been transferred to the village and the 14th-century castle made famous for its associations with Shakespeare's *Macbeth*.

Central A name selected by civil servants in 1975 to define the administrative region that took in all or parts of the former counties of Stirlingshire, Clackmannanshire and West Lothian until 1994.

Ceres (Fife) 'Western place'. *Siar* (Scottish Gaelic) 'western'; *ais* (Scottish Gaelic) 'place'. The resemblance to the name of the Greek goddess of crops seems coincidental.

Cessford (Borders) 'Cessa's enclosure'. *Cessa* (Old English proper name); *worth* (Old English) 'enclosed fields', replaced by 'ford'. Anglo-Saxon *-worth* names, so common in England, are rare in Anglian Scotland. By the time Anglians were moving in, *-worth* was obsolete and *-tun* or *-ham* were the normal forms.

Challoch (Dumfries & Galloway) 'Forge'. *Teallach* (Scottish Gaelic) 'anvil' or 'forge'.

Chanonry Point (Highland) 'Point of the canons'. The adjacent village of Rosemarkie was the site of an important abbey in Pictish times.

Chatelherault (South Lanarkshire) This entirely French name is part of the history of the Hamilton family. The Hamilton Earl of Arran was made Duke of Chatelherault in the early 16th century as a reward for giving up the regency of Scotland.

Chesters (Borders) 'Camps', from *castrum* (Latin) 'military camp', which became the Old English *ceaster*. There are a number of other Roman-related names in this region, just north of Hadrian's Wall.

Cheviot (Borders) The source of this name is unclear but it may be linked to a Pre-Celtic tribal name. *Cefn* (Brythonic) 'ridge' has also been suggested. Properly the name of the highest point in the range (on the English side and known as 'The Cheviot') it has been extended to signify the range of hills along which the border between Scotland and England runs for part of its way.

Clachan (Highland, Argyll & Bute) 'Place of stones'. *Clachan* (Scottish Gaelic) 'stones'. A clachan is a stone-built village.

Clachnacudden (Highland) 'Stone of the tubs'. *Clach* (Scottish Gaelic) 'stone'; *nan* (Scottish Gaelic) 'of'; *cudainn* (Scottish Gaelic) 'tubs'. Said to have been a stone on which the women of Inverness rested their wash-tubs on the way to the river, which became a sort of totem for the town.

Clachtoll (Highland) 'Hollow of stones'. *Clach* (Scottish Gaelic) 'stone'; *toll* (Scottish Gaelic) 'hollow' or 'hole'.

Clackmannan (Clackmannanshire) 'Stone of Manau or Manan'. *Clach* (Scottish Gaelic) 'stone'. *Manau* or *Manan* is an ancient personal name given to this area at the head of the Firth of Forth. The 'stone' is a large glacial erratic rock that now stands in the centre of the town of Clackmannan, once the county town of Clackmannanshire, Scotland's smallest county.

Clash, Loch (Highland) 'Loch of the trench'. *Clais* (Scottish Gaelic) 'trench' or 'deep furrow'. *Clash-* in names generally has this meaning.

Clashmore (Highland) 'Deep furrow'. *Clais* (Scottish Gaelic) 'trench' or 'furrow'; *mòr* (Scottish Gaelic) 'big'.

Clatt *see* **Clett**.

Cleghorn (South Lanarkshire) 'Clay house'. *Claeg* (Old English) 'clay'; *erne* (Old English) 'house'.

Cleish (Perth & Kinross) 'Furrow' or 'trench'. *Clais* (Scottish Gaelic) 'trench' or 'furrow'. The township is in the valley of the Gairney (possibly from *gearain* (Gaelic) 'to sigh') Water and presumably gave its name to the Cleish Hills rising behind. There is also a Cleish in West Lothian.

Clett (Shetland and Orkney Islands) 'Cliffs'. *Klettr* (Old Norse) 'cliffs'. There are many Clett names in the Shetland and Orkney Islands. Clatt in Aberdeenshire has the same origin.

Cleuch, Ben (Stirling) 'Gully mountain'. *Beinn* (Scottish Gaelic) 'mountain'; *cleuch* (Scots) 'gully'. At 2,364 feet/723 metres, this is the highest point of the Ochil Hills.

Clickhimin (Shetland Islands and other regions) 'Rock mouth'. *Klakk* (Old Norse) 'rock'; *minni* (Old Norse) 'mouth'. The Cleekhimin Burn flows into the Leader Water in the Borders.

Cloch (Inverclyde) 'By the stone'. *Cloiche* (Scottish Gaelic) 'by the stone'. Cloch Point opposite Dunoon, known to seamen as 'The Cloch', is an important navigational mark for vessels heading towards the Clyde docks.

Cloich Hills (Borders) 'Stone hills'. *Clach* (Scottish Gaelic) 'stone'.

Cluanie (Highland) 'Meadow'. *Cluain* (Scottish Gaelic) 'meadow' with *-ach* locative ending. Cluny in Badenoch and Clunie in Tayside have the same derivation.

Clyde, River, Strath and **Firth** (Renfrewshire, Inverclyde) 'Cleansing one'. A Brythonic river name derived from the root element, *clut*. The Roman name for this river was recorded in the 2nd century as Clota. The modern form Clutha is a poetic term for the Clyde.

Clydebank (West Dunbartonshire) A modern name, given to this industrial town when it was developed in the 19th century. It lies on the north bank of the Clyde, immediately to the west of Glasgow.

Clynder (Argyll & Bute) 'Red slope'. *Claon* (Scottish Gaelic) 'slope'; *dearg* (Scottish Gaelic) 'red'.

Clyne (Highland) 'Slope'. *Claon* (Scottish Gaelic) 'slope'; the locative form is *claoin*. Clynelish, a distillery name in the same east Sutherland locality, adds *lios* (Scottish Gaelic) 'garden'.

Coaltown (Fife) This name is prefixed to a number of localities in the former Fife coalmining area, to indicate a colliery or colliers' houses, as in Coaltown of Wemyss.

Coatbridge (North Lanarkshire) 'Bridge by the cottages'. The bridge was built in about 1800 as part of the development of the area as a coal-mining centre around the earlier small settlement of Cotts (*cot* [Old English] 'shelter' or 'cottage'). It is found as Coitts in 1582.

Coatdyke (North Lanarkshire) 'Cottage by the dyke'. *Cot* (Old English) 'hut' or 'cottage'; *dyke* (Scots) 'wall'.

Cockenzie (East Lothian) The meaning of this name is obscure but a personal name could be involved. Some authorities suggest 'Kenneth's nook'. *Cuil* (Scottish Gaelic) 'nook'. Recorded as Cowkany in 1590 and still pronounced today as 'Cockennie'.

Coigach (Highland) 'The place of fifths'. *Na cóigich* (Scottish Gaelic) 'fifths', implying some form of land division in times past. The same derivation applies to the area known as the Coigs of Strathdearn, south of Inverness.

Coire Cas (Highland) 'Steep corrie'. *Coire* (Scottish Gaelic) 'corrie'; *cas* (Scottish Gaelic) 'steep'. The corrie is in the centre of a popular climbing and ski-ing area.

Coldbackie (Highland) 'Cold bank'. *Kald* (Old Norse) 'cold'; *bakki* (Old Norse) 'bank'.

Coldstream (Borders) Before the bridge was built in 1766, the River Tweed was forded here and the name is a reference to the temperature of the river, which is a substantial stream at this point.

Coldingham (Borders) 'Village of the people at Colud'. *Colud* (Old English proper name); *inga* (Old English) affix with the sense of 'people of'; *ham* (Old English) 'village'.

Colinsburgh (Fife) This small village is named after Colin Lindsay, Earl of Balcarres, who founded it in 1705.

Colinton (Edinburgh) 'Colgan's farm'. Colgan is an Irish Gaelic personal name and it may have supplanted an earlier Anglian name. The suffix is from *tun* (Old English) 'farmstead'. It appears as Colgyntone in 1296.

Colintraive (Argyll & Bute) 'Swimming narrows'. *Caol* (Scottish Gaelic) 'strait' or 'kyle'; *nàimh* (Scottish Gaelic) genitive form of *snàmh*, 'swimming'. Cattle were swum across here from Bute to the mainland.

Collessie (Fife) 'Nook of the water'. *Cuil* (Scottish Gaelic) 'nook' or 'corner'; *eas* (Scottish Gaelic) 'waterfall', with the locative suffix *-ach*.

Coll (Argyll & Bute) Probably 'barren place'. *Kollr* (Old Norse) 'bald head' or 'bare top'. This description is apt for this Inner Hebridean island, which presents a bleak face of gnarled gneiss rock protruding through the heather, in contrast to its flat and fertile neighbour, Tiree.

Colonsay (Argyll & Bute) Possibly '(St) Columba's Isle'. Alternatively, some commentators suggest *Kolbein* (Old Norse) as a substitute personal name. The second part is derived from *ey* (Old Norse) 'island'.

Coltness (North Lanarkshire) 'Wood by the water (fall)'. *Coille* (Scottish Gaelic) 'wood'; *an* (Scottish Gaelic) 'by the'; *eas* (Scottish Gaelic) 'waterfall'.

Comiston (Edinburgh) 'Colman's farm'. *Colmàn* (Scottish Gaelic proper name, deriving from *Calum*, 'dove') and *tun* (Old English) 'farmstead'.

Comrie (Perth & Kinross) Place of the 'confluence'. *Comar* (Scottish Gaelic) 'river confluence'. Near here both the Water of Ruchill and the River Lednock meet with the River Earn in a convergence of valleys.

Con, Loch (Stirling) 'Loch of the dog'. *Con* (Scottish Gaelic) 'dog' or 'wolf'.

Condorrat (North Lanarkshire) Place of river confluence'. *Comh* (Scottish Gaelic) 'joining'; *dobhar* (Scottish Gaelic) 'water' or 'stream'; *ait* (Scottish Gaelic suffix indicating place).

Connel (Argyll & Bute) 'Whirlpool'. *Coingheall* (Scottish Gaelic) 'whirlpool', referring to the tidal rapids here at the entrance to Loch Etive. For a long time, the place was known as Connel Ferry, until the cantilever bridge was built over the rapids.

Conon, River, Strath and **Village** (Highland). 'Wolf or dog river'. The root-form appears to be *con* (genitive form of Old Irish *cu*) 'wolf' or 'dog'; the *-ona* (Pre-Celtic) 'water' suffix is frequently found in river names. The name appears in pre-20th-century sources as Conan.

Contin (Highland) Perhaps 'fort of the dog'. The root-form appears to be, as with Conon, *con* (genitive form of Old Irish *cu*) 'wolf' or 'dog'; *dainn* (Scottish Gaelic) 'rampart'.

Convinth, Glen (Highland) 'Glen of roaring'. *Confhadh* (Scottish Gaelic) 'howling' or 'rage'. The reference may be to the wind or water noise in this funnel-shaped glen.

Cora Linn (South Lanarkshire) 'Pool or falls of the boggy place'. *Corrach* (Scottish Gaelic) 'marshy place'; *linne* (Scottish Gaelic) 'pool' or 'falls'.

Corgarff (Aberdeenshire) 'Rough corrie'. *Coire* (Scottish Gaelic) 'corrie' or 'mountain hollow'; *garbh* (Scottish Gaelic) 'rough'.

Corpach (Highland) 'Corpse-place', from the fact that funerals from Fort William rested hear on their way to the church at Annat. *Corpach* (Scottish Gaelic) 'corpses'.

Corran (Highland) 'Low tapering cape'. *Còrr* (Scottish Gaelic) 'tapered' or 'drawn to a point', with *-an* diminutive ending. A derivation from *carran* (Irish Gaelic) 'reaping hook', indicating a curving spit of land, is also possible.

Corriehalloch (Highland) 'Foaming corrie'. *Coire* (Scottish Gaelic) 'mountain hollow' or 'corrie'; *salach* (Scottish Gaelic) 'turbulent', 'ugly' or 'dirty'. The unpronounced *s* in the Gaelic spelling has given rise to the English form 'Corrieshalloch'.

Corrievreckan (Argyll & Bute) 'Whirlpool of Brecon'. *Coire* (Scottish Gaelic) 'mountain hollow' or 'cauldron'; *Brychan* (a personal name) common to Celtic mythologies. In Gaelic legend, the hero, Brychan, perished with his fifty ships in this notorious whirlpool, which lies north of the island of Jura.

Corrieyairack, Pass of (Highland) 'Rising corrie'. *Coire* (Scottish Gaelic) 'mountain hollow'; *eirich* (Scottish Gaelic) 'rising'. There is an old military road over the pass from the Great Glen to Badenoch, linking Fort Augustus to the military barracks at Ruthven.

Corrour (Highland) 'Brown hollow'. *Coire* (Scottish Gaelic) 'corrie'; *odhar* (Scottish Gaelic) 'brown'.

Corsewall Point (Dumfries & Galloway) 'Cross well'. There is an ancient well-site here dedicated to St Columba.

Corstorphine (Edinburgh) Possibly 'cross of the fair hill'. *Crois* (Scottish Gaelic) 'cross'; *torr* (Scottish Gaelic) 'hill'; *fionn* (Scottish Gaelic) 'fair'. A cross did stand here by Corstorphine Hill in what is now a western suburb of Edinburgh. Other less well-founded derivations include one from 'Torphin' (personal name) or from the 11th-century Norse Earl Thorfinn. Records show Crostorfin in 1128 and Corstorphyne in 1508.

Coruisk, Loch (Highland) 'Water hollow'. *Coire* (Scottish Gaelic) 'mountain hollow' or 'corrie'; *uisge* (Scottish Gaelic) 'water'.

Coshieville (Perth & Kinross) 'By the trees'. *Cois* (Scottish Gaelic) 'beside'; *a* (Scottish Gaelic) 'the'; *bhile* (Scottish Gaelic) 'thicket'.

Coulter (South Lanarkshire) 'The back land'. *Cul* (Scottish Gaelic) 'back' or 'rear'; *tir* (Scottish Gaelic) 'land'. Also found as Culter.

Coupar Angus (Perth & Kinross) So named, when in the former county of Angus, to distinguish it from Cupar in Fife. Perhaps derived as Cupar, from *comphairt* (Scottish Gaelic) 'common grazing'.

Cove (Argyll & Bute, Aberdeenshire) 'Hut'. *Kofi* (Old Norse) 'hut'. Cove Bay in Cowal and south of Aberdeen are therefore not as tautologous as they sound.

Cowal (Argyll & Bute) The name of this Highland peninsula lying between Loch Fyne and the Firth of Clyde is a corruption of *Comhgall*, the name of one of King Fergus of Ulster's sons, who was also a chief of the Dalriad Scots in the 6th century.

Cowcaddens (Glasgow) 'Hazel nook'. *Cuil* (Scottish Gaelic) 'corner' or 'nook'; *calldainn* (Scottish Gaelic) 'of hazels'.

Cowdenbeath (Fife) Possibly 'Cowden's (land) by the birches'. *Cowden* (personal name) suggested by the earliest available record in 1626, which refers to the place as 'terris de Cowdounesbaithe'. The second element is certainly derived as *beith* (Scottish Gaelic) 'birch'.

Cowdenknowes (Borders) 'Hazel knolls'. *Calltuin* (Scottish Gaelic) 'hazel'; *knowes* (Scots) 'knolls'. Recorded in 1559 as Coldenknollis.

Cowie (Stirling) 'Wood'. *Coille* (Scottish Gaelic) 'wood'.

Coylum (Highland) 'Gorge leap'. *Cuing* (Scottish Gaelic) 'gorge'; *leum* (Scottish Gaelic) 'leap'.

Craigellachie (Moray) 'Rock of the stony place'. *Creag* (Scottish Gaelic) 'rock' or 'crag'; *ealeachaidh* (Scottish Gaelic from Old Irish *ailech*) 'stony'.

Craigendoran (Argyll & Bute) 'Rock of the waters'. *Creag* (Scottish Gaelic) 'rock'; *an t-* (Scottish Gaelic) 'of the'; *dobhráinn* (Scottish Gaelic) 'waters'.

Craigentinny (Midlothian) 'Rock of the fire'. *Creag* (Scottish Gaelic) 'rock'; *an* (Scottish Gaelic) 'of'; *teine* (Scottish Gaelic) 'fire', indicating a signal point. 'Fox's rock' has been suggested, from *an t-Sionnaich* (Scottish Gaelic) 'of the fox', but the Gaelic form, *Creag an Teine*, is against this derivation.

Craiglockhart (Edinburgh) 'Rock of the ship-station' or 'camp place'. *Creag* (Scottish Gaelic) 'rock'; *luing* (Scottish Gaelic) 'ship'; *phort* (Scottish Gaelic) 'landing-place'.

Craigmillar (Edinburgh) 'Rock of the bare height'. *Creag* (Scottish Gaelic) 'rock'; *maol* (Scottish Gaelic) 'bare' or 'bald'; *ard* (Scottish Gaelic) 'height'.

Craignure (Argyll & Bute) 'Yew tree rock'. *Creag* (Scottish Gaelic) 'rock'; *an* (Scottish Gaelic) 'of'; *iubhair* (Scottish Gaelic) 'yew tree'. The mention of the yew trees may indicate an old burial ground at this Mull ferry port.

Craigroyston (Argyll & Bute) 'Drostan's rock'. *Creag* (Scottish Gaelic) 'rock'; *Drostan* (Scottish Gaelic personal name from Pictish *Drust*). Drostan was reputed to be a 7th-century holy man. The 'roy' element appears to have been interpolated by popular etymology linking the name with the local hero, Rob Roy MacGregor.

Crail (Fife) 'Boulder rock'. *Carr* (Old Gaelic) 'boulder'; *ail* (Old Gaelic) 'rock'. This ancient port of the East Neuk of Fife was recorded as Caraile in 1153, showing the two elements of this apparent tautology. The dangerous Carr Rocks, guarded by a lightship, lie three miles offshore to the east in the Firth of Forth.

Cramond (Edinburgh) 'Fort on the River Almond'. *Caer* (Brythonic) 'fort'; and *see* **Almond**. There was a Roman fort here and evidence of a port town has been discovered.

Crarae (Argyll & Bute) Perhaps 'Boggy place'. *Cràthrach* (Scottish Gaelic) 'boggy place' but the Gaelic form of the name is *Carr-eibhe*, suggesting *carr* (Old Gaelic) 'boulder', and perhaps *eighe*, 'file'.

Crathie (Aberdeenshire) Perhaps 'shaking place', a reference to boggy ground. The Gaelic form is *Craichidh* but an older *Crathaigh* has been postulated, cognate with Cray in Glen Shee and with Achray.

Crawford (South Lanarkshire) 'Crow's ford'. *Craw* (Scots) 'crow', also a surname.

Crawfordjohn (South Lanarkshire) 'Crow's ford of John'. Recorded as Craufurd Johnne in 1275. John was the son-in-law of Baldwin, Sheriff of Lanark.

Creetown (Dumfries & Galloway) 'Town on the boundary stream'. *Crìoch* (Scottish Gaelic) 'boundary' – in this instance, the River Cree.

Creich (Highland, Dumfries & Galloway) 'Boundary place' or possibly 'tree place'. The Gaelic form is *Craoich*, which could derive from *craobh* (Scottish Gaelic) 'tree'; *critheach* (Scottish Gaelic) 'aspen' is also possible.

Crianlarich (Stirling) Possibly 'little pass'. *Crion* (Scottish Gaelic) 'little'; *lairig* (Scottish Gaelic) 'pass'. This would describe the situation of the village at the junction of Glen Dochart and Glen Falloch. Some authorities have suggested another Scottish Gaelic derivation, namely *critheann*, 'aspen tree' and *laraich*, 'house-site' or 'ruin'.

Crieff (Perth & Kinross) Place 'among the trees'. *Craobh* (Scottish Gaelic locative) 'tree'. An early record shows it as Craoibh.

Criffel (Dumfries & Galloway) 'Split fell'. *Kryfja* (Old Norse) 'to split'; *fjalr* (Old Norse) 'hill' or 'fell'. The name of this distinctive hill (1,868 feet/571 metres) near Dalbeattie was recorded in 1330 as Crefel.

Crimond (Aberdeenshire) 'Hill-mound'. *Crech* (Old Gaelic) 'hilltop'; *monadh* (Scottish Gaelic) 'hill' or 'mountain'. Older forms are Creithmo(n)de in the 14th century and Crechmond in the 16th century.

Crinan (Argyll & Bute) The derivation 'place of the Creones' has been tentatively suggested. This was one of the tribes identified by Ptolemy (AD 150). The Pre-Celtic root-form is *cre-* and the Gaelic form of the name is *Crìanan*.

Cromalt, River (Highland) 'Crooked river'. *Crom* (Scottish Gaelic) 'bending' or 'crooked'; *allt* (Scottish Gaelic) 'river'. The Cromalt gives its name to the surrounding rugged hills.

Cromarty (Highland) Perhaps 'little place by the bend'. *Crom* (Scottish Gaelic) 'crooked'; *ach* (Scottish Gaelic particle indicating place); *-an* (Scottish Gaelic diminutive suffix). The description suits this former county town lying in the hook-shaped bay formed by the South Sutor at the tip of the Black Isle Peninsula. Records show an earlier Old Gaelic form as Crumbathyn in 1263, which had altered to Cromardy by 1398, and Cromarte in 1565.

Cromdale (Moray) 'Bent haugh'. *Crom* (Scottish Gaelic) 'bent'; *dail* (Scottish Gaelic) 'meadow' or 'haugh'. The slopes here are known as the Haughs of Cromdale, the site of a battle, in 1690, when a government army defeated a Jacobite Highland force.

Crook of Devon (Perth & Kinross) 'Bend of Devon'. *Krókr* (Old Norse) 'crook' or 'bend'. The River Devon here takes a sharp turn westwards into Glen Devon. Crook of Alves in Moray has the same meaning. *See also* **Caldercruix**.

Crossmyloof (Glasgow) 'Cross of Malduff'. *Crois* (Scottish Gaelic) 'cross'; *Maolduibh* (Scottish Gaelic proper name) 'Malduff', literally 'bald dark one'. The similarity to 'Cross my palm' (*loof* [Scots] 'palm') is accidental.

Crossraguel (South Ayrshire) 'Cross of the bare fort'. 'Bare' probably means without a tower. *Crois* (Scottish Gaelic) 'cross'; *rathaig.* (Scottish Gaelic) 'small fort'; *maol* (Scottish Gaelic) 'bare'.

Croy (North Lanarkshire, Highland, South Ayrshire) 'Hard place'. *Cruadh* (Scottish Gaelic) 'hard'.

Cruachan, Ben (Argyll & Bute) 'The heaped or haunched mountain'. *Cruach* (Scottish Gaelic) 'pile' or 'stack'; *cruachann* (Scottish Gaelic) 'thigh' or 'haunch'. This steep mountain (3,695 feet/1,129 metres) rises above the Pass of Brander. Its name is often used without the prefix 'Ben', especially in Gaelic.

Cuillin (Highland) Possibly 'high rocks'. *Kiolen* (Old Norse) 'high rocks' or 'ridge'. Traditionally, this Skye mountain range, a favourite among rock-climbers, was thought to have been named after the Celtic hero Cuchulainn and earlier texts refer to the Cuchulin Hills. However, this is probably through late association of similar-looking names, even though the young Cuchulainn was said to have learned the art of war from the female warrior, Scathach, on Skye. A Norse origin, as with many other Hebridean mountains, is more likely. The mountains of Rum are also referred to as Cuillins.

Culbin (Moray) 'Back of the hill'. *Cul* (Scottish Gaelic) 'back'; *bheinne* (Scottish Gaelic) 'of the mountain'. Culbin is known for its extensive sand dunes, which cover a once-flourishing village.

Cullen (Moray) 'Holly'. *Culeann* (Scottish Gaelic) 'holly'.

Culloden (Highland) Possibly, at the 'back of the little pool'. *Cul* (Scottish Gaelic) 'back' or 'ridge'; *lodair* (Scottish Gaelic) 'little pool'. A document of 1238 records the name as Cullodyn. The moor here (also known as Drummossie) was the site, in April 1746, of the last full-scale battle fought in Scotland, in which the Jacobite army of Prince Charles Edward Stewart was defeated by Hanoverian Government troops under the Duke of Cumberland.

Culross [Koo-ross] (Fife) Possibly 'holly wood'. *Culeann* (Scottish Gaelic) 'holly'; *ros* (Scottish Gaelic) 'wood'. Records show Culenros in 1110.

Cults (Aberdeen) 'Woods'. *Coillte* (Scottish Gaelic) 'woods'. The terminal *-s* has been added in the Scots form to maintain the plural.

Culzean (South Ayrshire) 'Nook of birds'. *Cuil* (Scottish Gaelic) 'nook' or 'corner'; *ean* (Scottish Gaelic) 'of birds'.

Cumbernauld (North Lanarkshire) The 'meeting of the burns'. *Comar* (Scottish Gaelic) 'river confluence'; *na* (Scottish Gaelic) 'of the'; *allt* (Scottish Gaelic) 'stream' or 'burn'. Recorded as Cumyrnald in 1417. The original village here still has a burn flowing through it, which joins another nearby.

Cumbrae (North Ayrshire) Apparently 'island of the Cumbrians'. *Cymry* (Brythonic tribal name of the Cumbrian people who inhabited southern Scotland in early times); *ey* (Old Norse) 'island'. Recorded as Kumbrey in 1270 and Cumbraye in 1330.

Cuminestown (Aberdeenshire) 'Town of the Comyns or Cummings'. A reminder of the powerful Comyns of medieval times, Earls of Buchan and, at times, *de facto* rulers of the country.

Cumnock (East Ayrshire) Perhaps, 'crooked hill'. *Cam* (Scottish Gaelic) 'crooked' or 'sloping'; *cnoc* (Scottish Gaelic) 'hill'. It was recorded as Comnocke in 1297, Cunnok in 1461 and Canknok in 1548.

Cunningham (North Ayrshire, East Ayrshire) This Ayrshire district name is of obscure but probably Celtic origin. Attempts have been made to identify *cuinneag* (Scottish Gaelic) 'milk pail' (*see* **Quinag**) in the name. In 1153, it was recorded as Cunegan. It is also found as Cunninghame.

Cupar (Fife) Possibly, the 'common (land)'. *Comhpairt* (Scottish Gaelic) 'common pasture'. Some authorities believe that this ancient market town has a Pre-Celtic derivation. Recorded as Cupre in 1183.

Curly Wee (Dumfries & Galloway) The name of this hill (2,405 feet/729 metres) has been derived as 'windy bend'. *Cuir* (Scottish Gaelic) 'bend'; *le* (Scottish Gaelic) 'in the'; *gaoith* (Scottish Gaelic) 'wind'. *Cor* (Old Irish) 'hill' has also been suggested.

Currie (Midlothian) 'Boggy land'. *Currach* (Scottish Gaelic) 'bogland' or 'marshy area'. Now a south-western suburb of Edinburgh, the site of the original settlement was on low-lying land by the Water of Leith.

Cursetter (Orkney) 'Cow pasture'. *Ky-r* (Old Norse) 'cows'; *saetr* (Old Norse) 'pasture land'.

Cushnie (Aberdeenshire) 'Cold, frosty'. *Cuisneach* (Scottish Gaelic) 'frosty' or 'freezing'. This may be an example of an apotropaic place name, deliberately given to ward off the quality it describes.

D

Dairsie (Fife) The first part of the name appears to be 'oak', whether from *dairor* (Gaelic) or *derw* (Brythonic). The second part is uncertain. It has been tentatively identified with *beus* (Gaelic), which among other things means 'fornication'. If correct, it may refer to oak-grove rites. This is one of the few locations with an alternative name, here Osnaburgh, from an Old Norse personal name, with *burgh* (Scots, from Old Norse *borgr*) 'fort'.

Dalbeattie (Dumfries & Galloway) 'Meadow of the birch trees'. *Dail* (Scottish Gaelic) 'meadow'; *beitheach* (Scottish Gaelic) 'birch tree'. The town is enclosed by a bend in the River Urr. Recorded as Dalbaty in 1469.

Dalcross (Highland) 'Spit of the promontory'. *Dealg* (Scottish Gaelic) 'point'; *an* (Scottish Gaelic) 'of the'; *rois* (Scottish Gaelic) 'promontory'.

Dalgetty (Fife) 'Windy field'. *Dail* (Scottish Gaelic) 'field'; *gaoithe* (Scottish Gaelic) 'of the winds'. A suitable name for the exposed coastal setting of this residential township.

Dalguise (Perth & Kinross) 'Haugh of fir'. *Dail* (Scottish Gaelic) 'haugh' or 'meadow'; *giuthas* (Scottish Gaelic) 'fir'.

Dalkeith (Midlothian) 'Field by the wood'. *Dol* (Brythonic) 'field';

coed (Brythonic) 'wood'. Early documents show Dalkied in 1140, Dolchet in 1144 and Dalketh in 1145.

Dallas (Moray, Highland) 'Field by the waterfall'. *Dail* (Scottish Gaelic) 'field'; *eas* (Scottish Gaelic) 'waterfall'. Dallas near Edderton in Ross-shire (Gaelic, *Dalais*) has been derived from *dol* (Brythonic-Pictish) 'plateau'; and *-ais* (Brythonic-Pictish suffix denoting place).

Dalmally (Argyll & Bute) 'Site of Màillidh's church'. *Dail* (Scottish Gaelic) 'field', belonging specifically in this case to the church, from Old Gaelic *dol*; and *Màillidh* (Old Gaelic proper name). Màillidh appears to have been a holy man whose name is commemorated in a number of places.

Dalmarnock (Perth & Kinross) 'Site of Marnock's church'. *Dail* (Scottish Gaelic) 'field', belonging specifically in this case to the church, from Old Gaelic *dol*; and *Mernóc* (Old Gaelic proper name).

Dalmeny (West Lothian) Perhaps 'My Ethne's meadow'. *Dail* (Scottish Gaelic) 'meadow'; *mo* (Old Gaelic) 'my'; *Eithne* (Old Gaelic proper name). As the mother of St Columba, Ethne was a revered figure, though other saintly women also bore the name. *See* **Kilmany**. But older forms include Dumanie in 1180 and Dunmany in 1296, suggesting *dùn* (Scottish Gaelic) 'fort', from Brythonic *din*, perhaps with Brythonic *meini*, 'stones'.

Dalmuir (Dumbarton, Clydebank) 'The big field'. *Dail* (Scottish Gaelic) 'field'; *mòr* (Scottish Gaelic) 'big'.

Dalnacardoch (Highland) 'The tinker's field'. *Dail* (Scottish Gaelic) 'field'; *na* (Scottish Gaelic) 'of the'; *ceard* (Scottish Gaelic) 'tinker' or 'tinsmith'; *-ach* (Scottish Gaelic suffix denoting place).

Dalnaspidal (Perth & Kinross) 'Field of the refuge'. *Dail* (Scottish Gaelic) 'field; *nan* (Scottish Gaelic) 'of'; *spideal* (Scottish Gaelic) 'refuge' or 'hospice'. This place is located just south of the Pass of Drumochter, a natural site for a travellers' refuge.

Dalry (Dumfries & Galloway, Strathclyde) The derivation is not clear; it may be 'field of the heather'. *Dail* (Scottish Gaelic) 'field'; *fhraoich* (Scottish Gaelic) 'heather'; or the latter part may be *righ* (Gaelic) 'slope', as in Portree. It has also been suggested that the Dumfries-shire village, known in full as St John's Town of Dalry, had associations with King James IV and could be derived as 'the king's meadow', from *righ* (Scottish Gaelic) 'king'.

Dalserf (Fife) 'Place of St Serf's church'. *Dail* (Scottish Gaelic) 'field', in this case belonging specifically to the church, from *dol* (Old Gaelic); and *Serf* (a proper name from *servus* (Latin) 'slave'). St Serf, founder of the church at Culross, has strong associations with the Fife area.

Dalrymple (South Ayrshire) 'Field of the winding pool'. *Dail* (Scottish Gaelic) 'field'; *crom* (Scottish Gaelic) 'bent' or 'winding'; *poll* (Scottish Gaelic) 'pool'. The *c* of *crom* has been lost.

Dalswinton (Dumfries & Galloway) 'Field of the pig-farm'. *Dail* (Scottish Gaelic) 'field'; *swin* (Old English) 'pig'; *tun* (Old English) 'farmstead'. Noted in the 13th century as Dalswynton but earlier it must just have been 'Swynton'.

Dalwhinnie (Highland) Apparently the 'field of the champion'. *Dail* (Scottish Gaelic) 'field'; *cuingid* (Scottish Gaelic) 'champion'. This may refer to some historic or legendary contest.

Dalziel (North Lanarkshire) 'White meadow'. *Dail* (Scottish Gaelic) 'meadow'; *gheal* (Scottish Gaelic) 'white'. There are numerous Dalziels and Dalzells throughout the country. The *z,* as in many other cases, is actually a mis-written *y.*

Darvel (East Ayrshire) Perhaps 'stream by the township'. *Dobhar* (Brythonic-Scottish Gaelic) 'water'; *bhaile* (Scottish Gaelic) 'of the township'.

Dava (Highland) 'Ford of the stags or oxen'. *An* (Scottish Gaelic) 'the'; *damh* (Scottish Gaelic) 'ox' or 'stag'; *àth* (Scottish Gaelic) 'ford'.

Daviot (Highland, Aberdeenshire) It appears to be from an ancient tribal name, latinised as *Demetae.* Its Gaelic form is *Deimhidh*, from a root-form *dem* (Brythonic-Pictish) 'fixed' or 'sure'. It is cognate with the Welsh Dyfed. The two Daviots are small communities, one south of Inverness, the other in Formartine, north-west of Aberdeen.

Davoch of Grange (Moray) This place name, from near Keith, shows the old Scottish Gaelic land-measure term. An anglicised form of *dabhach* (Scottish Gaelic) 'vat', it indicated an area of land whose annual produce would fill a vat of standard size.

Dean, River (Midlothian) 'Valley or den'. *Denu* (Old English) 'dene', a name which corresponds to the steep-banked River Dean in Edinburgh.

Dearg, Ben (Highland, Moray) 'Red mountain'. *Beinn* (Scottish Gaelic) 'mountain'; *dearg* (Scottish Gaelic) 'red'. There are numerous mountains of this name throughout the Highlands and also Carn Deargs.

Dee, River and **Strath** (Aberdeenshire, Dumfries & Galloway) This ancient river name has a complex history, not yet fully explored. Its Gaelic name, *Dé*, has been related to *Dia*, 'god', though the river's gender is feminine. Its Pre-Celtic root is *Deua*, meaning a female divinity and it shares this with the Don. The Galloway Dee is also known as the Black Water of Dee.

Deer (Aberdeenshire, Dumfries & Galloway) 'Forest grove'. *Doire* (Scottish Gaelic) 'grove', normally of oaks, from *daur* (Old Irish Gaelic) 'oak'.

Delny (Highland) 'Place of thorns'. *Dealgan* (Scottish Gaelic) 'thorn'; *-ach* (Scottish Gaelic suffix indicating place).

Denholm (Borders, Dumfries & Galloway) 'Island in the valley'. *Denu* (Old English) 'valley'; *holmr* (Old English) 'river island'.

Denny (Falkirk) Presumably 'valley'. *Denu* (Old English) 'valley'. This industrial town lies in the Carron Valley near the site of the famous iron works. Nearby is Dennyloanhead, 'valley at the head of the lane'.

Deveron (Aberdeenshire) 'Black Earn'. This river was originally called *Eron*, perhaps from *Erin* (Old Irish), like several others, or more probably, from an older Pre-Celtic source. *See* **Earn**. *Dubh* (Scottish Gaelic) 'dark' is a later prefix, perhaps to distinguish this river from the Findhorn, as with the Adder rivers in the borders.

Devon, River and **Glen** (Perth & Kinross) 'Black stream'. *Dub* (Old Irish) 'black'; *-ona* (Pre-Celtic suffix) 'water' or 'river'. It has also been suggested that it may stem from a conjectured Brythonic word *domnona*, 'deep one' or 'mysterious one', cognate with -dovan names like Baldovan.

Diabaig (Highland) 'Deep bay'. *Djúp* (Old Norse) 'deep'; *vik* (Old Norse) 'bay'.

Dingwall (Highland) 'Parliament field'. *Thing* (Old Norse) 'parliament' or 'assembly'; *vollr* (Old Norse) 'field' or 'open space'. This indicates the site of an annual meeting to make laws and administer justice in the days of Viking occupation. Exact parallels to the name are found in other areas of Norse influence, for example Tynwald Hill on the Isle of Man, Tingwall on Shetland and Tinwald in Dumfries & Galloway.

Dinnet (Aberdeenshire) 'Place of refuge'. *Dìon* (Scottish Gaelic) 'shelter'; *ait* (Scottish Gaelic) 'place'.

Divie, River (Moray) 'Dark water'. The Gaelic name is *Duibhe*, 'dark'.

Dochart, River and **Glen** (Stirling) Perhaps 'high field measure'. *Dabhach* (Scottish Gaelic) 'field measure'; *ard* (Scottish Gaelic) 'high'.

Docharty, Glen (Highland) This may have the same derivation as Dochart. *Dochair* in current Gaelic means 'hurt', 'misery' or 'pain', and *dochairt* means 'sick' – possible but unlikely name sources.

Dochfour (Highland) 'Pasture area'. *Dabhach* (Scottish Gaelic field measure); *phùir* (Scottish Gaelic) 'pasture'.

Doll, Glen (Angus) 'Glen of the meadows'. *Dol* (Old Gaelic) 'meadow' or 'valley'.

Dollar (Clackmannanshire) Place by the 'ploughed field'. *Dol* (Brythonic) 'field'; *ar* (Brythonic) 'arable' or 'ploughed'. The name applies to the fertile lands here by the River Devon at the foot of the Ochil Hills. There is a local legend relating to the nearby Castle Campbell as 'Castle Gloom', between the burns of 'Dolour' and 'Grief' but with no etymological backing. 'Gloom' is *glòm* (Scottish Gaelic), *see* **Glomach**.

Dolphinton (Midlothian) 'Dolfin's place'. A charter of 1253 records this as Dolfinston. *Dolfin* was the brother of the first Earl of Dunbar.

Don, River (Aberdeenshire) The Gaelic name is *Deathan*, from the same root source as its neighbour the Dee. *Deua* (Pre-Celtic) 'god', with the suffix *-ona* indicating 'water' or 'river'. The belief in a river-spirit is indicated. *See* **Dee**.

Donibristle (Fife) 'Breasal's fort'. *Dùnadh* (Scottish Gaelic) 'camp'; *Breasail* (Old Irish personal name).

Doon, River and **Loch** (East Ayrshire, North Ayrshire) The same name as Don, from the same root, *deu-ona* (Pre-Celtic) 'river god'.

Dorain, Ben (Argyll & Bute) 'Hill of the streamlets'. *Dobhráinn* (Scottish Gaelic) 'of streams' and linked with *dobhar* (Brythonic) 'water' or 'stream'. Rising above Glen Orchy, this is the mountain (3,524 feet/1,077 metres) celebrated in the Gaelic verses of Duncan Bán MacIntyre.

Dores (Highland) 'Black woods'. *Dubh* (Scottish Gaelic) 'black'; *ros* (Old Gaelic) 'wood'.

Dorlinn (Argyll & Bute, Highland) 'Tidal isthmus'. *Doirlinn* (Scottish Gaelic) 'piece of land submerged by the tide'. Among the dorlinns are those joining Oronsay to Morvern and Erraid to the Ross of Mull (used by R L Stevenson in *Kidnapped*).

Dornie (Highland) Place of 'pebbles'. *Dornach* (Scottish Gaelic) 'with pebbles'. There is a pebbly spit here where Loch Long and Loch Duich join with Loch Alsh.

Dornoch (Highland) Place of 'pebbles'. *Dornach* (Scottish Gaelic) 'with pebbles' or 'fist-size stones'. The root-word *dorn* means 'fist'. Today, the beach here on the Dornoch Firth is mainly sandy. The name was recorded as Durnach in 1150.

Douglas (Dumfries & Galloway) 'Dark water'. *Dubh* (Scottish Gaelic) 'black'; *glas* (Scottish Gaelic) 'water'.

Doune (Stirling) 'Castle or fortified place'. *Dùn* (Scottish Gaelic) 'fortress'. The town, lying on the River Teith north-west of Stirling, is dominated by the 14th-century Doune Castle, although earlier fortifications existed here.

Dounby (Orkney) 'Township by the fort'. *Dùn* (Scottish Gaelic) 'fort'; *by* (Old Norse) 'township'.

Dounreay (Highland) Possibly 'fortified rath'. *Dùn* (Scottish Gaelic) 'fortified place'; *rath* (Scottish Gaelic) 'circular fort' or 'broch'. Britain's first experimental fast nuclear reactor, now decommissioned, is located here.

Dowally (Perth & Kinross) 'Black cliff'. *Dubh* (Scottish Gaelic) 'black'; *àille* (Scottish Gaelic) 'cliff'. Also found as a field or farm name in related forms, such as Dowald.

Dreghorn (Edinburgh) 'Dry house'. *Dryge* (Old English) 'dry'; *erne* (Old English) 'house'. This Edinburgh district is now the site of a large barracks.

Drem (East Lothian) 'Ridge'. *Druim* (Scottish Gaelic) 'ridge' or 'hump'.

Dron (Perth & Kinross) 'Ridge' or 'hump' from *dron* (Scottish Gaelic). Numerous names incorporate 'Dron' as an element, sometimes in the form Drungan (Dumfries & Galloway), from *dronnan* (Scottish Gaelic) 'little ridge'. *See also* **Drunkie**.

Drum (most regions) 'Ridge'. *Druim* (Scottish Gaelic) originally meaning 'back' and related to *dorsum* (Latin) 'back', is found as a local place name in many parts, as well as a prefix to many hill names.

Drumalban 'The ridge of Scotland'. This is the name of the great spinal watershed that runs from central to northern Scotland. *Druim* (Scottish Gaelic) 'ridge'; and *Albainn*, 'of Scotland', from *Alba* (Scottish Gaelic name for Scotland north of the Forth).

Drumchapel (Glasgow) 'Ridge of the horse'. *Druim* (Scottish Gaelic) 'ridge'; *chapuill* (Scottish Gaelic) 'horse'. This large housing estate was built in the 1950s on the western edge of Glasgow as part of the city's post-war 'overspill' programme to relieve overcrowding in the inner areas.

Drumbeg (Highland) 'Little ridge'. *Druim* (Scottish Gaelic) 'ridge' or 'hump'; *beag* (Scottish Gaelic) 'small'.

Drumbuie (Highland) 'Yellow ridge'. *Druim* (Scottish Gaelic) 'ridge' or 'hump'; *buidhe* (Scottish Gaelic) 'yellow'.

Drumclog (South Lanarkshire) 'Ridge of the rock' or 'of the bell'. *Druim* (Scottish Gaelic) 'ridge' or 'hump'; *clog* may be either 'rock' or 'crag' (Brythonic) or 'bell' (Scottish Gaelic).

Drumlanrig (Dumfries & Galloway) 'Bare ridge'. *Druim* (Scottish Gaelic) 'ridge' or 'hump'; *llanerch* (Brythonic) 'clear space'.

Drummond (Perth & Kinross, Highland) 'Humped mount'. *Druim* (Scottish Gaelic) 'ridge' or 'hump'; *monadh* (Scottish Gaelic) 'mountain'.

Drumnadrochit (Highland) 'Ridge by the bridge'. *Druim* (Scottish Gaelic) 'ridge'; *na* (Scottish Gaelic) 'of the'; *drochaid* (Scottish Gaelic) 'bridge'. An apt description of this place where there has long been a bridge over the River Enrick beneath a very steep ridge on the western bank of Loch Ness.

Drumochter (Highland, Perth & Kinross) 'Top of the ridge'. *Druim*

(Scottish Gaelic) 'ridge'; *uachdar* (Scottish Gaelic) 'the top of' or 'the upper part'. The name of the mountain pass carrying the main road and railway line from the South to Inverness and the highest point of a mainline railway in Britain (1,484 feet/454 metres).

Drumpellier (North Lanarkshire) 'Fort of spears'. Noted in 1203 as Dunpeleder. *Din* (Brythonic) 'fort'; *peledyr* (Brythonic) 'of spears'. The transformation of *din* to *drum* was presumably through association with other Gaelic or gaelicised names.

Drunkie, Loch (Stirling) 'Loch of the litle ridge'. *Loch* (Scottish Gaelic) 'lake' or 'loch'; *dronnaig* (Scottish Gaelic) 'little ridge' or 'knoll'.

Dryburgh (Borders) 'Fort town'. *Dryge* (Old English) 'fort'; *burh* (Old English) 'town', 'borough' or 'burgh'. Early records show Drieburh in 1160 and Dryburg in 1211. *Dryge* (Old English) 'dry' has also been suggested, though it does not seem particularly appropriate.

Dryhope (Borders) Perhaps 'fortified hollow' or 'dry hollow'. *Dryge* (Old English) 'fort' or 'dry'; *hop* (Old English) 'hollow' or 'land enclosed by hills'. Dryhope was a nest of Border Reivers.

Drymen (Stirling) 'On the ridge'. *Drumein* (Scottish Gaelic dative/locative of *druim)* 'on the ridge'. An apt description of the situation of this village to the north-west of Glasgow.

Duart (Argyll & Bute) 'Black point'. *Dubh* (Scottish Gaelic) 'black'; *àird* (Scottish Gaelic) 'cape' or 'point'. This is the promontory site of Duart Castle, the Maclean stronghold on Mull.

Duddingston (Edinburgh) 'Dodin's farmstead'. *Dodin* (Old English proper name); *tun* (Old English) 'farm' or 'village'.

Dufftown (Moray) Town founded and laid out in 1817 by James Duff (*dubh* [Gaelic] 'black'), the 4th Earl of Fife, after whom it is named.

Duffus (Moray) 'Black stance'. *Dubh* (Scottish Gaelic) 'black'; *fas* (Scottish Gaelic) 'stance' or 'station'. A place where a drover might rest his herd overnight.

Duich, Loch (Highland) 'Duthac's loch'. *Loch* (Scottish Gaelic) 'lake' or 'loch'; *Dubhthaich* (Scottish Gaelic personal name) 'of Duthac'. St Duthac was a venerated figure. *See* **Black Isle, Tain.**

Duirinish (Highland) 'Deer's ness'. *Dyr* (Old Norse) 'deer'; *nes* (Old Norse) 'point' or 'headland'. *See* **Durness.**

Duisk, River (South Ayrshire) 'Black water'. *Dubh* (Scottish Gaelic) 'black'; *uisge* (Scottish Gaelic) 'water'.

Dull (Perth & Kinross) 'Field or haugh'. *Dail* (Scottish Gaelic) 'meadow'. A very common prefix in place names but rarely appears on its own.

Dullatur (North Lanarkshire) 'Dark slopes'. *Dubh* (Scottish Gaelic) 'black'; *leitir* (Scottish Gaelic) 'hillside'.

Dulnain, River (Highland) 'Flood stream'. *Tuil* (Scottish Gaelic) 'flood', with *-ean* suffix indicating a stream. Rising in the Monadhliath Mountains, this swift river is liable to sudden floods.

Dumbarton (West Dunbartonshire) 'Stronghold of the Britons'. *Dùn* (Scottish Gaelic) 'fortified stronghold'; *Breatainn* (Scottish Gaelic) 'Britons'. Records from 1300 to 1450 show Dunbretane. This fort, on a steep rock, was the capital of the ancient kingdom of Strathclyde between the 5th and 11th centuries and played an important part in medieval Scottish history. The official and postal name of its county, Dunbartonshire, shows a more 'correct' form, though the change back from *m* to *n* was made in modern times.

Dumfries (Dumfries & Galloway) 'Fortress of the woodland'. *Dùn* (Scottish Gaelic) 'fortified stronghold'; *phris* (Scottish Gaelic genitive of *preas*) 'of the woodland copse'.

Dumfries & Galloway Official name of the south-western administrative region of Scotland, formed in 1975 and covering the former counties of Dumfries, Kirkcudbright and Wigtown.

Dumyat (Stirling) 'Hill of the Maeatae'. *Dùn* (Scottish Gaelic) originally indicated 'a hill', but so many hilltop sites were fortified that it acquired the sense of 'hill fort'. The name also incorporates the name of one of the tribes identified by the Romans, whose territory was close to the eventual line of Antonine's Wall. This hill (1,366 feet/418 metres) rises steeply above Bridge of Allan, controlling access north and east. Myot Hill, not far away, also appears to preserve the name of the Maeatae.

Dunadd (Argyll & Bute) 'Fortress of the Add'. *Dùn* (Scottish Gaelic) 'fort'. The etymology of *Add* is unclear, though it is presumably from the name of the adjacent River Add. The oldest recorded spelling is

Dun At. This was an important centre of the Dalriadic Scots, perhaps their capital, with a ritual stone still to be seen on its summit.

Dunbar (East Lothian) 'Fort on the height'. *Dùn* (Scottish Gaelic) 'fort'; *barr* (Scottish Gaelic) 'height'. A castle was built on the high rocks above the port's natural harbour but it was destroyed in 1650 by Cromwell's army, following their victory in battle here.

Dunbeath (Highland) 'Hill of birches'. *Dùn* (Scottish Gaelic) 'hill' or 'mound'; *beith* (Scottish Gaelic) 'birch tree'.

Dunblane (Stirling) 'Fort of St Blane'. *Dùn* (Scottish Gaelic) 'fort'; *Bláán* (Old Irish proper name) Blane. This was said to be St Blane's chief monastery and perhaps for that reason it is awarded the designation 'Dun-' rather than the more usual 'Kil-'.

Duncansby Head (Highland) 'Cape of Dungal's place'. *Dungal* (Old Gaelic proper name); *by* (Old Norse) 'village' or 'place'. Clearly Dungal made himself memorable to the Norsemen for his name to be preserved in this way.

Dundee Commonly derived as the 'fort of Daig'. *Dùn* (Scottish Gaelic) 'fortified place'; *Daig* (personal name of unknown connection). The fort presumably would have been on the high ground of Dundee Law, where the 13th-century Dundee Castle, long since destroyed, once stood. Other possible derivations include *Dun-dubh* (Scottish Gaelic) 'dark hill' or *Dun-Dè* (Scottish Gaelic genitive of *Dia*) 'hill of God'. The suggestion of Dun-Tay, 'fort on the Tay', has been discredited. There are various renderings in early records, from Donde in 1177 and Dunde in 1199 to Dundho and Dundo in 1200.

Dundonnell (Highland) 'Donald's fort'. *Dùn* (Scottish Gaelic) 'fort'; *Domhnuill* (Scottish Gaelic proper name) 'Donald'.

Dundurn (Perth & Kinross) 'Fort of the fist'. *Dùn* (Scottish Gaelic) 'fort'; *dorn* (Scottish Gaelic) 'fist'.

Dunedin *see* **Edinburgh**.

Dunfermline (Fife). The first part is *dùn* (Scottish Gaelic) 'hill' or 'fort'. The latter part is of uncertain derivation and may be a version of a Pictish proper name. Records show Dumfermelyn in 1100, Dumferlin in 1124 and Dunferlyne in 1375. The Gaelic name is *Dun Pharlain*, perhaps by association with the personal name Parlain, as in MacFarlane. The town became the capital of Malcolm Canmore's dynasty and its abbey, founded in 1072, is a royal burial place.

Dunipace (Falkirk) 'Hill of the pass'. *Din* (Brythonic) 'hill', rendered into the Gaelic *dùn*; *y* (Brythonic) 'of the'; *pás* (Brythonic) 'hill pass'.

Dunkeld (Perth & Kinross) 'Fort of the Caledonians'. *Dùn* (Scottish Gaelic) 'fort'; *Chailleainn* (Scottish Gaelic) 'Caledonians' – referring to the tribe of Picts who had a royal stronghold here in the first millennium. Early records reveal the name as Duincaillen in 865 and Dun-calden and Dunicallenn in 1000. In the 9th century, the town was the religious centre of the country, between the abandoning of Iona and the establishment of St Andrews, and it retains its cathedral.

Dunlop (East Ayrshire) 'Fort of the bend'. *Dùn* (Scottish Gaelic) 'fort'; *luib* (Scottish Gaelic) 'bend'.

Dunnet (Highland) 'Fort on the headland'. *Dùn* (Scottish Gaelic) 'fort'; *hofudr* (Old Norse) 'headland'. Dunnet Head is the most northerly point on the Scottish mainland.

Dunnichen (Angus) 'Nechtan's fort'. *Dùn* (Scottish Gaelic) 'fort'; *Nechtan* (Pictish proper name). Here, in 686, the army of Nechtan, the Pictish king, defeated the invading Angles.

Dunollie (Argyll & Bute) 'Ollach's Fort'. *Dùn* (Scottish Gaelic) 'fort'; *Ollaig* (Old Irish proper name). Strategically placed to control the Firth of Lorn and the Sound of Mull, it remained an important castle until relatively modern times.

Dunoon (Argyll & Bute) 'Fort (on) the river'. *Dùn* (Scottish Gaelic) 'fort'; *obhainn* (Scottish Gaelic adjectival variant of *abh*) 'river'. Recorded as Dunhoven in 1270 and Dunnovane in 1476. Traces of a 12th-century castle, and possibly an even earlier fort, can be found on a rock above the pier of this resort on the Clyde.

Dunottar (Aberdeenshire) 'Fort on the shelving ground'. *Dùn* (Scottish Gaelic) 'fort'; *faithir* (Scottish Gaelic) 'shelved or terraced slope'. The reference is to the slope on the landward side towards the castle on its rocky outcrop. The oldest reference is Duin-fother in 7th century.

Dunphail (Moray) 'Fort with the palisade'. *Dùn* (Scottish Gaelic) 'fort';

fàl (Scottish Gaelic) 'hedge' or 'palisade'. The reference is to an early fortification of wood rather than of stone.

Dunragit (Dumfries & Galloway) 'Fort of Rheged'. *Dùn* (Scottish Gaelic) 'fort'. A centre of the old Brythonic province of Rheged and a part of the kingdom of Strathclyde which stretched from Dumbarton to Westmorland. The motte of Dunragit shows the site of the fort.

Dunrobin (Highland) 'Robert's fort'. *Dùn* (Scottish Gaelic) 'fort'. The Robert in question is the third Earl of Sutherland. Dunrobin was their stronghold but there is the remnant of a broch close by which long antedates the castle.

Dunrossness (Shetland) 'Cape of the roaring whirlpool'. *Dynr* (Old Norse) 'loud noise'; *röst* (Old Norse) 'whirlpool'; *nes* (old Norse) 'cape' or 'point'. There are numerous tidal races called Roosts in the Northern Isles.

Duns (Borders) 'Fortified hill'. *Dùn* (Scottish Gaelic) 'hill' came to acquire the sense of 'fortified hill' and the *s* is a later addition, possibly meant as a plural. The former main town of Berwickshire, it lies at the foot of a hill called Duns Law. An older town, on the hill itself, was razed in 1542. The medieval scholar, Duns Scotus (*circa* 1265–1308), whose name gives the word 'dunce', is reputed to have been born here.

Dunsinane (Perth & Kinross) Perhaps 'hill of the paps or nipples'. *Dùn* (Scottish Gaelic) 'hill'; *sine* (Scottish Gaelic, plural *sineachan*) 'nipple'. Numerous hills and hill features are named after the female breasts.

Dunstaffnage (Argyll & Bute) 'Fort of the pillared cape'. *Dùn* (Scottish Gaelic) 'fort'; *stafr* (Old Norse) 'staff' or 'column'; *nes* (Old Norse) 'cape' or 'point'.

Duntocher (West Dunbartonshire) 'Causeway fort'. *Dùn* (Scottish Gaelic) 'fort'; *tóchar* (Scottish Gaelic) 'causeway' or 'road'. There was a Roman road here, near the end of the Antonine Wall.

Dunvegan (Highland) Possibly 'fort of the few'. *Dùn* (Scottish Gaelic) 'fort'; *beagain* (Scottish Gaelic) 'few in number' or 'small'. The significance is far from apparent. It may refer to an early siege but an old Norse personal name, *Began*, may be more likely. Recorded as Dunbegane in 1498, Dunveggane in 1517 and Dunnevegane in 1553. This castle, in north-west Skye, is the ancestral home of the chiefs of Macleod.

Durness (Highland) 'Headland of the deer'. *Dyr* (Old Norse) 'deer'; *nes* (Old Norse) 'headland'. The village is the most north-westerly on mainland Britain, situated on a remote headland where deer still roam.

Durno (Aberdeenshire) 'Pebbly place'. *Dornach* (Scottish Gaelic) 'pebbly'. The remains of a large Roman camp here suggest that this may have been Agricola's base for the Battle of Mons Graupius in AD 84.

Duror (Highland) 'Hard water'. The name comes from the river in Glen Duror. *Dur* (Scottish Gaelic) 'hard'; *dobhar* (Scottish Gaelic) 'water'.

Durris (Aberdeenshire) 'Black wood'. *Dubh* (Scottish Gaelic) 'black'; *ros* (Old Gaelic) 'wood'.

Durrisdeer (Aberdeenshire) 'Entrance to the forest'. *Dorus* (Scottish Gaelic) 'entrance' or 'entry'; *doire* (Scottish Gaelic) 'forest'.

Duthil (Highland) 'North side'. *Uathail* (Scottish Gaelic) 'north'.

Dyce (Aberdeenshire) Possibly 'southwards'. *Deis* (Scottish Gaelic locative of *deas*) 'to the south'. This may have been a reference to the location of the settlement here, on a south-facing slope. Alternatively, the meaning may be *dys* (Old Norse) 'cairn'.

Dysart (Fife) 'Desert place' or 'hermit's place'. *Diseart* (Scottish Gaelic) 'hermit's place'. The hermit was St Serf, who lived here in a cave for a time and had a conversation with the Devil.

E

Eaglesham (East Renfrewshire) Possibly 'church village'. *Eaglais* (Scottish Gaelic) 'church'; *ham* (Old English) 'village'. Recorded as Egilshame in 1158 and Eglishame in 1309.

Earlsferry (Fife) Established in the 12th century by the Macduff Earls of Fife as a ferry point across the Firth of Forth to North Berwick. Its Scots name suggests that by that time Gaelic names were no longer being given in Fife.

Earlston (Borders) Possibly 'Earcil's hill'. *Earcil* (personal name); *dun* (Old English) 'hill'. Early records show this clearly as Ercheldon in 1144 and Ercildune in 1180.

Earlstoun (Dumfries & Galloway) 'Earl's place'. This locality, with its loch, at the southern end of the Glenkens, takes its name from the Earls of Galloway.

Earn, River, Strath and **Loch** (Perth & Kinross) A Pre-Celtic river name, from a root-form *ar-* indicating flowing water, found in other river names, such as Deveron, and common in parts of France. This is a more likely source than the traditional one of *Erin*, an ancient name linking a mythical goddess-queen with the land itself. The name, *Eireann* (Old Irish) 'of Erin' in this context has been taken as evidence of an eastwards expansion by the Scots from Dalriada in the 6th and 7th centuries.

Eassie (Angus and other regions) 'Water'. *Eas* (Scottish Gaelic) 'water' or 'waterfall'. The *-ie* ending is often found with river names in regions where Pictish was spoken.

East Kilbride (South Lanarkshire) 'Church of (St) Brigid'. *Cill* (Scottish Gaelic) 'church'; *Brigid* (personal name). Brigid was a saint who took on many of the attributes of the legendary Celtic goddess of fire and poetry. East Kilbride was designated as Scotland's first New Town in 1947 but the old village here was recorded as Kellebride in 1180. The 'East' was added later to distinguish it from West Kilbride, 30 miles away, near the Ayrshire coast.

East Linton (East Lothian) 'Flax enclosure'. *Lin* (Old English) 'flax' (compare 'linen'); *tun* (Old English) 'enclosure' or 'village'. It was recorded as Lintun in 1127. The 'East' was added later to distinguish it from West Linton, 30 miles south-west, by the Pentland Hills.

Eathie (Highland) 'Ford' or 'ford stream', from *àth* (Scottish Gaelic) 'ford'. The Gaelic name is *Athaidh* and the *-aidh* suffix is common on stream names in Pictish parts of the country.

Ecclefechan (Dumfries & Galloway) Possibly 'church of (St) Fechin'.

Eaglais (Scottish Gaelic) 'church'; *Fechin* (Irish Gaelic personal name). Followers of this saintly, 7th-century Irish Abbot from Meath, helped in the evangelisation of Scotland. An alternative derivation is *eglwys-bychan* (Brythonic) 'little church'. The birthplace of the writer, Thomas Carlyle (1795–1881), whose home can still be visited.

Eck, Loch (Argyll & Bute) 'Horse loch'. *Loch* (Scottish Gaelic) 'lake' or 'loch'; *each* (Scottish Gaelic) 'horse'. The animal in question may have been a water kelpie or *each uisge*.

Eday (Orkney) 'Island of the isthmus'. *Eidh* (Old Norse) 'isthmus'; *ey* (Old Norse) 'island'.

Edderton (Highland) 'Place between mounds'. *Eadar* (Scottish Gaelic) 'between'; *dùn* (Scottish Gaelic) 'mound' or 'hillock', referring to the glacial drumlin hills of the area.

Eddleston (Borders) 'Edulf's place' from the late 12th century. *Edulf* (Old English proper name); *tun* (Old English) 'farmstead'. Previously recorded as first, *Penteiacob* (Brythonic) 'Headland of James's town', then as Gillemorestun, from *Gillemor* (Scottish Gaelic) 'Gilmour' (a follower of Mary) and *tun -*, indicating three proprietors, from three different language groups, before the name finally became fixed.

Eddrachillis (Highland) 'Place between two kyles'. *Eadar* (Scottish Gaelic) 'between'; *da* (Scottish Gaelic) 'two'; *chaolais* (Scottish Gaelic) 'kyles' or 'narrows'.

Eden, River (Fife, Borders) This river name, also found in Cumberland and Kent in England, is of uncertain origin.

Edinample (Highland) 'Face of the cauldron'. *Aodann* (Scottish Gaelic) 'face'; *ambuill* (Scottish Gaelic) 'of the cauldron' or 'of the vat', a reference to the waterfall at this location.

Edinburgh 'Fort of the rock face'. *Eideann* (Scottish Gaelic corrupted form of *aodann)* 'rock face'; *burh* (Old English) 'stronghold'. The latter element was a replacement for the original *dùn* (Scottish Gaelic) 'stronghold' or 'fort'. *Dún Eideann,* the Gaelic name for the city, is preserved also in Dunedin, New Zealand. The castle early became a royal stronghold. Long the *de facto* capital, its status was confirmed by the establishment of the Court of Session in 1532 and the building of Parliament House in 1632. Since1999, it has been again the seat of the Scottish Parliament.

Ednam (Borders) 'Place on the Eden'. Recorded as Hedenham in the early 14th century. *See* **Eden**.

Edradour (Perth & Kinross) 'Between two waters'. *Eadar* (Scottish Gaelic) 'between'; *dà* (Scottish Gaelic) 'two'; *dhobhar* (Brythonic-Scottish Gaelic) 'waters'.

Edrom (Borders) 'Township on the Adder'. This is one of the few Scottish places with the Old English *-ham* suffix, which seems to have become obsolete around the time the Anglians were establishing themselves in the south-east. The prefix is the river name, Adder.

Edzell (Angus) Perhaps 'running water dale'. From *áa* (Old Norse) 'running water' and *dalr* (Old Norse) 'valley'. Like Edale in the English Peak District but this is an odd location to find a Norse name.

Egilsay (Orkney) 'Church island'. *Eaglais* (Scottish Gaelic) 'church'; *ey* (Old Norse) 'island'.

Eglinton (North Ayrshire) 'Farm of Aegel's folk'. *Aegel* (Old English proper name); *ing* (Old English) 'of the people'; *tun* (Old English) 'farmstead'.

Eigg (Highland) Probably '(island with) the notch'. *Eag* (Scottish Gaelic) 'notch', 'nick' or 'gap'. On this Inner Hebridean isle, a wide rift or notch runs through from south-east to north-west, separating the northern plateau from the An Sgùrr ridge in the south. Recorded as Egge in 1292 and Egg in 1654.

Eighe, Beinn (Highland) In Scottish Gaelic, *eighe* can mean 'ice', 'file' or 'notch', any of which could fit this prominent Torridon mountain (3,309 feet/1,011 metres), though its long ridge makes 'file' more likely.

Eilean Donan (Highland) 'Donnan's isle'. *Eilean* (Scottish Gaelic) 'island'; *Donnan* (Old Gaelic proper name). The martyr, St Donnàn of Eigg, is commemorated in numerous places (mostly called Kildonan) from Kintyre to Sutherland. The castle of Eilean Donan played an important part in West Highland history until its destruction in the Jacobite Rising of 1719.

Eildon (Borders) This famous triple set of peaks (1,330 feet/407 metres), called *Trimontium* by the Romans, and of volcanic origin, may have a hybrid name, from *àill* (Scottish Gaelic) 'rock' and *dún* (Old English) 'hill'. Sir Walter Scott's favourite view of them was from the south. There is a Bronze Age hill fort here and a large Roman camp below at Newstead.

Eishort, Loch (Highland) 'Isthmus firth'. *Eidh* (Old Norse) 'isthmus'; *fjordr* (Old Norse) 'firth'.

Elcho (Perth & Kinross) 'Place of rocks'. *Aileach* (Scottish Gaelic) 'rocky'. Recorded as Elyoch in the 13th century.

Elderslie (Renfrewshire) 'Alder lea'. *Elloern* (Old English) 'alder'; *lí* (Old English) 'meadow'. This was the estate of William Wallace's father.

Elgin (Moray) The name has been derived as 'Little Ireland'. *Ealg* (Scottish Gaelic) an early name for Ireland; *-in* (Scottish Gaelic diminutive suffix) 'little'. Such a name may have been given by Gaelic-speaking settlers from Ireland to remind themselves of their mother country. However, *ealg* later came to also mean 'noble' or 'excellent' and the name may simply mean 'worthy place' with no direct links to Ireland or Dalriada.

Elgol (Highland) 'Fold of the stranger' has been suggested for this Skye location. *Fàl* (Scottish Gaelic) 'fold'; *a' ghoill* (Scottish Gaelic) 'of the Gall' or 'of the stranger'.

Elie (Fife) Place of 'the tomb'. *Ealadh* (Scottish Gaelic) 'tomb' or *ayle* (Scots) 'covered cemetery'. There was once such a cemetery here. Recorded as Elye in 1491 and Alie *circa* 1600.

Elliot (Angus) 'Mound'. This stream name seems to stem from *eileach* (Scottish Gaelic) 'mill-dam', 'weir' or 'mound' and to be cognate with Elliock near Sanquhar in Dumfries & Galloway.

Ellon (Aberdeenshire) Possibly 'green plain or meadow' from *àilean* (Scottish Gaelic) 'green place' or 'meadow'. This derivation suits the location in the Ythan valley but as there are islands in the river here, *eilean* (Scottish Gaelic) 'island', is just as appropriate. It was recorded in the mid-12th century as Eilan, which suggests the latter form.

Elphin (Highland) 'Rocky peak'. *Ailbhinn* (Scottish Gaelic) 'rock peak'.

Elrick (Highland, Aberdeenshire) This name is found in a number of localities. It is cognate with Elrig (Dumfries & Galloway) and is also found as Eldrick. A derivation has been proposed, from Scottish Gaelic *eilerg*, derived by metathesis of *r* and *l*, from the Old Irish Gaelic *erelc*, 'ambush', with the sense here of 'deer trap' – a cul-de-sac into which hunted deer were driven for slaughter. This was a frequent practice.

Elvan Water (South Lanarkshire) 'Bright stream'. *Al-gwen* (Brythonic) 'very white'. It joins the Clyde at Elvanfoot.

Embo (Highland) 'Eyvind's steading'. *Eyvin* (Old Norse personal name); *bol* (Old Norse, shortened form of *bolstadr*) 'farmstead'.

Enard Bay (Highland) 'Eyvind's bay'. *Eyvind* (Old Norse personal name); *fjordr* (Old Norse) 'fjord' or 'bay'.

Enzie (Dumfries & Galloway, Grampian) 'Angled nook'. *Eang* (Scottish Gaelic) 'point of land' or 'gusset'.

Eoropaidh (Western Isles) 'Beach village'. The name of this most northerly village on Lewis is a Gaelicised form of *eyrar-by* (Old Norse) 'shore settlement'.

Erbusaig (Highland) 'Erp's bay'. *Erp* (Old Norse personal name, originally Pictish and related to the Old Gaelic *erc-aig* a Gaelic form of *vik* (Old Norse) 'bay'.

Erchless (Highland) 'Place on the Glass'. *Air* (Scottish Gaelic) 'on the'; *glais* (Scottish Gaelic river name). The castle here is the seat of the Clan Chisholm. *See* **Glass**.

Eriboll (Highland) 'Township on the ridge'. *Eyri* (Old Norse) 'tongue of land'; *ból* (Old Norse) 'building' or 'steading'. The name appears cognate with the Scottish Gaelic *earball*, nowadays 'tail' but with a toponymic sense of 'ridge'. There is a ridge between Lochs Eriboll and Hope.

Ericht, River and **Loch** (Highland, Perth & Kinross) Perhaps 'beauteous', from *eireachdas* (Scottish Gaelic) 'beauteous', which can refer to landscape. Apart from the Badenoch Ericht, another River Ericht flows into the Isla above Coupar Angus.

Eriskay (Western Isles) 'Eric's island'. *Erik* (Old Norse personal name); *ey* (Old Norse) 'island'.

Erisort, Loch (Western Isles) 'Eric's firth'. *Erik* (Old Norse personal name); *fjord*, 'firth'.

Errol (Perth & Kinross) This name has been tentatively associated with Airlie, from *ar ole* (Brythonic-Pictish) 'on the ravine', but there is no ravine here on the Carse of Gowrie. The Hay family, hereditary Constables of Scotland, take their title of Earls of Errol from here.

Erskine (Renfrewshire) Possibly 'high marsh'. *Ard* (Scottish Gaelic) 'high'; *sescenn* (Scottish Gaelic) 'marsh'. A derivation, from *ir ysgyn* (Brythonic) 'green ascent', has also been put forward.

Esk, River (Angus, Dumfries & Galloway, Midlothian) 'Water' – a basic river name. *Uisge* (Scottish Gaelic) 'water'. The numerous Esks testify to its currency. Derived from a Pre-Celtic root *esc.* and Welsh Usk is related. It seems a favourite name for rivers reaching the sea close to each other, such as the North and South Esks which flow into the Montrose basin and those which flow between the Pentland and Moorfoot Hills to reach the sea at Musselburgh.

Eskdalemuir (Dumfries & Galloway) 'Moor of the the Esk valley'. *See* **Esk**.

Esslemont (Aberdeenshire) 'Hill of spells'. *Eoisle* (Scottish Gaelic) 'spells' or 'charms'; *monadh* (Scottish Gaelic) 'mountain' or 'hill'. The name has also been derived from a Brythonic word cognate with *iselfynnydd* (Welsh) 'low hill'.

Etive, River and **Loch** (Argyll & Bute) The Gaelic name is *Eitche*, which has been taken to be from *Eitig* (Old Irish feminine proper name) 'foul one', indicating a malevolent tutelary spirit, inspired perhaps by the turbulent Falls of Lora at the entrance to the loch. A connection with *éite* (Scottish Gaelic) 'white pebble' has also been suggested.

Ettrick (Borders, Argyll & Bute) The name of this Borders village is taken from the river on which it stands, the Ettrick Water. This also applies to other nearby places – Ettrick Forest, Ettrick Pen, Ettrickbridge and so on. The first part may be related to *eadar* (Scottish Gaelic) 'between'. Another suggestion is *atre* (Brythonic) 'playful', as an apt description of the river here. However, there is no definite origin established for this name, which may be from an ancient Pre-Celtic root.

Evanton (Highland) 'Evan's town'. This village on the shore of the

Cromarty Firth was founded around 1810 by a landowner named Evan Fraser.

Evie (Orkney) This Orkney parish name, Efju in the *Orkneyinga Saga* (*circa* 1225), has been suggested as 'eddy', from *efja* (Old Norse) 'backwater' or 'eddy'.

Ewe *see* **Kinlochewe**.

Eye, Loch (Highland) 'Loch of the isthmus'. *Eidh* (Old Norse) 'isthmus', giving Scottish Gaelic *uidh*. The Gaelic name is *Loch na h-uidhe*. The Eye Peninsula in Lewis also has the 'isthmus' sense.

Eyemouth (Borders) 'At the mouth of the Eye Water'. The river name is tautologically derived from *éa* (Old English) 'river'. 'Water' was added when the old meaning was lost.

Eynhallow (Orkney) 'Holy isle'. In the *Orkneyinga Saga* of *circa* 1225, it is recorded as Eyin Helga, from (Old Norse) *ey* (Old Norse) 'island' and *heilag-r* (Old Norse) 'saint'.

F

Fair Isle (Shetland) 'Sheep Island'. *Faer* (Old Norse) 'sheep'; 'isle' (probably English translation of Old Norse *ey*) 'small island'. A record of 1529 shows the 'isle' as Faray. The remote Fair Isle, lying midway between Shetland and Orkney, was settled by the Vikings as a staging post to which they brought sheep. A place name exactly parallel to it is found in that of the Faeroe Islands and for the same reasons.

Fala (Borders) 'Sheepfold'. *Fàl* (Scottish Gaelic) 'pen' (for strayed sheep or cattle) or 'wall', with -*ach* (Scottish Gaelic) 'field' ending.

Falkirk 'Speckled church'. *Fawe* (Scots) 'speckled'; *kirke* (Scots) 'church'. This is a translated version of the original Egglesbreth, from *eaglais*, 'church' and *breac*, 'speckled', first recorded in the early 12th century. It is presumed that the early settlement here, predating the industrial town by more than a thousand years, had a church that was built of variegated stone. It was recorded as Faukirke in 1298, Falkirk from 1458 and is now the centre of a unitary authority.

Falkland (Fife) The origin of the name remains uncertain. Possible associations with falconry have been made, from *falca* (Old English) 'falcon'. One authority has drawn another connection with the town's regal status in proposing the derivation *folc* (Old English) 'people's' and 'land' (English), that is 'Crown property'. These suggestions, influenced by Falkland's royal palace, may be wide of the mark. Early records show Falleland in 1128 and Falecklen in 1165.

Falloch, Glen (Stirling) Possibly 'Glen of hiding'. *Gleann* (Scottish Gaelic) 'valley'; *falach* (Scottish Gaelic) 'place of concealment'.

Fannich, River, Loch and **mountain group** (Highland) *Fàn* (Scottish Gaelic) indicates a gentle slope, and the name may stem from this. It may alternatively be a water name, cognate with the verb *gwanegu* (Welsh) 'to rise in waves'.

Fare, Hill of (Aberdeenshire) 'Watch hill'. *Faire* (Scottish Gaelic) 'watchfulness' or 'sentinel', with 'hill' substituted for the Gaelic *cnoc* in the post-Gaelic era. This Midmar hill rises 1,545 feet/487 metres above Strath Dee, with a wide outlook.

Farg, Glen (Perth & Kinross) 'Ferocious glen'. *Gleann* (Scottish Gaelic) 'valley' or 'glen'; *fearg* (Scottish Gaelic) 'anger', perhaps with reference to the steepness of the glen.

Farigaig *see* **Farr**.

Farr (Highland) Most likely 'upper ground'. *For* (Scottish Gaelic) 'superior'. However, an Old Gaelic prefix, *far*, 'lower', has also been suggested for such 'Farr-' names as Farigaig, from *far* (Scottish Gaelic) 'below' and *gàg* (Scottish Gaelic) 'cleft' or 'ravine'.

Farrar, River and **Strath** (Highland) First recorded on Ptolemy's map of Scotland in AD 150 as *Varar*, this much-discussed name has sometimes been taken to indicate a non-Celtic but Indo-European language spoken in Pre-Celtic Scotland. Its origins remain unclear.

Faskally (Perth & Kinross) 'Stance by the ferry'. *Fas* (Scottish Gaelic) is an obsolete term for 'house' or 'dwelling' but in place names it has the sense of 'stance' (*see* **Duffus**); *calaidh* (Scottish Gaelic) 'ferry'. The location of a former ferry across the Tummel. The modern dam at Pitlochry has created Loch Faskally here. The 'Fas-' element in many local place names indicates the extent of sheep and cattle-droving across the countryside in former days.

Faslane (Argyll & Bute) 'Stance on the enclosed land'. *Fas* (Scottish Gaelic) 'stance'; *lainne* (Scottish Gaelic locative form of *lann)* 'enclosed ground' or 'field'.

Fasnakyle (Highland) 'Stance in the wood'. *Fas* (Scottish Gaelic) 'stance', *na* (Scottish Gaelic) 'of''; *coille* (Scottish Gaelic) 'wood'.

Fassiefern (Perth & Kinross) 'Stance of the alder tees'. *Fas* (Scottish Gaelic) 'stance'; *fearna* (Scottish Gaelic) 'of the alders'.

Fauldhouse (West Lothian) 'House on the fallow land'. *Falh* (Old English) 'fallow land'; 'house' (Modern English, from Old English *hus*).

Fearn (Highland) 'Place of the alders'. *Feàrna* (Scottish Gaelic) 'alder'.

Ferintosh (Highland) 'The chief's holding'. *Fearann* (Scottish Gaelic) 'land' or 'estate'; *toisich*' (Scottish Gaelic) 'chief'. This was the principal whisky-distilling centre in the Highlands up to the 18th century.

Ferniehirst (Aberdeenshire) 'Alder wood'. *Feàrna* (Scottish Gaelic) 'alder tree'; *hirst* (Old English) 'wood'.

Ferryport-on-Craig (Fife) There were several ferries across the Firth of Tay from Fife to Dundee and its environs and this name appears to have been current from around the 16th century. The 'Craig' (*carraig* [Scottish Gaelic] 'rock') affirms the steep cliff-bound aspect of the Fife side.

Feshie, River and **Glen** (Highland) 'Boggy meadowland'. *Féith* (Scottish Gaelic) 'boggy place'; *-isidh* (Scottish Gaelic suffix denoting pasture-land, derived from *innse* (Scottish Gaelic) meaning 'meadow' as well as 'island').

Fetlar (Shetland) The derivation of the island's name has been suggested as coming from *fetill* (Old Norse) 'belt'.

Fettercairn (Aberdeenshire) 'Wooded slope'. *Faithir* (Scottish Gaelic) 'terraced slope' or 'gradient'; *cardden* (Brythonic-Celtic) 'wood' or 'copse'. Recorded in the *Pictish Chronicle* around AD 970 as Fotherkern.

Fetteresso (Aberdeenshire) 'Watery slope'. *Faithir* (Scottish Gaelic) 'terraced slope' or 'gradient'; *easach* (Scottish Gaelic) 'water-logged' or 'watery'.

Fiddich, River and **Glen** (Moray) Fidach was one of the ancient province names of Pictland and it seems likely that it is preserved in this name. The root element *fid* is likely to be from a personal name. The glen lies at the heart of the Speyside whisky-distilling area.

Fife The name of this ancient kingdom, former county and present administrative region has been attributed to the personal name Fib, a legendary precursor of the Picts, one of the seven sons of Cruithne who gave their names to the provinces of Pictland. Recorded as Fib in 1150 and Fif in 1165. *See* **Fyvie**.

Findhorn (Moray) 'White water'. *Fionn* (Scottish Gaelic) 'white'; *eren* (Pre-Celtic river name). This name, with others, has sometimes been seen as a form of the Irish Gaelic *Erin*. *See* **Earn**. The village derives its name from the river, at whose mouth it stands.

Findochty (Moray) 'House on the fair or bright land-measure'. *Fionn* (Scottish Gaelic) 'fair' or 'bright'; *davach* (Scottish Gaelic land measure); *taigh* (Scottish Gaelic) 'house'. The local pronunciation is 'Finnechtie'.

Findon (Aberdeenshire, Highland) 'Fair hill'. (Scottish Gaelic) *Fionn* (Scottish Gaelic) 'fair' or 'bright'; *dùn* (Scottish Gaelic) 'hill'.

Finnan, River and **Glen** (Highland) 'Fingon's Glen'. *Gleann* (Scottish Gaelic) 'glen'; *Fhionghuin* (Scottish Gaelic proper name). The clan name, MacKinnon, derives from Fingon. Here the Stewart standard was raised in August 1745, signalling the start of the last Jacobite Rising.

Finnart (Argyll & Bute) 'Bright height'. *Fionn* (Scottish Gaelic) 'fair' or 'bright'; *àird* (Scottish Gaelic) 'height'. The site of a tanker terminal on Loch Long.

Finnieston (Glasgow) Dating from 1768, the name commemorates John Finnie, tutor to the landowner, Matthew Orr.

Finstown (Orkney) 'Finn's place'. *Finn* (old Norse proper name); *ton* (Scots, from Old English *tun*) 'settlement' or 'place'. It has been suggested that David Phin, an Irish drummer, set up an inn here in 1811 but inns tend to be where there are already settlements.

Fintaig, River and **Glen** (Highland) 'White river'. *Fionn* (Scottish Gaelic) 'white'; *t-àg* (Scottish Gaelic diminutive suffix indicating a 'stream').

Fintry (Stirling, Aberdeenshire) 'White house'. *Fionn* (Scottish Gaelic) 'white'; *tref* (Brythonic) 'house' or 'homestead'.

Fionnphort (Argyll & Bute) 'White harbour'. *Fionn* (Scottish Gaelic) 'white'; *phort* (Scottish Gaelic) 'harbour' or 'beaching place'. This Mull township is the ferry-port for Iona.

Firth (Orkney) 'Sea inlet'. *Fjordr* (Old Norse) 'sea inlet' or 'fjord'.

Fishnish (Argyll & Bute) 'Fish point'. *Fisk* (Old Norse) 'fish'; *nes* (Old Norse) 'point'. The unnecessary English 'Point' has been added to this Mull name in modern times, in ignorance of the original meaning.

Fitful Head (Shetland) 'Cape of the web-footed birds (sea birds). *Fit* (Old Norse) 'foot'; *fugl* (Old Norse) 'bird'. 'Head' is an English translation of *hofud* (Old Norse) 'headland'.

Fiunary (Highland) 'Fair shieling or hill-pasture'. *Fionn* (Scottish Gaelic) 'bright' or 'fair'; *airidh* (Scottish Gaelic) 'shieling' or 'hill pasture'.

Five Sisters of Kintail (Highland) A modern name given to the mountain group at the head of Loch Duich. In Gaelic, it is *Beinn Mhòr*, 'big mountain', though the peaks are also individually named.

Fladda (Western Isles) 'Flat island'. The numerous Fladdas are from *flat-ey* (Old Norse) 'flat island'.

Flanders Moss (Stirling) This wide, level, once-marshy expanse west of Stirling is presumably named after the low-lying country of Flanders, translated from the Gaelic *a' Mhòine Fhlanrasach*, or possibly after the 17th-century Flemings, who brought the techniques to drain it.

Flannan Isles (Western Isles) 'St Flannan's isles' (in Gaelic, *na h-Eileanan Flannach*). All three of the island lighthouse-keepers mysteriously vanished here in 1900.

Fleet, River (Dumfries & Galloway) 'Estuary'. *Fleot* (Old English) 'estuary'.

Fleet, River and **Loch** (Highland) 'Flooding stream'. *Fljotr* (Old Norse) 'fleet' or 'flood'.

Flodigarry (Highland) 'Fleet garth'. *Flotr* (Old Norse) 'fleet'; *gearraidh* (Scottish Gaelic) 'land between machair and moor'.

Flotta (Orkney) 'Fleet island'. *Flotr* (Old Norse) 'fleet'; *-ey* (Old Norse) 'island'. Flotta lies in the vast natural harbour of Scapa Flow.

Fochabers (Moray) The name 'lake marsh' has been suggested. *Fothach* (Brythonic) 'lake'; *aber* (Brythonic) 'confluence', with the sense of 'marsh'. The village is close to the flood-plain of the Spey and has a small loch nearby. The terminal *-s* found in Fochabris (1514) is not in earlier sources.

Foinaven (Highland) This has been derived as 'wart mountain'. *Foinne* (Scottish Gaelic) 'warts'; *bheinn* (Scottish Gaelic) 'mountain'. In some sources, it is shown as *fionn*, 'white', but whether or not 'wart' is correct, 'white' is definitely wrong. This stark mountain (2,980 feet/911 metres) is in the far north-west.

Fonab (Highland) 'Abbot's land'. *Fonn* (Scottish Gaelic) 'land'; *aba* (Scottish Gaelic) 'abbot'.

Footdee (Aberdeen, Fife) 'Peaty place'. *Fòid* (Scottish Gaelic) 'peat'; *ait* (Scottish Gaelic locative suffix). Despite its harbour-side location, this Aberdeen district name has nothing to do with the River Dee.

Fordun (Aberdeenshire) 'On the hill above the fort'. *Faithir* (Scottish Gaelic) 'shelved or terraced slope'; *dùn* (Scottish Gaelic) 'fort'. The earlier spelling is Fordoun. John Fordun (mid-14th century), one of the country's early historians, is associated with here.

Fordyce (Aberdeenshire) 'South-facing slope'. *Faithir* (Scottish Gaelic) 'shelved or terraced slope'; *deas* (Scottish Gaelic) 'south'. A favoured place.

Forfar (Angus) Possibly 'watching hill'. *Faithir* (Scottish Gaelic) 'terraced slope'; *faire* (Scottish Gaelic) 'watchfulness' or 'sentinel'. The nearby Hill of Finhaven would have been a suitable place for such a lookout. It was recorded as Forfare in a document *circa* 1200. The county town of Angus, also known as Forfarshire, was once an important weaving centre and is still a market and textile town.

Formartine (Aberdeenshire) 'Martin's land'. *Fearann* (Scottish Gaelic) 'holding' or 'estate'; *Mhartainn* (Scottish Gaelic personal name) 'Martin's'. This district of central Aberdeenshire was recorded in 1433 as Fermartyn.

Forres (Moray) 'Below the bushes'. *Far* (Scottish Gaelic) 'below' or 'under'; *ras* (Scottish Gaelic) 'shrubs' or 'underwood'. Recorded as Fores in 1187 and Forais in 1283. The Gaelic name is *Farrais*. The name is likely to be a reference to the town's situation at the foot of thickly wooded hills.

Forsinard (Highland) 'Waterfall on the height'. *Fors* (Old Norse) 'waterfall'; *an* (Scottish Gaelic) 'of the'; *àird* (Scottish Gaelic) 'height'.

Forss (Highland) 'Waterfall'. *Fors* (Old Norse) 'waterfall'. The River Forss has a waterfall here.

Fort Augustus (Highland) Formerly known as Kilchomain (St Colman's church), the town was renamed after the Jacobite Rising of 1715 in commemoration of William Augustus, Duke of Cumberland, when the old fortification was rebuilt. The fort is now the site of a Benedictine abbey.

Fort George (Highland) Fort and village named after King George II. The fort is one of the best preserved 18th-century military installations in Europe.

Fort William (Highland) The original settlement was known as Inverlochy (*see* **Lochy**). A fort was established here by General Monk in 1655, at which time the place was called Gordonsburgh, after the Duke of Gordon on whose land it had been built. Shortly afterwards, its name changed briefly to Maryburgh, after Queen Mary II, cosovereign of King William II. Finally, in 1690, the fort was rebuilt as a major garrison and renamed Fort William, after the king.

Forteviot (Perth & Kinross) This ancient royal centre by the Earn appears to have as its first element *fathair* (Scottish Gaelic) 'terraced or shelved slope'. The second part is of unclear derivation, perhaps a personal name. It is not related to the Borders Teviot.

Forth (Stirling, Fife, South Lanarkshire) Tacitus's first-century account of Caledonia calls the Forth, *Bodotria*, which is not the source of the present name. A source has been traced to *voritia* (Brythonic) 'slow-running', giving an Old Gaelic form, *foirthe*, though there is no clear evidence that this name was a river name. The form 'Forth' is recorded from the 12th century. An alternative source has been suggested in *fjordr* (Old Norse) 'sea loch' or 'firth', though it seems unlikely that a name would not have been fixed well before the Viking period.

Fortingall (Perth & Kinross) 'Fortified church'. *Fartair* (Old Gaelic) 'fortress' (from the same Celtic root as the Welsh *gwerthyr*); *cill* (Scottish Gaelic) 'church'. The yew tree here is of a great age and there is a local legend that Pontius Pilate spent his last years in this place.

Fortrose (Highland) 'Beneath the headland'. *Foter* (Scottish Gaelic) 'beneath'; *ros* (Scottish Gaelic) 'cape'. This small town, with the ruins of its medieval cathedral, lies beneath the Rosemarkie Headland on the Black Isle.

Foss (Perth & Kinross) 'Stance or cattle station'. *Fas* (Scottish Gaelic) 'stance'.

Foubister (Orkney) 'Fua's farm'. *Fua* (Old Norse proper name); *bolstadr* (Old Norse) 'farmstead'.

Foula (Shetland) 'Bird Island'. *Fugl* (Old Norse) 'fowl' or 'bird'; *ey* (Old Norse) 'island'. This remote and isolated small island, lying 14 miles/23 kilometres due west of the Shetland mainland, is famed for its very high and sheer cliffs, still teeming with sea birds.

Foulis (Highland, Tayside) 'Small stream'. *Foghlais* (Scottish Gaelic) 'lesser stream'. Foulis Castle is the seat of the chief of the Clan Munro. The same derivation applies to Easter and Wester Fowlis, in Perthshire.

Foyers (Highland) 'Terraced slope'. *Fothair* (Scottish Gaelic) 'terraced slope' or 'stepped gradient'. This name describes the situation of this village on the steeply terraced east side of Loch Ness. There is a famous cataract here, the Falls of Foyers, harnessed for hydroelectric production.

Fraserburgh (Aberdeenshire) 'Fraser's town'. This major fishing port on the north coast of Buchan, originally called Faithlie, was renamed in 1592 to honour Sir Alexander Fraser, the then new landowner and developer of the town. The second element is derived from *burh* (Old English and adapted Scots *burgh*) 'town'. It is known to locals as 'the Broch'.

Frendraught (Aberdeenshire) 'Land by the bridge'. *Fearann* (Scottish Gaelic) 'land' or 'estate'; *drochaid* (Scottish Gaelic) 'bridge'.

Freuchie (Fife) 'Heathery place'. *Fraochach* (Scottish Gaelic) 'heathery'.

Frew, Fords of (Stirling) 'Current or swift current'.(Brythonic) *friú*

(Brythonic) 'current'. This lowest fording point on the River Forth was strategically important until modern times. The Gaelic name is *na Friùthachan*, a gaelicised rendering of the original.

Friockheim (Angus) Originally known simply as Friock Feus (apparently after a bailie from Forfar, by the name of Freke) *Heim* (German) 'home' or 'village', was added in 1830 by the landowner, John Anderson, who had spent some time in Germany.

Fruin, River and **Glen** (Argyll & Bute) Possibly 'Raging stream'. *Freoine* (Scottish Gaelic) 'rage'. Recorded as Glenfrone in the 13th century.

Furnace (Argyll & Bute) Kilns were set up here on Loch Fyneside for iron-smelting in the 18th century, using local wood fuel, hence the name. In Gaelic, it is *An Fhùirneis*.

Fyne, River and **Loch** (Argyll & Bute) 'Stream of wine or virtue'. *Fine* (Scottish Gaelic) 'wine'. The reference is to an ancient holy site, perhaps Kilmorich at the foot of Glen Fyne.

Fyvie (Aberdeenshire) Possibly a 'path'. *Fiamh* (Scottish Gaelic) 'path'. Some commentators consider that the origin of Fife comes from the same root.

G

Gairloch (Highland) 'Short loch'. *Gearr* (Scottish Gaelic) 'short'; *loch* (Scottish Gaelic) 'lake' or 'loch'. The village situated at the head of this short sea loch has usurped the name and the loch is often called Loch Gairloch. Gareloch on the Firth of Clyde has the same derivation.

Gairsay (Orkney) 'Garek's isle'. *Garek* (Old Norse personal name); *ey* (Old Norse) 'island'.

Galashiels (Borders) 'Shielings by the Gala Water'. The latter part of the name comes from *skali-s* (Old Norse) 'sheilings' (sheds or huts used by shepherds as temporary shelters on summer pastures) The source of Gala has been suggested as *galga* (Old English) 'gallows', but river names are generally older than place names and the origin may be *gal gwy* (Brythonic) 'clear stream'. The name was recorded as Galuschel in 1237 and Gallowschel in 1416. This town has long been the main centre for the Borders woollen trade.

Galloway (Dumfries & Galloway) 'Land of the stranger Gaels'. *Gall* (Scottish Gaelic) 'stranger'; *Ghaidhil* (Scottish Gaelic) 'Gaels'. This tribal name was given by the Scots to the extreme south-west part of Scotland, which was once settled by Gaels of mixed Irish and Norse origins, who were thus regarded as 'foreigners'.

Galston (East Ayrshire) 'Village of the strangers'. *Gall* (Scottish Gaelic) 'stranger'; *tun* (Old English) 'village'. As in the case of Galloway, the reference here to strangers would have been to settlers of a tribe different from the native Scots.

Gamrie (Aberdeenshire) Possibly 'cold place'. *Geamhradh* (Scottish Gaelic) 'winter'.

Garbost (Western Isles) 'Geirr's farm'. *Geira* (Old Norse proper name); *bolstadr* (Old Norse) 'farmstead'.

Gardenstown (Aberdeenshire) Literally, 'Garden's town'. This fishing port on the Banff-shire coast was set up in 1720 by Alexander Garden of Troup, who gave it his family name.

Garelochhead (Argyll & Bute) 'At the head of the short loch'. *Gearr* (Scottish Gaelic) 'short'; *loch* (Scottish Gaelic) 'lake' or 'loch'. The English suffix suggests a modern name. The village is situated on the Gareloch, a short fiord-like indentation off the Firth of Clyde, at present Britain's nuclear submarine base.

Gargunnock (Stirling) Possibly 'rounded hill'. *Garradh* (Scottish Gaelic) 'enclosure' or 'place'; *cnuic* or *duin-ock* (Scottish Gaelic) 'rounded hill' or 'mound'. The village of this name lies at the base of the Gargunnock Hills.

Garioch (Aberdeenshire) 'Rough ground'. *Garbh* (Scottish Gaelic) 'roughness'; *-ach* (Scottish Gaelic suffix) 'field' or 'place'.

Garmouth (Moray) 'Short plain'. *Gearr* (Scottish Gaelic) 'short', here in the sense of 'narrow'; *magh* (Scottish Gaelic) 'plain'.

Garnkirk (North Lanarkshire) 'Hen run'. *Gart* (Scottish Gaelic) 'enclosure' or 'field'; *cearc* (Scottish Gaelic) 'hen'. Such is the apparent sense of the Gaelic name. However, a 12th-century form,

Leyngartheyn, suggests the present name is a scotticised version of *lann* (Brythonic) 'church' become *kirk* (Scots) and *gartan* (Scottish Gaelic) 'little field'.

Garry, River, Loch and **Glen** (Highland, Perth & Kinross) 'Rough river'. The name comes from a Celtic root *garu,* as does *garbh* (Scottish Gaelic) 'rough'. There are two Glen Garrys, in Perthshire and Inverness-shire respectively; the latter being the ancient territory of the MacDonnells, from whom we have the distinctive 'Glengarry' bonnet.

Garscadden (Glasgow) 'Herring yard'. *Gart* (Scottish Gaelic) 'enclosure'; *sgadain* (Scottish Gaelic) 'herring'.

Garscube (Glasgow) 'Corn-yard or field'. *Gart* (Scottish Gaelic) 'enclosure' or 'field'; *sguab* (Scottish Gaelic) 'sheaf'.

Garten, River (Highland) 'River of thickets'. *Cardden* (Brythonic) 'thicket'. *See* **Boat of Garten** and **Pluscarden**.

Garth (Perth & Kinross) 'Cornfield'. *Gart* (Scottish Gaelic) 'standing corn' or 'cornfield'. 'Gart-' and 'Garty-' are common prefixes for local and field names, with the sense of 'field', especially 'cornfield'.

Gartmore (Stirling) 'Big cornfield'. *Gart* (Scottish Gaelic) 'standing corn' or 'cornfield'; *mòr* (Scottish Gaelic) 'big'.

Gartnavel (Glasgow) 'Apple field'. *Gart* (Scottish Gaelic) 'enclosure' or 'field'; *n'* (Scottish Gaelic) 'of the'; *abhal* (Scottish Gaelic) 'apples'.

Gartness (Stirling) 'Field (probably cornfield) by the water or stream. *Gart* (Scottish Gaelic) 'standing corn' or 'cornfield'; *nan* (Scottish Gaelic) 'of the'; *eas* (Scottish Gaelic) 'water'.

Gartney, Strath (Stirling) 'Gartan's strath'. *Gartán* (Scottish Gaelic personal name, perhaps related to Pictish *Gartnait*); *srath* (Scottish Gaelic) 'wide valley'. The use of *srath* here, by the side of Loch Katrine, is more akin to the Irish Gaelic sense of 'lakeside meadowland', than the usual Scottish Gaelic sense of a 'wide river valley'.

Gartocharn (West Dunbartonshire) 'Place of the humped hill'. *Garradh* (Scottish Gaelic) 'enclosure' or 'place'; *chairn* (Scottish Gaelic corrupt form of *carn*) 'humped hill'. This village is situated beneath the isolated Duncryne Hill ('hill of the aspen tree', from *crithionn* [Gaelic] 'aspen') on the southern shore of Loch Lomond.

Gartsherrie (North Lanarkshire) 'Colt field'. *Gart* (Scottish Gaelic) 'enclosure' or 'field'; *searraigh* (Scottish Gaelic) 'colts'.

Garve (Highland) 'Rough ground'. *Garbh* (Scottish Gaelic) 'rough'. This village is situated in a rocky, hummocky valley, at the end of the loch of the same name.

Garvelloch Isles (Argyll & Bute) 'Rough or rocky isles'. *Garbh* (Scottish gaelic) 'rough'; *eileach* (Scottish Gaelic) 'rock'.

Gask (Aberdeenshire, Highland, Perth & Kinross) 'Tongue or tail of land'. *Gasg* (Scottish Gaelic) 'tail' or 'point of land extending from a plateau'. 'Gask' is an element in numerous place names.

Gatehouse of Fleet (Dumfries & Galloway) 'Roadhouse on the (Water of) Fleet'. *Geata-hus* (Old English) 'roadhouse'; 'Fleet' (Old English river name – *fleot*, 'stream' or 'estuary'). The town was not founded until 1790 but the name is older. Such roadhouses were monastic in origin and therefore pre-16th-century.

Gauldry (Fife) 'Wood of the Galls'. *Gall* (Scottish Gaelic) 'strangers' or 'foreigners'; *doire* (Scottish Gaelic) 'grove' or 'wood'.

Gaur, River (Perth & Kinross) 'Winter river'. *Geamradh* (Scottish Gaelic) 'winter'. This river, flowing into Loch Rannoch, is at its height with the melting of winter snow.

Georgemas (Highland) There was a cattle market here on St George's Day, April 23rd, and the name simply means 'St George's mass or feast'. It is the most northerly railway junction in the country, where the Thurso branch joins the Highland line to Wick.

Giffnock (East Renfrewshire) 'Little ridge'. *Cefn* (Brythonic-Celtic) 'ridge'; *oc* (Brythonic diminutive suffix) 'little'. An accurate description of the situation of this place, now a southside suburb of Glasgow.

Gifford (East Lothian) The name of the locality appears to come, from the Norman family name, *Gyffard*. The village was established in the 18th century.

Gigha (Argyll & Bute) Possibly 'God's isle'. *Gud* (Old Norse) 'God'; *ey* (Old Norse) 'island'. A derivation, from the Old Norse *gjá*, 'gape', has also been proposed, relating either to features of the island or to the sound separating it from Kintyre. Recorded as Gudey in 1263, Geday in 1343, Gya in 1400 and Giga in 1516.

Gilmerton (Edinburgh and other regions) 'Gilmour's farm'. *Gille Moire* (Scottish Gaelic proper name) 'Servant of Mary'; *tun* (Old English) 'farm'. Shown as Gillmuristona in the 12th century.

Girnigoe (Highland) 'Gaping geo'. *Gjá* (Old Norse) 'gape'; *geo* (Old Norse) 'sea cleft'.

Girvan (South Ayrshire): 'Short river'. *Gearr* (Scottish Gaelic) 'short'; *abhainn* (Scottish Gaelic) 'river'. It was recorded as Girven in 1275.

Glamis (Angus) 'Wide gap'. *Glamhus* (Scottish Gaelic) 'wide gap' or 'vale'. Records show Glammes in 1187 and Glammis in 1251. The name describes the situation of this village, with its famous 14th-century castle, lying in the centre of the broad vale of Strathmore between the Sidlaw Hills and the edge of the Highlands.

Glasgow 'Place of the green hollow' or 'dear green place'. *Glas* (Brythonic) 'green'; *cau* (Brythonic) 'hollow'. The Gaelic form is *Glaschu*. Some authorities consider that there is a 'familiarative' sense implied in the derivation and hence the popular rendering 'dear green place'. The name was recorded as Glasgu in 1116. An ecclesiastical centre, founded by St Kentigern in the 6th century, Glasgow's growth as a factory town and port began in the 17th century and by 1840 it had become, as it remains, Scotland's largest city.

Glass, River, Glen, Loch (Highland, Dumfries & Galloway) The noun *glas* in Scottish Gaelic has the primary meanings of 'lock' or 'green surface' but also 'water'. There are several Glass rivers.

Glassary (Argyll & Bute) 'Grey shieling'. *Glas* (Scottish Gaelic) 'grey'; *airidh* (Scottish Gaelic) 'shieling'.

Glen An anglicised form of the Scottish Gaelic *gleann*, the conventional term for a river valley in mountain or hill country. It is cognate with the Welsh *glyn*. Glens are generally steeper and narrower than straths. *See* glens under defining name (for example, **More**) except when the two are normally combined.

Glenalmond (Perth & Kinross) 'Glen of the river'. *Gleann* (Scottish Gaelic) 'glen' or 'valley'. *See* **Almond**.

Glenbrittle *see* **Brittle, Glen**.

Glencoe (Highland) Probably the 'narrow glen'. *Gleann* (Scottish Gaelic) 'glen' or 'valley'; *comhann* (Scottish Gaelic) 'narrow'. This spectacular, deep, glaciated valley with its many sheer rock faces is famed today for mountain climbing and notorious for the massacre of the Macdonalds that took place here in 1692. The modern village of Glencoe lies at the west end, near where the River Coe flows into Loch Leven.

Glendaruel (Argyll & Bute) There are differing explanations for this name. It may be that the original form has become too distorted to be recognisable. The elements *Gleann* (Scottish Gaelic) 'glen' and *dà* (Scottish Gaelic) 'two' are clear but the third part has been variously derived from *ruadhail* (Scottish Gaelic) 'red spots' and *ruadha* (Scottish Gaelic) 'points' or 'headlands'.

Gleneagles (Perth & Kinross) 'Glen of the church'. *Gleann* (Scottish Gaelic) 'glen'; *eaglais* (Scottish Gaelic) 'church'. It was recorded as Gleninglese *circa* 1165. Famous for the luxury hotel and golf courses at its open end, this narrow Ochil glen still has the remains of an old chapel and a 'St Mungo's Farm' indicating its past history as a church property.

Glenelg (Highland) This has been taken for 'glen of Ireland'. *Gleann* (Scottish Gaelic) 'glen'; *Ealg* (Scottish Gaelic) early name for Ireland. As with Elgin and Blair Atholl, the reference here to Ireland would be one of commemoration of the motherland by early Gaelic-speaking settlers to this place on the west coast of Scotland. It has also been derived from *eilg* (Old Gaelic) 'noble', which stems from the same root.

Glenfinnan (Highland) Possibly 'glen of (St) Finan'. *Gleann* (Scottish Gaelic) 'glen'; *Finan* (Irish Gaelic personal name from *fionn*, 'fair') a 7th-century abbot from Iona and a contemporary of St Columba.

Glenkens, The (Dumfries & Galloway) 'Glen of the white river'. *See* **Ken**. The plural ending has been ascribed to the four parishes forming the district.

Glenlivet (Moray) Apparently 'glen of the slippery smooth place'. *Gleann* (Scottish Gaelic) 'glen'; *liobh* (Scottish Gaelic) 'slimy', 'slippery' or 'smooth'; *ait* (Scottish Gaelic) 'place'. According to one authority, the name of the River Livet has possibly been back-formed from that of the glen, an unusual occurrence.

Glenrothes (Fife) A modern name created when this new town was established in 1948 as a modern mining centre. The mines have now closed down. The second part acknowledges the Earls of Rothes as local landowners and the former Rothes Colliery.

Glomach (Highland) 'Place of the chasm'. *Glòm* (Scottish Gaelic) 'abyss' or 'chasm'; *-ach* (Scottish Gaelic suffix) 'place'. Here in Kintail, the Falls of Glomach (370 feet/113 metres) are the highest in the country.

Goat Fell (North Ayrshire) 'Goats' hill'. At 2,868 feet/874 metres, this is the highest peak on Arran. *Geitar* (Old Norse) 'goats'; *fjall* (Old Norse) 'hill'.

Goil, Loch (Argyll & Bute) Perhaps 'loch of the Gall or stranger'. *Loch* (Scottish Gaelic) 'lake' or 'loch'; *goill* (Scottish Gaelic) 'of the stranger'. Glen Gyle would seem to have the same origin.

Golspie (Highland) Apparently 'Gulli's farm'. *Gulli* (Old Norse personal name); *byr* (Old Norse) 'farmstead'. Recorded as Goldespy in 1330 and Golspi in 1448.

Gometra (Argyll & Bute) 'Godmund's isle'. *Godmundr* (Old Norse personal name); *ey* (Old Norse) 'island'. This island lies immediately west of Ulva, from which it is separated by a narrow sound.

Gorbals (Glasgow) The meaning of the name of this former slum area of Glasgow remains uncertain. One authority has suggested a derivation with reference to *gorr balk-r* (Old Norse) 'built walls'. It is recorded in a document of 1521 as Gorbalis.

Gordon (Borders, Aberdeenshire) 'Great fort'. *Gor* (Brythonic prefix to intensify the meaning of what follows); *dun* (Brythonic and Gaelic) fort.

Gordonstoun (Moray) 'Gordon's town'. Renamed in 1638 after Sir Robert Gordon, the estate, now a boarding school, had previously been called the Bog of Plewlands.

Gorebridge (Midlothian) Possibly the 'bridge at the wedge-shaped land'. *Gora* (Middle English) 'triangular piece of land' or 'bridge' (English). For a Scots form *see* **Gushetfaulds**.

Gorgie (Edinburgh) The name of this western district probably means 'broad field'. *Gor* (Brythonic) 'broad'; *cyn* (Brythonic) 'field'.

Gowrie (Perth & Kinross) Perhaps 'Gabràn's carseland'. *Gabràin* (Old Gaelic proper name) 'of Gabràn'. Gabràn was a 6th-century King of Dalriada, reigning from about 537, but it is probable that he had close connections with this more eastern district. Other districts, like Cowal and Lorn, are named after kings of this period. A derivation, from *gabhar* (Scottish Gaelic) 'goat', is also suggested, though *Gabràn* and *gabhar* may both be from the same root. Gowrie, linked with Atholl, was one of the seven major divisions of Pictland.

Gourock (Inverclyde) Probably the 'place of the hillocks'. *Guirec* (Scottish Gaelic) 'pimple' or 'hillock'. The local terrain here is noticeably made up of steep hillocks plunging straight into the Firth of Clyde. Gourock is the ferryport for Dunoon, across the firth.

Govan (Glasgow) 'Ridge'. *Cefn* (Brythonic) 'ridge'. *See* **Giffnock**. Alternative derivations include 'dear rock', from *cu* (Brythonic) 'dear' and *faen* (Brythonic mutated form of *maen*) 'stone', as well as '(place of the) smith', from *gobhann* (Scottish Gaelic) 'blacksmith'. Names indicating a smithy are not unusual, though most have the place prefix 'Bal-' in front. It was recorded as Guven in 1147, Gvuan in 1150 and Gwuan in 1518.

Graemsay (Orkney) 'Grim's isle'. *Grim* (Old Norse personal name); *ey* (Old Norse) 'island'.

Grahamston (Falkirk) A relatively modern name following urbanisation of the area, close to Falkirk, and using the well-established suffix '-ton', indicating a township. The old name was Graham's Muir, after Sir John Graham, killed in the Wars of Independence, 1298.

Grampian Mountains (Highland, Perth & Kinross, Moray) The name seems to be a version of Graupius (Mons Graupius, site of a battle between the Romans and Caledonians in AD 84) first written by Hector Boece in 1526 in his *History of Scotland*. The derivation of 'Graupius' is unknown. The correct name of this mountain massif is 'The Mounth' from *monadh* (Scottish Gaelic) 'mountain'.

Grandtully (Perth & Kinross) 'Thicket on the hill'. *Cardden* (Brythonic) 'thicket'; *tulach* (Scottish Gaelic) 'hill'.

Grange (Fife and other regions) This name indicates the presence of a pre-Reformation grange or barn, used for storing produce belonging to an abbey. Many parishes in Scotland were chartered to abbeys and 'grange' occurs as an element in many names.

Grangemouth (Stirling) 'Mouth of the Grange Burn'. This industrial port on the south side of the Firth of Forth, founded in 1777, stands at the mouth of the Grange Burn, itself named after the nearby grange for Newbattle Abbey.

Granton (Edinburgh) 'Green hill'. *Gren* (Old English) 'green'; *dun* (Old English) 'hill' or 'rise'. Names like Grendon in England are cognate. Once a coastal fishing village outside Edinburgh, now incorporated into the city.

Grantown-on-Spey (Highland) 'Grant's town by the River Spey'. This town beside the River Spey was originally built in 1766 as a model planned village for the then local landowner, Sir James Grant, after whom it is named. *See also* **Spey**.

Grantshouse (Borders) A modern name used for a former North British Railway station adjacent to an inn kept by one Tammy Grant.

Great Glen *see* **More, Glen**.

Greenan (Argyll & Bute) 'Sunny place'. *Grianan* (Scottish Gaelic) 'sunny place'. A frequent local name for a sun-facing slope. Grenan in Bute has the same source, as do Grennan and Bargrennan in Dumfries & Galloway, the latter incorporating *barr* (Scottish Gaelic) 'height'. In Lewis, the name is found in its original Gaelic form.

Greenlaw (Midlothian) 'Green hill'. *Law* (Scots) 'hill'.

Greenock (Inverclyde) Place of the 'sunny hillock'. *Grian-aig* (Scottish Gaelic) 'sunny'; most authorities attribute the last syllable to meaning 'hilly place' or 'hillock'. Certainly, as is the case for the neighbouring town of Gourock, the terrain here rises steeply from the Firth of Clyde and Lyle Hill is a notable landmark.

Gretna Green (Dumfries & Galloway) Possibly place of the 'gravelly haugh'. *Greoten* (Old English) 'gravelly'; *halth* (Old English) 'haugh' or 'fertile land enclosed by the bend of a river'. The village takes its name from the adjacent village of Gretna, both settlements being beside the River Sark. Records show Gretenho in 1223, Gretenhowe in 1376 and Gretnay in 1576. This village, 'first and last' in Scotland, was the wedding place of many eloping English couples, taking advantage of Scotland's relaxed marriage laws.

Grimshader (Western Isles) 'Grim's farm'. *Grimr* (Old Norse proper name); *seadair* (Scottish Gaelic from Old Norse *saetr*) 'farm'.

Gruinard [Green-yard] (Highland) 'Split firth'. *Grein* (Old Norse) 'split' or 'divided'; *fjordr* (Old Norse) 'firth'. Now known as Gruinard Bay and divided by Gruinard Isle in the centre.

Guard Bridge (Fife) 'Bridge by the enclosure'. *Gart* (Scottish Gaelic) 'enclosure' or 'field'.

Guay (Perth & Kinross) 'Boggy plain'. *Gaoth* (Scottish Gaelic) 'marsh'; *magh* (Scottish Gaelic) 'plain'.

Guildtown (Perth & Kinross) This 'new' township on the left bank of the Tay, north of Perth, was founded in 1818 on land owned by the Perth Guildry.

Gullane [Gull-an] (East Lothian) The name of this Lothian resort east of North Berwick has been derived from *guallan* (Scottish Gaelic) 'shoulder', perhaps with the local hill, Gullane Law, in mind. The emphasis on the first syllable makes a *-linn*, 'lake' ending unlikely.

Gushetfaulds (Glasgow) 'Cattle or sheep-folds in the gore'. *Gushet* (Scots) 'triangular corner', 'gusset' or 'gore'; *fauld* (Scots) 'fold'.

Gyle, Glen *see* **Goil.**

H

Haddington (East Lothian) 'Hada's people's farm'. *Hada* (personal name); *inga* (Old English) 'people's'; *tun* (Old English) 'farm'. The former county town of East Lothian and a busy market centre. Recorded as Hadynton in 1098 and Hadintun and Hadingtoun in 1150.

Haddo (Aberdeenshire) 'Half-davoch', an agricultural measure of land reckoned by the number of beasts that worked it. The name is derived as 'half' (Old English) and *dabhach* (Scottish Gaelic) 'land measure'. Apart from Haddo House, there is another Haddo near Rattray Head. Many names, especially field and farm names, come from land-measurement terms. *See* **Arrochar, Kirriemuir, Pennyghael** and **Pinmill.**

Hailes (Edinburgh) 'Hall'. *Heal* (Old English) 'hall' – a place of assembly is implied.

Halbeath (Fife) 'Wood of birches'. *Coille* (Scottish Gaelic) 'wood'; *beath* (Scottish Gaelic) 'of birches'.

Halkirk (Highland) 'High church'. *Há* (Old Norse) 'high'; *kirkju* (Old Norse) 'church'. The Gaelic name is *Hacraig*, presumably from a change in pronunciation of the original form from *kirk* to *krik*. Early Bishops of Caithness had their seat here.

Halladale, River and **Strath** (Highland) Either 'Helgi's dale' or 'holy dale'. The latter from *helg* (Old Norse) 'hallowed' and *dalr* (Old Norse) 'valley'. The Gaelic form, *Healadal*, suggests the first interpretation. Recorded in 1222 as Helgadal.

Hamilton (South Lanarkshire) The name comes from the Norman-French name *de Hameldon*. Originally a village by the name of Cadzow, it was renamed by the first Lord Hamilton when he moved here from England in the 15th century. *See* **Cadzow**.

Hamar (Shetland) This name is found in a number of steep locations. *Hamar-r* (Old Norse) 'hammer' or 'crag'.

Hamnavoe (Shetland) 'Harbour of the bay'. *Hamn* (Old Norse) 'harbour'; *vagr* (Old Norse) 'bay'. There are two fishing villages of this name on Shetland, one on West Burra and the other on Yell. It is also an old name for Stromness.

Handa (Highland) 'Sand island'. *Handr* (Old Norse) 'sand'; *ey* (Old Norse) 'island'. Nowadays, this island off the Sutherland coast is a bird sanctuary.

Handwick (Shetland) 'Sand bay'. *Handr* (Old Norse) 'sand'; *vik* (Old Norse) 'bay'.

Hare Law (Dumfries & Galloway, Borders) Possibly 'Hares' hill'. *Hara* (Old English) and *heri* (Old Norse) 'hare'; *law* (Scots from Old English *hlaw*) 'hill'. An alternative possibility comes from *hára* (Old English with a similar form in Old Norse) 'old' or 'hoary', which is normally used in conjunction with *stan* (Old English) 'stone', indicating a boundary stone.

Hare Ness (Aberdeenshire) 'Higher ness'. *Har* (Scots from Old English *hiera*) 'higher'; *nes* (Old Norse) 'cape'.

Harlaw (Aberdeenshire) 'Hare hill'. *Law* (Scots from Old English *hlaw*) 'hill'. This Scots name may be a translated version of a Gaelic name, since prior to Robert Bruce's 'herschip' of Buchan in 1307, names in this region would have been Pictish, Gaelic or Norse. *See* **Hare Law** and **Hare Ness** above for alternative possibilities. In 1411, the armies of the Lord of the Isles and the Earl of Buchan met in a fierce but inconclusive battle here.

Harray (Orkney) 'High island'. *Hár* (Old Norse) 'high'; *ey* (old Norse) 'island'.

Harris (Western Isles) 'Higher island'. *Haerri* (Old Norse from *hár*) 'higher' seems the likeliest derivation, though the *-s* ending is a problem. The Gaelic rendering is *Na h-Earrad*, with the definite article. It does seem probable that the name is descriptive of a topography of high hills, especially as compared with the lower-lying Lewis. Recorded as Heradh in 1500, The Harrey in 1542 and Harreis in 1588. Harris is not a separate island but the southerly and more mountainous part of the island which also forms Lewis to the north.

Hartfell (Dumfries & Galloway, Borders) 'Stag's hill'. *Hart* (Old English) 'stag'; *fell* (Old English) 'hill'.

Hasker (Western Isles) 'Deep sea skerry'. *Hafr* (Old Norse) 'open sea'; *sker* (Old Norse) 'reef' or 'skerry'. Heisker has the same derivation.

Hatton (Aberdeenshire and other regions) 'Hall farm'. *Hall* (Old English) 'manor house'; *tun* (Old English, giving Scots *toun*) 'farm-stead'. This was a common name in the 16th and 17th centuries for the large farmhouse in which the laird lived. As with many Scots words ending in *-all*, the *-l* sound has been lost.

Hawick [Haw-ick] (Borders) 'Hedged enclosure settlement'. *Haga* (Old English) 'hedge'; *wic* (Old English) 'settlement' or 'farm'. It was recorded as Hawic in the 12th century.

Hawthornden (Borders) 'Hawthorn dale'. *Denu* (Old English) 'valley'. This was the estate of William Drummond, the leading Scottish poet of the 17th century.

Hebrides (Western Isles) *Haebudes*, the name given to the Inner Hebrides by the Romans, has also been applied to the 'Long Island' or Outer Hebrides. It is found in the writings of Pliny in the first century and Ptolemy (*circa* 150) has the Greek form *Eboudai*. The present name is the product of a misreading of *ri* for *u* in the transcription of ancient manuscripts.

Hecla (Western Isles) This mountain in South Uist (2,000 feet/612 metres) shares its name with a famous volcano in Iceland. *Hekla* (Old Norse) 'cowl' or 'hooded cloak'.

Helensburgh (Argyll & Bute) 'Helen's town'. This carefully planned residential town of 1776, on the north shore of the Firth of Clyde, was named in honour of Lady Helen Sutherland, wife of Sir James Colquhoun of Luss, who bought land here in 1752.

Hell's Glen (Argyll & Bute) English translation of *Gleann* (Scottish Gaelic) 'valley' or 'glen'; *Ifrinn* (Scottish Gaelic) 'Hell'. But it is likely, with the original Gaelic *aifrionn* meaning 'chapel' or 'place of offerings', that the meaning is the complete opposite.

Helmsdale (Highland) 'Hjalmund's dale'. *Hjalmund* (Old Norse personal name) 'helmet'; *dalr* (Old Norse) 'valley' or 'dale'. Recorded in the *Orkneyinga Saga* (*circa* 1225) as Hjalmunddal.

Heriot (Borders) Perhaps 'strategic pass'. *Here* (Old English) 'army'; *geat* (Old English) 'hill-pass'. An alternative is *here-geatu*, 'army equipment', perhaps a form of service required from the tenant. *Heriot* remains a Scots law term for the landlord's claim to part of a deceased tenant's estate (usually the best cow).

Hermiston (Edinburgh) 'Herd's place'. *Hirdmannis* (Old English) 'herdsman's'; *tun* (Old English) 'settlement' or 'place'. The name was borrowed for literary use in Robert Louis Stevenson's unfinished novel *Weir of Hermiston*.

Highland Since 1975 this word, properly an adjective and not a noun, has been the name of the northernmost administrative region of mainland Scotland. The correct term is 'Highlands'.

Highlandman (Perth & Kinross) The road here was known as Highlandman's Loan, since it was the route south for Highland cattle drovers, coming from the Crieff cattle tryst.

Hirta (Western Isles) This, as *Hirt* or *Hiort*, is the Scottish Gaelic name of the St Kilda Islands but in English it has become the name of the main island. Its derivation has been variously explained as *hirtir* (Old Norse) 'stags', recorded from 1202 and presumably a reference to the horn-like peaks of the islands; as *hjorth-ey* (Old Norse) 'herd island'; and as *hirt* (Old Irish) 'death' with the sense that this remote archipelago was the gateway to the western underworld. *See* **St Kilda.**

Hobkirk (Borders) 'Church in the valley'. *Hop* (Old Norse) 'shelter' or 'valley'; *kirkja* (Old Norse) 'church'. Formerly known as Hopekirk and recorded as Hopechirke in 1220; Hopeskirk in 1586 and Hoppkirck *circa* 1610. *See* **Kirkhope.**

Holburn Head (Highland, Aberdeenshire) Probably 'beacon cape'. *Holl* (Old Norse) 'hill'; *bruni* (Old Norse) 'burning'.

Holy Loch (Argyll & Bute) English form of the Scottish Gaelic *An Loch Seunnta*. *Seunnta* (Scottish Gaelic) 'sacred'. Apparently so called from its association with St Mund, follower of St Columba and an early Christian missionary at work in this area of the Cowal Peninsula. *See* **Kilmun.**

Holyrood (Edinburgh) 'Holy cross'. *Halig* (Old English) 'holy'; *rod* (Old English) 'cross'. This name, associated with the royal palace of Holyroodhouse in Edinburgh, was originally that of the 12th-century abbey founded by King David I and containing the 'black rood' (said to hold part of the True Cross, brought to Scotland by his mother, St Margaret).

Holywood (Dumfries & Galloway) Literally 'holy wood' but originally Darcongall or 'wood of St Congal'. *Doire* (Scottish Gaelic) 'copse'. An abbey was founded here in the 12th century.

Hope, Ben and **Loch** (Highland) 'Bay'. *Hop* (Old Norse) 'bay' or 'shelter place'. The mountain (3,040 feet/929 metres) takes its name from the loch, as does the township of Hope.

Hopeman (Moray) This relatively recent (1805) fishing village seems to derive its name from Haudmont, a local estate name. *Haut* (French) 'high'; *mont* (French) 'hill'.

Hourn, Loch (Highland) 'Furnace, kiln or gully'. *Sòrn* (Scottish Gaelic) 'snout', 'furnace' or 'concavity'. The latter meaning seems most apt to this deeply incised mountain sea loch, whose Gaelic form is *Loch Shuirn*. The *s* has given way to *h* in pronunciation in the same way as Corriehalloch.

Houston (Renfrewshire) 'Hugo's farmstead'. *Hugo* (Old English personal name); *tun* (Old English) 'farmstead'. This residential village has grown up around the 12th-century farmstead property of Hugo de Paduinan.

Howe o' the Mearns (Aberdeenshire) This district, between Laurencekirk and Stonehaven, is literally 'the hollow of the Mearns', from *howe* (Scots) 'hollow'. It is a direct translation of the Gaelic *Lag na Maoirne. See* **Mearns**.

Howgate (Midlothian) Perhaps 'road of the howe'. *Howe* (Scots) 'hollow'; *gait* (Scots) 'road'.

Hoy (Orkney) 'High island'. *Hár* (Old Norse) 'high'; *ey* (Old Norse) 'island'. Hoy is much higher than than any of the other Orkney Islands and has lofty cliffs and the celebrated rock stack (450 feet/138 metres) known as 'The Old Man of Hoy'. It was recorded as Haey in the *Orkneyinga Saga* (*circa* 1225). *See* **Harray**.

Humbie (Fife, East Lothian) 'Dog's town'. *Hund* (Old English) 'dog', probably used as a nickname; *by* (Old Norse) 'settlement' or 'place'.

Huntly (Aberdeenshire) 'Huntsman's wood'. *Hunta* (Old English) 'huntsman'; *leah* (Old English) 'wood'. Originally a Borders place name (there is still a Huntlywood to be found near Earlston), it was transferred north by the Gordon family who became landholders here. Alexander Gordon, 4th Duke of Gordon and Earl of Huntly, founded the present town in 1769 at the confluence of the Deveron and Bogie rivers.

Hutchesontown (Glasgow) The land in this Glasgow area was purchased by the Hutcheson brothers, founders of Hutcheson's Hospital (1639) and developed in the 1790s.

Hyndland (Glasgow) 'Back land'. Hyndland (Scots) 'back land' is a precise translation of the Gaelic form *cul tir. See* **Culter**.

I

Ibrox (Glasgow) 'Ford of the badger'. *Ath* (Scottish Gaelic) 'ford'; *bruic* (Scottish Gaelic) 'badger'. *See* **Broxburn**. Ibrox Park is the home ground of Glasgow Rangers FC.

Inchaffray (Perth & Kinross) 'Isle or water-meadow of the chapel'. *Innis* (Scottish Gaelic) 'island' or 'water-meadow'; *aifrionn* (Scottish Gaelic) 'chapel' or 'place of offering'. Situated on the Pow (Scots, 'sluggish stream') Water, east of Crieff, this was an important monastery in medieval times.

Inchard, Loch (Highland) 'Meadow-fjord'. *Engi* (Old Norse) 'meadow'; *fjordr* (Old Norse) 'firth'. As in many other cases, 'Loch' is a superfluous later addition, made when the sense of the Norse suffix was lost.

Inch Cailleach (Argyll & Bute) 'Isle of the Old Woman'. *Innis* (Scottish Gaelic) 'island'; *cailleach* (Scottish Gaelic) 'old woman'. One of the islands in Loch Lomond.

Inchcape (Highland, Angus) 'Isle or water-meadow of the block or head'. *Innis* (Scottish Gaelic) 'island'; *ceap* (Scottish Gaelic) 'block' or 'head'. In the case of the Inchcape Rock off Arbroath, famous for its one-time warning bell and present lighthouse, the 'block' is the rock itself.

Inchcolm (Fife) 'Island of (St) Columba'. *Innis* (Scottish Gaelic) 'island'; *Columba* (Latin 'dove' giving Gaelic *Colum*). This small island in the Firth of Forth is the site of the now ruined abbey dedicated to St Columba and founded in 1123 by King Alexander I.

Inchinnan (Renfrewshire) 'Isle of St Finnan'. *Innis* (Scottish Gaelic) 'island'; *Finnén* (Old Gaelic proper name). St Finnan is remembered in numerous place names. *See* **Kilwinning**.

Inchmahome (Stirling) 'Isle of St Colman'. *Innis* (Scottish Gaelic) 'island'; *mo* (Scottish Gaelic) 'my'; *Colmóc* (Old Irish proper name, form of Colmán). This island in the Lake of Menteith still has the ruins of its monastery.

Inchkeith (Midlothian) The first part of this island name from the Firth of Forth is *innis* (Scottish Gaelic) 'island'. The latter part does not appear to have any connections with *coed* (Brythonic) 'wood'. St Bede's *History of the English Church* (*circa* 720) refers to 'Giudi', which may be a personal or tribal name.

Inchmarnock (Argyll & Bute) 'Island of dear little St Ernan'. *Innis* (Scottish Gaelic) 'island'; *mo* (Scottish Gaelic) 'my'; *Iarnan* (Irish Gaelic personal name with *-oc* Gaelic diminutive suffix) 'little Ernan'.

St Ernan, said to be St Columba's uncle, is commemorated in several different parts of the country. This island lies to the west of Bute. *See* **Kilmarnock**.

Inchmurrin (Argyll & Bute) 'Island of St Mirin'. *Innis* (Scottish Gaelic) 'island'; *Mirin* (personal name). St Mirin was a 7th-century Irish abbot who founded a monastery at Paisley where his name is also commemorated in that of the local football team, St Mirren. On Inchmurrin, the largest island in Loch Lomond, there are the ruins of his chapel.

Inchnadamph (Highland) 'Isle or water meadow of the oxen'. *Innis* (Scottish Gaelic) 'water meadow'; *na* (Scottish Gaelic) 'of the'; *daimh* (Scottish Gaelic) 'stag' or 'oxen'. The 'isle' sense here could refer to its being an area of arable limestone soil in the midst of a vast wilderness of infertile older rocks.

Inchture (Perth & Kinross) Possibly 'hunting meads'. *Innis* (Scottish Gaelic) 'water meadow'; *a* (Scottish Gaelic) 'of the'; *thòire* (Scottish Gaelic) 'pursuit'.

Inchtuthil (Perth & Kinross) 'Thwart-lying meadow'. *Innis* (Scottish Gaelic) 'meadow' or 'island'; *tuathal* (Scottish Gaelic) 'thwart-placed' or 'leftwards-bending'. This is the site of one of the largest Roman camps in Scotland.

Ingliston (Edinburgh) 'Ingialdr's farm'. *Ingialdr* (Old Norse personal name); *tun* (Old English) 'farm'. Though *Inglis* (Scots) 'of the English(man)' is equally possible. This area to the west of Edinburgh is now the permanent site of the Royal Highland Show.

Innellan (Argyll & Bute) 'Place of islands'. *An-eilean* (Scottish Gaelic) 'island place'.

Innerleithen (Borders) 'Confluence of the River Leithen'. *Inbhir* (Scottish Gaelic) 'confluence'; *Leithen* (Scottish Gaelic river name) is related to *leathann*, 'broad', with the sense of broad surrounding slopes. Recorded as Innerlethan in 1160. This Borders woollen-manufacturing town is sited where the River Leithen meets the River Tweed.

Insch, also **Insh** (Aberdeenshire, Highland) 'Meadow'. *Innis* (Scottish Gaelic) 'water-meadow' or 'island'. Sometimes the local topography is the best guide and at Insch in Aberdeenshire, 'meadow' is more likely.

Inver (Highland, Perth & Kinross) 'River mouth or confluence (where a small river flows into a larger or into a loch or the sea.)'. *Inbhir* (Scottish Gaelic) 'river mouth' or 'confluence'. In the villages of Ross-shire and Perthshire, the name is used on its own (though Inver was once Inverlochslin). However, in hundreds of other places, it is a prefix to a river name or some other designatory term.

Inveraray (Argyll & Bute) 'Mouth of the River Aray'. *Inbhir* (Scottish Gaelic) 'river mouth'; *Aray* (Pre-Celtic river name) probably means 'smooth-running'. This river name is widely found throughout Europe in many variant forms: Aar, Ahr, Ahre, Aire, Ara, Ayr, Oare, Ohre, Ore. Rebuilt in the later 18th century, this was the administrative centre of the powerful Earls and Dukes of Argyll, whose seat remains Inveraray Castle.

Inverbervie (Aberdeenshire) 'Mouth of the Bervie Water'. *Inbhir* (Scottish Gaelic) 'river mouth'; *bervie* (probably Celtic river name similar to Welsh *berw*) 'boiling' or 'seething'. The original settlement here was Aberbervie, the Brythonic *Aber-* form more correctly reflecting the strong Brythonic-Pictish influence on the place names of the north-east part of Scotland.

Inverewe (Highland) 'Mouth of the River Ewe'. The site of a celebrated garden of temperate and sub-tropical plants. *See* **Kinlochewe**.

Invergarry (Highland) 'Mouth of the River Garry'. *Inbhir* (Scottish Gaelic) 'river mouth'; *Garry* (Scottish Gaelic river name derived from *garbh*) 'rough'. The village is sited where the river tumbles into Loch Oich, cutting through the steep-sided Great Glen.

Invergordon (Highland) This town has a fabricated name given in around 1760 to honour its founder, Sir Alexander Gordon, who was the landowner at the time. Previously, the name of the small village here, at the mouth of the local Breckie (from *breac* (Gaelic) 'speckled') Burn, was Inverbreckie. Invergordon was an important naval base in the two 20th-century world wars and today it repairs oil rigs.

Invergowrie (Perth & Kinross) 'Mouth of the Gowrie'. *See* **Gowrie**.

Inverkeilor (Angus) 'Mouth of the clay stream'. *Inbhir* (Scottish Gaelic) 'river mouth'; *cil* (Scottish Gaelic) 'red clay'; *dobhar* (Brythonic-Gaelic) 'stream'. *See* **Rankeillor**.

Inverkeithing (Fife) 'Mouth of the Keithing Burn'. *Inbhir* (Scottish Gaelic) 'river mouth'; *Keithing* (Brythonic river name derived from *coed*, 'wood'). Early records show Hinhirkethy *circa*.1050, Innerkethyin 1114 and Inverchethin *circa* 1200.

Inverkip (Inverclyde) 'River mouth by the crag'. *Inbhir* (Scottish Gaelic) 'river mouth'; *ceap* (Scottish Gaelic) 'block' or 'head'.

Inverkirkaig (Highland) 'Mouth of the kirk-bay stream'. *Inbhir* (Scottish Gaelic) 'river mouth'; *kirkja* (Old Norse) 'church'; *vik* (Old Norse) 'bay'. In this case, the settlement has untypically given its name to the river.

Invermoriston *see* **Moriston, River** and **Glen.**

Inverness (Highland) 'Mouth of the River Ness'. *Inbhir* (Scottish Gaelic) 'river mouth'; *Nis* (Pre-Celtic river name of undetermined origin). Situated where the River Ness, having flowed out of the nearby Loch Ness, discharges into the Moray Firth. Always the largest town in the Highlands, this town is the main commercial and administrative centre for a vast region of northern and north-west Scotland. *See* **Ness.**

Inveroran (Highland) 'Mouth of the stream'. *Inbhir* (Scottish Gaelic) 'mouth' or 'confluence'; *dhobhran* (Brythonic-Scottish Gaelic) 'water' or 'stream'.

Inversnaid (Stirling) 'Mouth of the needle-stream'. The name of this stream flowing into Loch Lomond appears to be connected with *snàthad* (Scottish Gaelic) 'needle'.

Inveruglas (Argyll & Bute) 'Mouth of the dark stream'. *Inbhir* (Scottish Gaelic) 'mouth' or 'confluence'; *dubh* (Scottish Gaelic) 'dark'; *glais* (Scottish Gaelic) 'water'. After the *r* the *d* of *dubh* is lost.

Inverurie (Aberdeenshire) 'Confluence of the River Urie'. *Inbhir* (Scottish Gaelic) 'river mouth' or 'confluence'; *Urie* (Scottish Gaelic river name), *see* **Urie**. Here the Urie flows into the River Don.

Iona (Argyll & Bute) This small island off the south-west coast of Mull was probably a sacred site long before its association with the Celtic church. There is no doubt that the original form was *Ioua*, and manuscript writers supplanted the *u* with an *n*. The most probable derivation is from *eo* (Old Irish) 'yew'. The yew has always been associated with holy places. From the late 6th century, the island was closely associated with the fame of St Columba. When the area passed into Norse control, the name appears to have undergone some confusion with -*ey* (Norse) 'island'. A document around 1100 records the name of Hiona-Columcille and until about 1800 the island was known as Icolmkill, from *ey* (Old Norse) 'isle' and *Columcille* (Scottish Gaelic) 'dove of the church'.

Irongray (Dumfries & Galloway) 'Land portion of the horse stud'. *Earran* (Scottish Gaelic) 'portion'; *na* (Scottish Gaelic) 'of'; *greigh* (Scottish Gaelic) 'the horse herd' or 'stud'.

Irvine (North Ayrshire) Possibly place of 'the white (river)'. *Yr* (Brythonic) 'the'; *(g)wyn* (Brythonic) 'white'. Early records show Yrewyn *circa* 1140 and Irvin in 1230.

Isbister (Orkney) 'Ine's farm'. *Ine* (Old Norse proper name); *bolstadr* (Old Norse) 'farmstead'.

Isla, River and **Strath** (Moray, Perth & Kinross) The derivation has been tentatively traced back to a Pre-Celtic root-form *il* or *eil*, with the meaning of 'rapid-moving'.

Islay (Argyll & Bute) Possibly 'Ile's island'. *Ile* (personal name); *ey* (Old Norse) 'island'. The name of this large and most southerly of the Inner Hebrides has at least in part a Norse origin, in common with most of the major islands off the west coast of Scotland. The insertion of the *s* is relatively recent. Recorded as Ilea *circa* 690 and Ile in 800.

J

Jarlshof (Shetland) 'Earl's Court'. *Jarl* (Old Norse) 'earl'; *hof* (Old Norse) 'court'. The name of this important archaeological site at the southern tip of Shetland's mainland was devised by Sir Walter Scott in 1816. Its original name is not recorded.

Jedburgh (Borders) 'Town by the Jed Water'. The first element of the name of this Borders town, with its famous ruined abbey, is that of its river, the Jed, probably derived from a version of *gweden* (Brythonic) 'winding' or 'twisting' (as of a river meander). The second element has its origins as *burh* (Old English) 'town'. Prior to its establishment as a burgh, the settlement name was Jed-worth, signifying 'enclosure by the Jed Water' and still found in Bonjedward, a three-language hybrid of *Bonn* (Scottish Gaelic) 'foot'; *jed* and *worth* (Old English) 'enclosure'. Jedworth is also preserved in the form 'Jeddart'. Records confirm Gedwearde *circa* 800, Geddewrde in 1100, Gedword in 1130, Jaddeuurd *circa* 1145 and Jeddeburgh in 1160.

Jemimaville (Highland) A 'new' 18th or early 19th century village, named after the wife of the laird, Sir George Munro, *circa* 1830. The '-ville' termination is an effort towards something more sophisticated than the old '-ton'.

John o' Groats (Highland) Wrongly supposed by many to be the most northerly place in mainland Britain (actually Dunnet Head). It was named after John de Groot, a Dutchman who came to live in Caithness in the late 15th century under the patronage of King James IV. The final *s* of the name is a reminder that the original form was 'John o' Groat's House', still preserved in a children's nursery rhyme.

Johnstone (Renfrewshire, Dumfries & Galloway) 'John's settlement'. *John* (personal name); *tun* (Old English) 'farm' or 'settlement'. The names go back to the 13th and 12th centuries respectively.

Joppa (Edinburgh) Biblical names are not uncommon in Scotland from the 16th century on, though usually applied to farms or even fields rather than larger communities. The name of this district of Edinburgh, on the shore of the Firth of Forth, came in the 1780s from that of a farm called after the Biblical Joppa (now Jaffa). The name itself is thought to be derived as *yapho* (Hebrew) 'beautiful'.

Jordanhill (Edinburgh, Glasgow) For these names and for Edinburgh's Jordan Burn, a landowner's religious feeling seems the most likely explanation.

Juniper Green (Edinburgh) A 19th-century name. This south-west residential district of Edinburgh was formerly a small isolated settlement having the name of Curriemuirend, the next place to the west being the village of Currie. First recorded in 1812, the name is probably an accurate description of the locality at the time.

Jura (Argyll & Bute) Apparently 'Doirad's island'. *Doirad* (Scottish Gaelic personal name); *ey* (Old Norse) 'island'. The latter Old Norse ending may have substituted the earlier Gaelic form, recorded as *Doirad Eilinn* in a document of AD 678.

K

Kames (Inverclyde, Orkney, other regions) The Kameses in Strathclyde and in the Northern Isles have separate derivations: *camas* (Scottish Gaelic) 'landing creek' or 'bay' in the south; and *kambr* (Old Norse) 'crest' in the north. Thus the Kames of Hoy is a hill. But there is also a Kaim Hill in Renfrewshire. There are numerous other Kameses in localities throughout the country, sometimes spelt Kaimes, as in south-east Edinburgh.

Katrine, Loch (Stirling) Although the river flowing out of Loch Katrine is the Achray Water, the name may nevertheless be a river name, from *cet* (Brythonic) 'wood', cognate with *coed* (Welsh) and the same archaic river name as may be found in 'Earn', making 'wood river'. Since the 1850s this loch has been the prime source of Glasgow's water supply.

Keil (Argyll & Bute) 'Church (place)'. *Cill* (Scottish Gaelic) 'church'.

Keiss (Highland) 'Jutting place'. *Keisa* (Old Norse) 'protrude'. Tang (from *tange* [Old Norse] 'tongue') Head does protrude into the sea by this Caithness village.

Keith (Moray) The etymology is unclear. It has been associated with the Pictish proper name Cait but may more probably be from *coit* (Brythonic and Old Gaelic) 'wood', cognate with *coed* (Welsh) as in Dalkeith. Recorded in 1203 as Ket. Fife Keith, beside the old town and laid out in 1817, commemorates James Duff, 4th Earl of Fife. The town was referred to as Kethmalruf ('of St Maelrubha') in 1220 and as Ketmariscalli ('of the marischal') in 1250, the latter noting its association with the Keiths, hereditary Earls Marischal of Scotland.

Kellie (Fife) Perhaps 'holly'. *Celyn* (Brythonic) 'holly'. Compare **Cullen**.

Kells (Dumfries & Galloway) Perhaps 'wells' or 'springs'. *Kell* (Old Norse) 'spring'.

Kelso (Borders) Place of the 'chalk hill'. *Calc* (Old English) 'chalk'; *how* (Old English) 'hill'. There is still a part of the town known as 'the chalkheugh'. Early records show Calkou in 1126, Kelcou in 1158 and Kelsowe in 1420. This Tweedside town preserves the ruins of a fine Romanesque abbey, founded in 1128.

Kelty (Fife) 'Woods'. *Coilltean* (Scottish Gaelic) 'woods'. A record of 1250 shows Quilte.

Kelvinside (Glasgow) 'Narrow river'. *Caol abhainn* (Scottish Gaelic) 'narrow river'. This leafy district of the West End of Glasgow takes its name from the River Kelvin, a north bank tributary of the River Clyde. Certainly, 'narrow river' is descriptive of the deep gorge that the Kelvin cuts through this area of the city.

Kemnay (Aberdeenshire) 'Head of the plain'. *Ceann* (Scottish Gaelic) 'head'; *a'* (Scottish Gaelic) 'of the'; *maigh* (Scottish Gaelic) 'plain'. The transposing of the *n* and *m* goes back at least to the 14th century, in the early years of which the region was forcibly scotticised by Robert Bruce.

Ken, River and **Loch** (Dumfries & Galloway) 'White (stream)'. *Càin* (Scottish Gaelic) 'white'.

Kenmore (Perth & Kinross) 'Great head'. *Ceann* (Scottish Gaelic) 'head'; *mòr* (Scottish Gaelic) 'big'.

Kenmure (Dumfries & Galloway) 'Moor of the Ken'. *See* **Ken**.

Kennethmont (Aberdeenshire) 'St Alcmund's church'. Alcmund was an early Bishop of Hexham. This name is recorded from the 12th century as Kylalcmund with *cill* (Scottish Gaelic) 'church'. Kynalcmund is also an old form. As memory of Alcmund faded, the name was misinterpreted and modelled with a false etymology on the more familiar name 'Kenneth'.

Kennoway (Fife) 'Head field'. *Ceann* (Scottish Gaelic) 'head'; *achadh* (Scottish Gaelic) 'field'. A small agricultural town lying a few miles inland from the coastal plain. Recorded as Kennachyn in 1250.

Kentallen (Argyll & Bute) 'Head of the inlet'. *Ceann* (Scottish Gaelic) 'head'; *an t'* (Scottish Gaelic) 'of the'; *saileinn* (Scottish Gaelic) 'small inlet'. *See* **Kintail.**

Keppoch (Highland) 'Block or top'. *Ceap* (Scottish Gaelic) 'block' or 'top'; with *-ach* (Scottish Gaelic suffix) 'field'. There are several locations of this name, the best known being that in Lochaber, associated with the Macdonalds of Keppoch.

Kerrera (Argyll & Bute) Perhaps 'copse island'. *Kjarbr* (Old Norse) 'copse'; *ey* (Old Norse) 'island'. This island in Oban Bay is where Alexander II died suddenly on his campaign to reclaim the Hebrides from the Norwegians.

Kerry (Highland) 'Fourth part'. *Ceathraimh* (Scottish Gaelic) 'quarter', relating to early land divisions. *See* **Kirriemuir.**

Kershopefoot (Borders) 'Foot of Kerr's hollow'. *Kerr* (proper name from *càrr* [Scottish Gaelic] 'marsh'); *hop* (Old English) 'hollow'. *Kerse* (Scots) 'carse' has been suggested as an alternative for *Kerr*.

Kessock (Highland) 'St Kessoc's place'. Kessoc was a Pictish saint of whom little is known. North and South Kessock mark the former ferry points from Inverness across to the Black Isle.

Kilbarchan (Renfrewshire) Probably the place of 'St Berchan's church'. *Cill* (Scottish Gaelic) 'church'; *Berchan* (personal name) of a 7th-century Irish saint).

Kilbirnie (North Ayrshire) Probably the place of 'St Brendan's church'. *Cill* (Scottish Gaelic) 'church'; *Brénaind* (Irish Gaelic personal name) of either of two 6th-century Irish saints of this name, both with genuine Scottish links.

Kilbowie (Renfrewshire) 'Yellow back'. *Cùl* (Scottish Gaelic) 'back', perhaps here implying 'of the hill'; *buidhe* (Scottish Gaelic) 'yellow'. 13th-century forms of the name show the *cùl* prefix, as in Cullbuthe.

Kilbrandon (Argyll & Bute) 'Church of St Brandon'. *Cill* (Scottish Gaelic) 'church'; *Brénaind* (Irish Gaelic personal name). This was 'Brendan the Voyager', who founded a church on the isle of Hinba, off Mull.

Kilbrannan (Argyll & Bute) 'Strait of Brandon'. *Caol* (Scottish Gaelic) 'strait' or 'kyle'; *Brénaind* (Irish Gaelic personal name). Ignorance of the Gaelic meaning has prompted the addition of 'Sound' to the name of this sea channel between Arran and Kintyre.

Kilbride (Argyll & Bute) 'St Bride's church'. *Cill* (Scottish Gaelic) 'church'; *Brìd* (Irish Gaelic proper name) 'Bride' or 'Bridget'. Fifteen saints bore the name of Brìd and the name is spread across Scotland. *See also* **East Kilbride**.

Kilchoan (Highland) 'St Comgan's church'. *Cill* (Scottish Gaelic) 'church'; *Chomhghain* (Scottish Gaelic personal name, giving modern Cowan). Comgan was a holy man of the 8th century.

Kilchomain *see* **Fort Augustus**.

Kilchurn (Argyll & Bute) 'Strait of the cairn'. *Caol* (Scottish Gaelic) 'strait' or 'kyle'; *chùirn* (Scottish Gaelic) 'of the cairn'. This castle-island is dramatically situated in Loch Awe.

Kilconquhar (Fife) 'Church of Conchobar'. *Cill* (Scottish Gaelic) 'church'; *Conchubair* (Old Irish proper name). The name later became compressed to Conchar. At one time the name was spelled Kinyuchar, which suggests *ceann* (Scottish Gaelic) 'head' and *uachdair* (Scottish Gaelic) 'of the upper ground' and implies a false assumption as to the Gaelic etymology. The *Kil-* references predate the *Kin-* ones.

Kilcreggan (Argyll & Bute) 'Church on the little crag'. *Cill* (Scottish Gaelic) 'church'; *creag* (Scottish Gaelic) 'rock' or 'crag'; *-an* (Scottish Gaelic diminutive suffix).

Kildalton (Argyll & Bute) 'The daughter church'. *Cill* (Scottish Gaelic) 'church'; *daltain* (Scottish Gaelic) 'of the foster child'. The name implies a church set up by a mother foundation, a common practice in the Celtic church. The Kildalton Cross is one of the finest carved Celtic crosses.

Kildary (Highland) The *Kil-* of this Easter Ross village is *caol* (Scottish Gaelic) 'narrow' prefixed to *daire* (Scottish Gaelic) 'oak wood'. Cognate with Kildare in Ireland.

Kildonan (Highland) 'Church of St Donnán'. *Cill* (Scottish Gaelic) 'church'; *Donnán* (Irish Gaelic proper name). Little is known of St Donnán, though he is associated with Eigg and is said to have been martyred by a queen. Legend gives him the sobriquet of 'the Great'. This district of Sutherland was the scene of a 'gold rush' in the 1880s when gold was found in the stream.

Kildrummy (Aberdeenshire) 'Head of the ridge'. *Ceann* (Scottish Gaelic) 'head'; *druim* (Scottish Gaelic) 'ridge'. Known earlier as Kindrummie, the village and the ruined 13th-century keep are on the edge of the Correen Hills.

Kilkerran (Argyll & Bute) 'Church of St Ciaran'. *Cill* (Scottish Gaelic) 'church'; *Chiaráin* (Old Irish proper name). This is probably St Ciaran of Clonmacnoise in Ireland, who died in AD 549. Kilkerran was a former name of present-day Campbeltown.

Killiecrankie (Perth & Kinross) 'Wood of aspen trees'. *Coille* (Scottish Gaelic) 'wood'; *creitheannich* (Scottish Gaelic) 'aspens'. Just south of the village is the still heavily wooded Pass of Killiecrankie, where in 1689 the troops of King William II were defeated by the Jacobites led by Graham of Claverhouse.

Killin (Stirling) Possibly place of the 'white church'. *Cill* (Scottish Gaelic) 'church'; *fionn* (Scottish Gaelic) 'white'. Alternatively, it may be derived from *cilltean* (Scottish Gaelic) 'burying ground', as this has long been a sacred place for the MacNab clan. This picturesque village is a tourist centre for Loch Tay.

Kilmacolm (Inverclyde) 'Church of my Columba'. *Cill* (Scottish Gaelic) 'church'; *mo* (Scottish Gaelic) 'of my'; *Coluim* (personal name) referring to St Columba, the famous early Irish-Scots saint. The addition of *mo* here denotes dedication. Kilmacolme is recorded in 1205.

Kilmahog (Stirling) 'Church of Cùg'. *Cill* (Scottish Gaelic) 'church'; *mo* (Scottish Gaelic) 'of my'; *Chùg* (Scottish Gaelic personal name from Islay, anglicised to Cook).

Kilmallie (Highland) 'Church of Màillidh'. *Cill* (Scottish Gaelic) 'church; *Màillidh* (Old Gaelic personal name). Màillidh is one of the many early holy men about whom little is known.

Kilmaluag (Argyll & Bute) 'Church of Mo-Luoc'. *Cill* (Scottish Gaelic) 'church'; *mo* (Scottish Gaelic) 'of my'; *Lugaidh* (Old Irish proper name). He was one of the pioneer missionary saints whose name was often given wrongly as Moluag, the 'mo' element not being part of it.

Kilmannan (West Dunbartonshire) The name of a reservoir in the Kilpatrick Hills, just north of Old Kilpatrick, seems to preserve the name *Manau*, an ancient Brythonic personal name given to the region at the head of the Firth of Forth (*see also* **Slammannan**). *Kil* here may be a form of *cùl* (Gaelic) 'back', as in Kilbowie, and indicate the westernmost extent of the territory.

Kilmany (Fife) 'Eithne's Church'. *Cill* (Scottish Gaelic) 'church'; *m'*, abbreviated form of *mo* (Scottish Gaelic) 'my'; *Eithne* (Irish Gaelic feminine personal name). This was the name of Columba's mother but there is no definite indication that she is the dedicatee. The name is cognate with Kilmeny in Islay.

Kilmarnock (East Ayrshire) 'Church of my dear little St Ernan'. *Cill* (Scottish Gaelic) 'church'; *mo* (Scottish Gaelic) 'of my'; *Iarnan* (personal name, reputedly of the priest and uncle of St Columba); *-oc* (diminutive suffix). The name was recorded as Kelmernoke in 1299. This Ayrshire market town was once synonymous with the blue bonnet worn by the Scottish countryman.

Kilmaronock (Stirling) 'Church of my little St Ronan'. Apart from the different personal name, the derivation is the same as that of Kilmarnock.

Kilmartin (Argyll, Highland) 'Church of St Martin'. *Cill* (Scottish Gaelic) 'church'; *Mhàrtuinn* (Gaelic form of 'Martin'). St Martin of Tours, who taught St Ninian, was widely venerated in Gaelic Scotland.

Kilmaurs (East Ayrshire) 'Church of St Maurice'. *Cill* (Scottish Gaelic) 'church'; *Mauruis* (Scottish Gaelic form of 'Maurice'). Noted in the 15th century as Sancte Maure.

Kilmelfort (Argyll & Bute) 'Church of the sandy bay'. *Cill* (Scottish Gaelic) 'church'; *melr* (Old Norse) 'sand'; *fjordr* (Old Norse) 'bay' or 'loch'.

Kilmorack (Highland) 'Church of St Barr'. *Cill* (Scottish Gaelic) 'church'; *mo* (Scottish Gaelic) 'of my'; *Bharróc* (Irish Gaelic proper name of the saint most often met as Finbarr, from *fionn-barr*, 'white head').

Kilmore (Highland, Argyll & Bute) 'Great church'. *Cill* (Scottish Gaelic) 'church'; *mòr* (Scottish Gaelic) 'big'.

Kilmuir (Highland) 'Mary's church'. *Cill* (Scottish Gaelic) 'church'; *Mhuire* (Scottish Gaelic proper name) 'Mary's'. Kilmory has the same derivation.

Kilmun (Argyll & Bute) 'Church of St Mund'. *Cill* (Scottish Gaelic) 'church'; *Mundu* (Irish Gaelic personal name of a disciple and friend of St Columba). Recorded as Kilmun in 1240 and Kilmond in 1410. *See* **Holy Loch**.

Kilninver (Argyll & Bute) 'Church at the confluence'. *Cill* (Scottish Gaelic) 'church'; *an* (Scottish Gaelic) 'of the'; *inbhir* (Scottish Gaelic) 'confluence' or 'river mouth'.

Kilpatrick *see* **Old Kilpatrick.**

Kilravock (Highland) 'Church on the fort-place'. *Cill* (Scottish Gaelic) 'church'; *ràth* (Scottish Gaelic) 'ring-fort'; *-aig* (Scottish Gaelic suffix denoting place). The castle here is the seat of the chief of the Clan Rose.

Kilrenny (Fife) 'Church of the bracken'. *Cill* (Scottish Gaelic) 'church'; *reithneach* (Scottish Gaelic) 'bracken'.

Kilsyth (North Lanarkshire) Possibly 'church of St Syth'. *Cill* (Scottish Gaelic) 'church'; *Syth* (personal name). However, there is no recorded saint of such a name. Some authorities consider there may be an alternative derivation in *saighde* (Scottish Gaelic) 'arrows'. The place was recorded as Kelvesyth in 1210 and Kelnasythe in 1217, possibly suggesting some connection with the River Kelvin whose source is nearby at Kelvinhead.

Kiltarlity (Highland) 'Church of Talorcan'. *Cill* (Scottish Gaelic) 'church'; *Taraghlain* (Scottish Gaelic form of Pictish personal name) 'Talorcan's'. In the 13th century, the name was recorded as Kyltalargy. Talorcan may mean 'fair-browed'.

Kiltearn (Highland) 'Church of the Lord'. *Cill* (Scottish Gaelic) 'church'; *Tighearna* (Scottish Gaelic) 'Lord'.

Kilwinning (North Ayrshire) 'Church of St Finnian'. *Cill* (Scottish Gaelic) 'church'; *Finnian* (Irish Gaelic personal name). St Finian or Finnian learned under St Ninian and, in turn, taught St Columba.

Kinbrace (Highland) 'Seat of the chief (literally, of the brooch)'. *Ceann* (Scottish Gaelic) 'head' or 'head place'; *na* (Scottish Gaelic) 'of'; *bhraiste* (Scottish Gaelic) 'brooch'. A reference to the chief of the Clan Gunn and his possession of a distinctive heirloom.

Kincardine (Fife, Aberdeenshire, Highland) 'At the head of the wood'.

Cinn (Scottish Gaelic locative of *ceann*) 'at the head of'; *cardden* (Brythonic-Pictish) 'wood' or 'thicket'. This frequently found descriptive place name was adopted as that of the former county and present district of Kincardine in the Mearns area of eastern Scotland, after the 12th-century Kincardine Castle. Kincardine in Fife was the lowest road bridging-point of the Forth until the building of the Forth Road Bridge.

Kincardine o' Neil (Aberdeenshire) 'Kincardine of the O'Neils'. The name is to distinguish it from Kincardine in the Mearns and refers to the monastery of Banchory-Ternan, founded by descendants of the Uí Néill clan of Ulster, and of which this parish was a property.

Kincraig (Highland) 'End of the crag'. *Ceann* (Scottish Gaelic) 'head' or 'end'; *na* (Scottish Gaelic) 'of'; *creige* (Scottish Gaelic) 'crag' or 'rock'. Recorded in the 17th century as Kyncragye but the *-ie* ending has not stuck.

Kinfauns (Perth & Kinross) 'Head of the coltsfoot'. *Ceann* (Scottish Gaelic) 'head'; *fathan* (Scottish Gaelic) 'coltsfoot'. The termination is the Brythonic-Pictish *-ais*, indicative of place, and found only in the formerly Pictish area.

King Edward (Aberdeenshire) 'End of the (land) division'. *Cinn* (Scottish Gaelic) 'at the head of'; *eadaradh* (Scottish Gaelic) 'division'. Although the English kings Edward I and III ventured far into Scotland, the origin of the name has no connection with them and merely shows an attempt, when Gaelic was forgotten, to relate the Gaelic sound to something apparently meaningful. The locality has also given its name to a species of potato, a major crop in the region.

Kinghorn (Fife) 'At the head of the muddy ground'. *Cinn* (Scottish Gaelic) 'at the head of'; *gronn* (Scottish Gaelic) 'muddy land' or 'marshland'. The 'king' associations made by some, on account of the fact that it was on the cliffs near here that King Alexander III died after falling from his horse in 1286, are incorrect. It was recorded as Kingorn as early as 1140.

Kingoldrum (Angus) 'At the head of the wooded ridge'. *Cinn* (Scottish Gaelic) 'at the head of'; *coille* (Scottish Gaelic) 'wood'; *druim* (Scottish Gaelic) 'ridge'.

Kinglass, Glen (Stirling) 'Glen of the dog stream'. The Gaelic form is *Conghlais*, from *con*, 'dog' or 'wolf' and *glas*, 'stream'.

Kingshouse (Stirling) This remote settlement in the Moor of Rannoch was established as a government base and staging-post on the route between Stirling and Fort William.

Kingskettle (Fife) Possibly 'Ketil's point or head'. *Ceann* (Scottish Gaelic) 'head'; *Ketil* (Old Norse proper name). On the other side of the Firth of Forth is Kirkettle, another Gaelic-Norse hybrid meaning 'Ketil's cairn'.

Kingston (Moray) Originally Kingston-upon-Spey, this village at the mouth of the Spey was named after the English city of Kingston-upon-Hull by two expatriate timber merchants who set up their establishment here in 1784.

Kingussie (Highland) 'At the head of the pine wood'. *Cinn* (Scottish Gaelic) 'at the head of'; *ghiuthsaich* (Scottish Gaelic) 'pine wood' or 'fir wood'. Records show Kinguscy in 1210 and Kyngucy in 1380. Forests of fir trees and outcrops of the Scots Pine from the old Caledonian Forest are still very much a feature of the Strathspey landscape. This resort village has the Highland Folk Museum.

Kinlochbervie (Highland) 'Head of Loch Bervie'. *Ceann* (Scottish Gaelic) 'head' or 'end'; *Loch Biorbhaidh* (Scottish Gaelic) 'boiling or stormy loch'. As the only pier in the far north-west, it is an important landing-place for deep-sea fishing vessels. *See* **Inverbervie**.

Kinlochewe (Highland) 'Head of Loch Ewe'. *Ceann* (Scottish Gaelic) 'head' or 'end'; *Loch Lù* (Scottish Gaelic) possibly 'loch of the yew trees' or 'loch of the isthmus'. 'Loch of the isthmus' is from *eidh* (Old Norse) 'isthmus', which fits the short level stretch through which the river flows but seems etymologically less likely. Loch Ewe is a sea loch, whose name comes from the short River Ewe, which flows from the inland loch now known as Loch Maree but which formerly bore the name Loch Ewe. This explains why Kinlochewe is situated on Loch Maree but it remains unusual in that it is not at the end but midway on the south side. *See* **Maree**.

Kinlochleven (Highland) 'Head of Loch Leven'. *Ceann* (Scottish Gaelic) 'head'; *loch* (Scottish Gaelic) 'lake' or 'loch'; *léan* (Scottish Gaelic) 'swampy place'. *See* **Leven**, **Lomond**. The availability of hydroelectric power led to the establishment of the aluminium works in this remote spot.

Kinloss (Moray) Possibly 'head of the garden'. *Ceann* (Scottish Gaelic) 'head'; *lios* (Scottish Gaelic) 'garden'. This may have some reference to the abbey founded here in 1151, probably on an earlier religious site. It is now the site of an important military airfield and a centre for air-sea rescue operations.

Kinnaber (Angus) 'Head of the estuary'. *Ceann* (Scottish Gaelic) 'head'; *aber* (Brythonic-Pictish) 'mouth of a river'. This refers to the location near Montrose, above the estuaries of the North and South Esk rivers. The former railway junction here, where the east and west coast routes from London to Aberdeen merged, marked the winning post of the 'Race to the North' of the 1890s.

Kinnaird (Aberdeenshire) 'Hill head'. *Ceann* (Scottish Gaelic) 'head'; *àird* (Scottish Gaelic) 'height'. At Kinnaird Head, by Fraserburgh, the first lighthouse of the Commissioners for Northern Lights was erected in 1787. It is now a lighthouse museum.

Kinneil (West Lothian) 'Wall's end'. *Ceann* (Scottish Gaelic) 'head' or 'end'; *fhaill* (Scottish Gaelic) 'wall'. The location, a former colliery site, is close to the east end of the Antonine Wall.

Kinross (Perth & Kinross) 'Head of the promontory'. *Ceann* (Scottish Gaelic) 'head'; *ros* (Scottish Gaelic) 'promontory'. The name was recorded as Kynros in 1144. This historic former county town stands on a promontory that protrudes into Loch Leven.

Kintail (Highland) 'Head of the sea-water'. *Ceann* (Scottish Gaelic) 'head'; *an t-saille* (Scottish Gaelic) 'of the salt water inlet'. This dramatic, mountainous area of the north-west Highlands lies at the end of the long sea loch, Loch Duich. Once Clan Mackenzie territory, it includes the peaks known as the 'Five Sisters of Kintail'. *See* **Five Sisters of Kintail, Kentallen.**

Kintore (Aberdeenshire) 'At the head of the hill'. *Cinn* (Scottish Gaelic) 'at the head of'; *torr* (Scottish Gaelic) 'steep hill'.

Kintyre (Argyll & Bute) 'Head of the land'. *Ceann* (Scottish Gaelic) 'head'; *tire* (Scottish Gaelic) 'of land'. Records indicate Ciuntire in 807 and Cantire in the 18th century. The termination of this long, and in places fertile, peninsula is the Mull of Kintyre from *maol*

(Scottish Gaelic) 'headland'. Boldly claimed by the Norwegian King Magnus 'Barelegs' in 1098, Kintyre became the territory of the MacRanalds and later of the Campbells.

Kippen (Stirling) Place of 'the little stump'. *Ceap* (Scottish Gaelic) 'stump' or 'block'; *-an* (Scottish Gaelic diminutive suffix). This village sits on an elevated stump of the Gargunnock Hills overlooking Flanders Moss.

Kirkbister (Shetland) 'Church farm'. *Kirkja* (Old Norse) 'church'; *bolstadr* (Old Norse) 'farm'. Kirbister in Orkney has the same derivation.

Kirkcaldy (Fife) 'Fort on the hard hill'. *Caer* (Brythonic) 'fort'; *caled* (Brythonic) 'hard'; *din* (Brythonic) 'hill'. The fort here presumably was on the elevated site of the present Ravenscraig Castle, above the town. Records show Kircalathin in 1150. This town was the world's main centre of linoleum manufacture in the late 19th and early 20th centuries. Like a number of other Scottish towns, it is known as 'the lang toun' because of its straggling growth along the coastal road.

Kirkconnel (Dumfries & Galloway) 'Connal's church'. *Kirk* (Scots, from *cirice* [Old English] or *kirkja* [Old Norse]) 'church'; *Conall* (Old Irish proper name). Conall was a pupil of St Mungo.

Kirkcudbright [Kirk-oobrie] (Dumfries & Galloway) 'Church of St Cuthbert'. *Kirk* (Scots, derived from *cirice* [Old English] or *kirkja* [Old Norse]) 'church'; *Cudberct* (Old English personal name meaning 'famous-bright') 'Cuthbert'. County town of the former Kirkcudbrightshire, it lies at the heart of MacLellan country. It was recorded as Kirkcutbrithe in 1291. The great 7th-century ascetic, St Cuthbert, was born in the Borders. He was Prior of Melrose and later Bishop of Lindisfarne.

Kirkgunzeon (Dumfries & Galloway) 'Finnian's church'. *Cirice* (Scottish Gaelic) 'church'; *Guinneain* (Scottish Gaelic) 'Finnian's'.

Kirkhope (Borders) 'Church in the valley'. *Kirk* (Scots, derived from *kirkja* (Old Norse) 'church'; *hop* (Old Norse) 'shelter' or 'valley'. *See* **Hobkirk**.

Kirkintilloch (East Dunbartonshire) 'Fort at the head of the hill'. *Caer* (Brythonic) 'fort'; *cinn* (Scottish Gaelic) 'at the head of'; *tulaich* (Scottish Gaelic) 'hill'. The name is recorded around 1200 as

Kirkintulach. Its origin lies in the existence of a 2nd-century Roman fort, built as part of the Antonine Wall system, on a small hill in what is now the old part of the town.

Kirkmichael (Perth & Kinross, South Ayrshire) 'Church of St Michael'. *Kirk* (Scots, from *cirice* [Old English]) 'church'.

Kirkness (Orkney) 'Church on the headland'. *Kirkja* (Old Norse) 'church'; *nes* (Old Norse) 'headland'.

Kirk o' Shotts (North Lanarkshire) 'Church on the steep slopes'. *Kirk* (Scots, from *cirice* [Old English] or *kirkja* [Old Norse]) 'church'; *sceots* (Old English) 'steep slopes'. *See* **Shotts**.

Kirkoswald (South Ayrshire) 'Church of St Oswald'. *Kirk* (Scots, from *cirice* [Old English] or *kirkja* [Old Norse]) 'church'; *Oswald* (Old English personal name). The 7th-century missionary, King Oswald of Northumbria, had links with this part of ancient Strathclyde.

Kirkpatrick (Dumfries & Galloway) 'Church of St Patrick'. There are several places of this name. By the time a village had been established, an additional name was sometimes supplied to make its identity clear, as in Kirkpatrick Fleming ('Patrick's church of the Fleming(s)'). The 'Fleming' was added in the 13th century at a time when much land was being granted to incomers from Flanders.

Kirkwall (Orkney) 'Church on the bay'. *Kirkja* (Old Norse) 'church'; *vagr* (Old Norse) 'bay'. The Orkney capital is situated at the head of a small sheltered bay, off the Wide Firth. The name was recorded as Kirkiuvagr in the *Orkneyinga Saga* around 1225 and later as Kirkvaw in a text of 1400. The kirk has, since its founding in 1138, been the splendid cathedral of St Magnus. Kirkwall also retains the ruins of the palace of the Stewart Earls of Orkney.

Kirk Yetholm *see* **Yetholm**.

Kirriemuir (Angus) 'The great quarter'. *Ceathramh* (Scottish Gaelic) a land measure that was a fourth of a *dabhach*: (192 Scots acres); *mòr* (Scottish Gaelic) 'great' or 'big'. *See* and compare **Arrochar**, **Haddo**. This Angus town, birthplace of J M Barrie, is the 'Thrums' of his stories.

Kishorn (Highland) 'Protruding cape'. *Keisa* (Old Norse) 'protrude'; *horn* (Old Norse) 'cape'. *See* **Keiss**.

Kittybrewster (Aberdeen) 'Brewing green'. *Cèide* (Scottish Gaelic) 'green' or 'hillock'; *browster* (Scots) 'brewing'.

Knapp (Angus, and other regions) 'Lump or hill'. *Knappr* (Old Norse) 'knob' or 'lump', indicating a low but distinctive hill. The name is often found as a particle, as in Knap of Trowglen ('hill of the trolls' glen').

Knapdale (Argyll & Bute) 'Hill and dale country'. *Knappr* (Old Norse) a protuberant, knob-like small hill; *dalr* (Old Norse) 'dale' or 'valley'. The name suits this northern part of the Kintyre Peninsula, where hills rise and fall in parallel folds.

Knock (Moray) 'Hill or hillock'. *Cnoc* (Scottish Gaelic) 'hill'. Both in its scotticised and Gaelic forms, it occurs in very many local and hill names (usually hills under 1,000 feet/300 metres). The 'Knock-' form is very common in the Galloway area but is found throughout the country.

Knockan (Highland) 'Little hill'. *Cnocan* (Scottish Gaelic) 'small hill'.

Knockando (Moray) 'Hill of the market'. *Cnoc* (Scottish Gaelic) 'hill'; *cheannachd* (Scottish Gaelic) 'of the market'.

Knoydart (Highland) 'Cnut's fiord'. *Cnut* (Old Norse personal name); *fjordr* (Old Norse) 'firth' or 'sea loch'. This remote area of mountain wilderness is situated on the west coast of Scotland between Loch Nevis and Loch Hourn.

Kyle (North Ayrshire, East Ayrshire) The old central division of Ayrshire. Although the name has been linked to a Brythonic King Coel, the source is more likely to be from the Water of Coyle, which flows to join the Ayr and whose name probably derives from *caol* (Gaelic) 'narrow'.

Kyleakin (Highland) 'Narrows of Haakon'. *Caol* (Scottish Gaelic) 'straits' or 'narrows'; *Haakon* (Old Norse personal name) Several kings of Norway bore this name and it may also be called after a local magnate. Most people take the source as Haakon IV, who ravaged this stretch of coast before his rebuff at the Battle of Largs in 1263. There was a ferry crossing here until the Skye bridge was built in the 1990s.

Kyle of Lochalsh (Highland) 'Narrows of Loch Alsh'. *Caol* (Scottish

Gaelic) 'narrows'. This village, the railhead and former ferry terminal for Skye, is situated at the narrow sea entrance into Loch Alsh opposite Kyleakin. *See* **Alsh, Loch**.

Kylerhea (Highland) 'Reith's strait'. *Caol* (Scottish Gaelic) 'strait' or 'kyle'; *Réithainn* (Old Gaelic proper name, perhaps stemming from *reidh* [Scottish Gaelic] 'smooth').

Kylesku (Highland) 'The narrow narrows'. *Caolas* (Scottish Gaelic) 'narrows' or 'strait'; *cumhann* (Scottish Gaelic) 'narrow' or 'thin'. This name, with an apparent tautology, describes the narrow sea entrance at the junction of three lochs. There was formerly a ferry crossing here but the narrows have now been bridged.

L

Ladder Hills (Aberdeenshire) 'Hills of the slopes'. *Leitir* (Scottish Gaelic) 'hill slope'. 'Hills' is a later addition.

Ladybank (Fife) 'Boggy slope'. *Leathad* (Scottish Gaelic) 'slope'; *bog* (Scottish Gaelic) 'moist'.

Ladywell (West Lothian) 'Our Lady's well', the site of a well dedicated to the Virgin Mary. There are many other local 'Lady-' names, all dating back to before the Reformation of 1560 and most, but not all, with the same derivation. *See* **Ladybank**.

Lagavulin (Argyll & Bute) 'Hollow by the mill'. *Lag* (Scottish Gaelic) 'hollow'; *a'mhuilinn* (Scottish Gaelic) 'by the mill'.

Laggan (Highland) 'Hollow place' or 'place of hollows'. *Lag* (Scottish Gaelic) 'hollow'.

Laide (Highland) 'Slopes'. *Leathad* (Scottish Gaelic) 'slope'.

Lairg (Highland) 'The pass'. *Lairig* (Scottish Gaelic) 'pass' or 'beaten path'. The name defines this spot inland from the Dornoch Firth where routes from West and North Sutherland converge. It is still the site of important annual lamb sales.

Lairig Ghru (Highland, Moray) 'The gloomy pass'. *Lairig* (Scottish Gaelic) 'pass'; *ghru* (Scottish Gaelic) 'gloomy'. The pass forms a deep gash through the Cairngorms at a maximum height of 2,750 feet/840 metres. It is part of a popular, though tough, hill-walking route.

Lake of Menteith *see* **Menteith, Lake of.**

Lamancha (Borders) A Spanish name given to the locality by the proprietor, Admiral Cochrane, in the 1730s. Formerly Grange of Romanno. *Rath* (Scottish Gaelic) 'ring fort'; *manaich* (Scottish Gaelic) 'of the monk'.

Lamberton (Borders) 'Lambert's farm'. *Lambert* (Norman French proper name); *tun* (Old English) 'farm'. Lamberton Toll, north of Berwick, now marks the border with England.

Lamlash (North Ayrshire) 'Isle of Mo-Laise'. *Eilean* (Scottish Gaelic) 'island'; *Malaise* (Scottish Gaelic proper name, incorporating *mo*, 'my' or 'my dear' and *las*, 'flame'). The 7th-century saint Mo-Laise had a cave on Holy Island in Lamlash Bay.

Lammermuir (Borders, Midlothian) Possibly 'lambs' moor'. *Lombor* or *lambre* (Old English) 'lamb'; *muir* (Scots version of Old English *mor*) 'moorland'. Nowadays known as the Lammermuir Hills. A number of hills within this range have sheep-related names, including Lamb Hill, Lammer Law, Wedder Law and Hog Law. In an early 9th-century document the area was called Lombormore and in a later text Lambremor.

Lanark (South Lanarkshire) 'The glade'. *Llanerc* (Brythonic) 'forest glade'. The name is recorded as Lannarc in 1188 and Lanerch in 1430. This historic market and former county town is located on an early forest clearing settlement site at the top of the steep east bank of the River Clyde, some 50 miles/80 kilometres upstream from its estuary. Lanark has associations with William Wallace, who opened his campaign in the War of Independence by killing the English sheriff here. New Lanark, a well-preserved 'model' mill town set up by Robert Owen and David Dale in 1784, lies below Lanark in the river valley near the Falls of Clyde. It was so named to distinguish it from the older settlement.

Lane (Dumfries & Galloway) 'River'. *Linne* (Scottish Gaelic) 'pool' or 'stream'. The term is found in a number of stream names, notably in Carrick around Loch Doon, into which the Carrick Lane flows.

Langbank (Renfrewshire) Presumably 'long bank'. *Lang* (Scots) 'long'; 'bank' (English). This simple name is apt for this straggling village on the raised banks of the Firth of Clyde.

Langholm (Dumfries & Galloway) 'Long water-meadow'. *Lang* (Scots) 'long'; *holm* (Scots elided form of Old Norse *holmr*) 'water meadow' or 'haugh'. Located on level ground by the meandering River Esk, this name was recorded in its present form in 1376. It well describes the situation of this border wool-manufacturing town, birthplace of Scotland's famous 20th-century poet, Hugh MacDiarmid (1892–1978).

Laphroaig (Argyll & Bute) 'Hollow by the big bay'. *Lag* (Scottish Gaelic) 'hollow'; *a'mhor* (Scottish Gaelic) 'by the big'; *aig* (Scottish Gaelic from Old Norse *vik*.) 'bay'. 'Loud bay' has also been suggested, from *labhar* (Scottish Gaelic) 'loud'.

Larbert (Falkirk) Possibly 'half wood'. *Lled* (Brythonic) 'half' or 'part'; *pert* (Brythonic) 'wood'. Recorded as Lethberth in 1195 and Larbert in 1251.

Largo (Fife) 'Steep place'. *Leargach* (Scottish Gaelic) 'steep slope'. The name may first have been applied to the hill of Largo Law. It was recorded as Largaugh in 1250, Largaw in 1279 and Largo in 1595. This town was the birthplace of Alexander Selkirk, the model for Defoe's Robinson Crusoe.

Largs (North Ayrshire) 'Hillside'. *Learg* (Scottish Gaelic) 'hillside'. This resort town on the Firth of Clyde sits on the shore under the immediate slopes of the Renfrewshire hills. The *s* ending of the name would appear to have been a later addition as part of the anglicisation process. It was documented Larghes in 1140. A famous battle was fought here in 1263 between the Norsemen and the Scots.

Lasswade (Midlothian) Probably 'the ford by the meadow'. *Leas* (Old English) 'meadow'; *gewaed* (Old English) 'ford'. The town, south-west of Dalkeith, lies on the North Esk river. A record of 1150 shows the name as Leswade.

Latheron (Highland) 'Miry place'. *Làthach* (Scottish Gaelic) 'miry', giving the Gaelic form *Latharn*.

Latheronwheel (Highland) 'Miry place of the pool'. *Latharn* (Scottish

Gaelic from *làthach*) 'miry'; *a' Phuill* (Scottish Gaelic) 'of the pool' or 'of the hole'.

Lauder (Borders) This small town lies on the Leader Water and presumably takes its name from this river. *Lou* (Brythonic) 'wash'; *dobhar* (Brythonic) 'water'. *Lòthur* (Old Irish) means 'trench'. The name is recorded as Louueder in 1208, Lawedir in 1250 and Loweder in 1298. *See also* **Lowther**.

Laurencekirk (Aberdeenshire) 'St Laurence's kirk'. This small market town was founded by Lord Gardenstone in 1770 and named Kirkton of St Laurence, the latter being a reference to the patron saint of its church, St Laurence of Canterbury. Previously, it was called Conveth, from *coindmed* (Old Irish) 'billetting', indicating a place where the warriors of a chief were lodged with the people.

Laurieston (Falkirk) This small town to the east of Falkirk was originally known as Langtoune, a name recorded in 1393, which still aptly describes its straggling form along the old Edinburgh road. It was briefly called Merchistown in 1774, then Laurenceton after its owner, Sir Lawrence Dundas of Kerse, before finally assuming its current form.

Lawers (Perth & Kinross) Possibly 'loud, resounding stream'. *Labhar* (Scottish Gaelic) 'loud'. The name was extended from the stream to Ben Lawers (3,984 feet/1,214 metres) and to the surrounding area, which is divided into three (hence the plural form): *Labhar Sìos*, 'East Lawers; *Labhar Suas*, 'West Lawers' and *Labhar na Craoibhe*, 'Lawers of the Trees'. Although this derivation has been contested, it remains the most probable.

Laxford, Loch (Highland) 'Salmon fiord'. *Laks* (Old Norse) 'salmon'; *fjord* (adaptation of Old Norse *fjordr*) 'sea loch' or 'firth'. The River Laxford, flowing from Loch Stack, has been named from the sea loch.

Leader, River *see* **Lauder**.

Leadburn (Midlothian) 'Bernard's stone'. *Leac* (Scottish Gaelic) 'stone'; *Bernard* (Old English personal name). The name is found as Lecbernard around 1200.

Leadhills (South Lanarkshire) Simply 'the place in the lead hills'.

This Scots name reflects that this former mining village was once an important site for the extraction of lead, as well as gold and silver.

Lecht, The (Moray) 'The declivity'. *Leachd* (Scottish Gaelic) 'declivity' – a downward hillslope as in a mountain pass. The derivation is certainly descriptive of this high pass in the Cairngorms, where the old 18th-century military road (now a modern highway) rises to over 2,000 feet/635 metres and is frequently mentioned in the winter road reports as being 'blocked by snow'. In recent years, a ski centre has been developed here.

Ledi, Ben (Stirling) Traditionally taken as 'mountain of God'. *Beinn* (Scottish Gaelic) 'mountain'; *le* (Scottish Gaelic) 'in possession of'; *Dia* (Scottish Gaelic) 'God'. The principal meaning of the prefix *le* is 'with', though a possesive sense may have been stronger in earlier times. The significance of the name probably goes back to a pre-Christian holy site on the mountain (2,882 feet/881 metres). A more likely alternative has been suggested in *leathad* (Scottish Gaelic) 'slope'.

Ledmore (Highland) 'Big slope'. *Leathad* (Scottish Gaelic) 'slope'; *mòr* (Scottish Gaelic) 'big'. Ledbeg conversely means 'small slope' from *beag* (Scottish Gaelic) 'small'.

Leith (Edinburgh) Possibly 'wet place'. *Lleith* (Brythonic) 'moist'. The Gaelic form is *Lìte*. Records show Inverlet in 1145 and Leth in 1570. Inverleith is still used as a local district name. This long-time port of Edinburgh, an independent burgh until 1920, lies at the mouth of the Water of Leith on the Firth of Forth and is the new home of the Scottish Civil Service.

Lendrick (Stirling) 'Clear space or glade'. *Lanerc* (Brythonic) 'forest glade'. The process of metathesis has transposed the latter part of the name, as with Lanrick. *See also* **Lanark.**

Lennoxtown (East Dunbartonshire) This small town to the north of Glasgow was named after the local family of Dukes and Earls of Lennox, who took their title in turn from the ancient territory of Lennox that encompassed the former county of Dumbartonshire, much of Stirlingshire and parts of Perthshire and Renfrewshire. The name Lennox was originally Leven-ach ('field of the River Leven') and elided through Levenax. It is probably derived as *leamhanach* (Scottish Gaelic) 'covered in elms'. *See* **Leven**.

Leny, River and **Pass** (Stirling) 'Narrow cattle path'. *Lànaig* (Scottish Gaelic) 'narrow cattle path'.

Lenzie (East Dunbartonshire) This name has the same derivation as Leny. The *z*, as very often in Scottish names, is actually a *y* (a confusion caused by old writing styles) but modern usage sounds the *z* in this case.

Lerwick (Shetland) 'Mud bay'. *Leir* (Old Norse) 'mud'; *vik* (Old Norse) 'bay'. The name of the bay is Old Norse but there was no town here until about 1600, several centuries after the end of the Viking era. Previously, the capital of the islands was Scalloway.

Leslie (Fife, Aberdeenshire) Possibly 'garden by the pool'. *Lios* (Scottish Gaelic) 'enclosure' or 'garden'; *linn* (Scottish Gaelic) 'pool'. Both the Leslies are located by streams. An alternative derivation of *llys* (Brythonic) 'court' and *celyn* (Brythonic) 'holly' has also been advanced. The Fife name was recorded in the late 12th century as Lesslyn.

Lesmahagow (South Lanarkshire) 'Church of Mahagow'. *Eaglais* (Scottish Gaelic form of *ecclesia* [Latin]) 'church'; *Mahagow* (from an Irish Gaelic personal name *Machute*, not known as such but perhaps a form of the Breton *Maclovius* or *Malo* or the Gaelic *Mo-Fhegu* ['my Fechin']). Records show Lesmahagu in 1130, Ecclesia Machuti in 1144 and Lesmachute in 1316.

Letham (Angus, Fife, Stirling) 'Village of the barns'. *Hlatha* (Old English) 'barns'; *ham* (Old English) 'village'.

Letterewe [Letter-you] (Highland) 'Hillside above the River Ewe'. *Leitir* (Scottish Gaelic) 'hillside'; *Lù* (Scottish Gaelic river name). *See* **Kinlochewe**.

Letterfinlay (Highland) 'Hill of the fair soldier'. *Leitir* (Scottish Gaelic) 'hillside'; *fionn* (Scottish Gaelic) 'fair'; *laoich* (Scottish Gaelic) 'soldier's'.

Letters (Highland) 'Hill slopes'. *Leitir* (Scottish Gaelic) 'hillside'.

Leuchars (Fife) Probably place of 'the rushes'. *Luachair* (Scottish Gaelic) 'rushes'. This village, with a modern military airfield, is situated in north-east Fife close to the estuary of the River Eden.

Leven (Fife, Highland, West Dunbartonshire) Probably 'elm river'.

The Fife town and loch take their names from the River Leven, which flows from Levenmouth on the loch to the sea at Innerleven (*inbhir* Scottish Gaelic] 'river mouth') by Methil. The river name derives here, as in the case of the River Leven flowing from Loch Lomond, from *leamhain* (Scottish Gaelic) 'elm'. The West Highland Loch Leven also takes its name from its river, perhaps with the same derivation as above, though *lèan* (Scottish Gaelic) 'swampy place' has also been suggested.

Leverburgh (Western Isles) A modern hybrid name joining the family name of Lord Leverhulme, proprietor of Lewis in the 1920s, with *burgh* (Scots) 'town'. The village was developed as a fishing port and processing station.

Lewis (Western Isles) 'Homes of the people'. *Ljod* (Old Norse) 'people' but also 'music'; *hus* (Old Norse) 'house' or 'home'. In Scottish Gaelic, it became *Leòdhas* and it has been confused with *leoghuis* (Scottish Gaelic) 'marshiness'. It was recorded as Leodus and Lyodus *circa* 1100, Liodhus in the *Orkneyinga Saga* around 1225 and Leoghuis in 1449. This northern and larger part of the largest Outer Hebridean island is a vast tract of mainly low-lying peatland with hundreds of small lochs.

Lhanbryde (Moray) 'Church-place of St Bride'. The prefix, common in Wales, is most unusual and perhaps unique in Scotland, though *làn* is attested as a rare Gaelic word for church. Older forms include Lamanbride in 1215 and Lambride in the late 14th century.

Liathach (Highland) 'The grey one'. *Liath* (Scottish Gaelic) 'grey'; -*ach* (Scottish Gaelic suffix denoting place). A distinctive, steep-faced mountain (3,456 feet/1,056 metres) in the Torridon range.

Liberton (Edinburgh) Perhaps 'lepers' place'. *Liber* (Old English) 'leper'; *tun* (Old English) 'place'. This may have referred to a location beyond the town wall, where lepers were segregated from the main population.

Liddesdale (Borders) 'Dale of the Liddel Water'. The likely derivation is from the Old Norse *hly*, 'shelter' or *dalr*, 'dale', in which case the stream takes its name from the valley, an unusual event; and the 'dale' is unnecessarily repeated. This was the territory of the reiving Armstrongs.

Liff (Angus) Perhaps '(place of) herbs'. *Luibh* (Scottish Gaelic) 'plant' or 'herb'. *See* **Luce, Luss.**

Lincluden (Dumfries & Galloway) 'Pool on the Cluden stream'. *Linn* (Scottish Gaelic) 'pool' or 'fall'; *Cluden* (Brythonic) a river name, etymologically linked to *Cluaidh*, 'Clyde'.

Lindifferon (Fife) 'Field by the water'. *Lann* (Scottish Gaelic) 'field'; *dyffryn* (Brythonic) 'watercourse' or 'valley'.

Lindores (Fife) 'Field of the black wood' or 'lake of the black wood'. *Lann* (Scottish Gaelic) 'field' or *llyn* (Brythonic) 'lake'; *dubh* (Scottish Gaelic) 'black'; *ros* (Scottish Gaelic) 'wood'. *Lann* normally had the sense of 'belonging to the church' and there was a well-known monastery here.

Linlithgow (West Lothian) Place by 'the lake in the moist hollow'. *Llyn* (Brythonic-Celtic) 'lake'; *lleith* (Brythonic) 'moist'; *cau* (Brythonic) 'hollow'. Recorded in 1147 as Linlitcu. This historic royal burgh takes its name from Linlithgow Loch, which lies immediately below the ruins of its 16th-century palace.

Linnhe, Loch (Highland) Literally 'the pool'. *Linne* (Scottish Gaelic) 'pool'. The seaward end, past the Corran narrows, is known in Gaelic as *An Linne Sheileach*. *Seileach* (Scottish Gaelic) is explained variously as 'salty', and 'of the willows'. The inner loch is *An Linne Dubh*, from *dubh* (Scottish Gaelic) 'black'.

Linton (East Lothian) 'Flax-farm'. *Lín* (Scottish Gaelic) 'lint' or 'flax'; *tun* (Old English) 'farmstead'. There are East and West Lintons.

Linwood (Renfrewshire) Hybrid name meaning 'wood by the pool'. *Llyn* (Brythonic) 'pool'; *wudu* (Old English) 'wood'.

Lionel (Western Isles) 'Flax hill'. *Lín* (Scottish Gaelic) 'flax'; *hóll* (Old Norse) 'hill'. In the era before industrial production of clothes, flax was a widely grown crop.

Lismore (Argyll & Bute) 'Big garden'. *Lios* (Scottish Gaelic) 'garden' or 'enclosure'; *mòr* (Scottish Gaelic) 'big'. This fertile island in Loch Linnhe had a flourishing monastic community set up by St Moluag in the 6th century and, for a time in the 13th century, it was the seat of the See of Argyll.

Livingston (West Lothian) Place of 'Leving's village'. *Leving* (Old English personal name) an early Saxon landowner; *tun* (Old

English) 'village'. Recorded as Leuinistun in 1250 and Levyngestone in 1297. The old village is now incorporated in Livingston New Town, created in 1962.

Lix (Highland, Angus) 'Place of flagstones'. *lic* (Scottish Gaelic *leac* in the locative form) flagstone. The English form represents the (English) plural.

Loanhead (Midlothian) 'At the top of the lane'. *Loan* (Scots) 'lane'; head (English) 'at the top of'. Recorded as Loneheid in 1618. This former coal-mining town is situated just south-east of Edinburgh by the attractive environs of the North Esk's glen. It was for a long time a summer retreat for inhabitants of the city. The original loan here would have been one that climbed up from the river.

Loch *see* under specific names (**Achray**, for example) except where the names have been run into one. There is a Loch Loch below Beinn a'Ghlo in Perthshire. The first 'Loch' is from *loch* (Scottish Gaelic) 'lake' and the second from *lòch* (Old Irish Gaelic) 'dark'.

Lochaber (Highland) Probably 'area of the loch confluence'. *Loch* (Scottish Gaelic) 'sea loch' or 'lake'; *aber* (Brythonic) 'at the confluence of'. This is a region where several lochs join (Loch Eil and Loch Linnhe, for example) or almost join (Loch Arkaig and Loch Lochy). The suffix position of *-aber* is unusual but not unique (*see* **Kinnaber**). However, the word itself is very rare on the west coast.

Lochaline (Highland) 'Beautiful loch'. *Loch* (Scottish Gaelic) 'lake' or 'loch'; *alainn* (Scottish Gaelic) 'beautiful'.

Locharbriggs (Dumfries & Galloway) *Lochar* is from *luachar* (Scottish Gaelic) 'rushes', presumably referring to the reedy moss through which the Lochar river runs. *Briggs* has been assumed to be *brig* (Scots) 'bridge' but the plural form is odd and it is perhaps more likely to reflect the plural of *brig* (Scottish Gaelic) 'heap' or 'pile', referring to the gathered rushes used for thatching.

Lochay, Glen *see* **Lochy.**

Lochboisdale (Western Isles) *Loch* (Scottish Gaelic) has been added to a name already indicative of a coastal feature, namely *bug* (Old Norse) 'bay', indicating something less indented than a *vik*. The termination is *dalr* (Old Norse) 'dale'.

Lochcarron (Highland) Formerly known as Jeantown, this village takes its name from the loch on which it is situated. *See* **Carron**.

Lochearnhead (Stirling) Anglicised version of Kinlochearn, the place at the head of Loch Earn. *See* **Earn**.

Lochee (Dundee) 'Corn loch'. *Loch* (Scottish Gaelic) 'lake' or 'loch'; *iodh* (Scottish Gaelic) 'corn'.

Lochgelly (Fife) Place of 'the shining loch'. *Loch* (Scottish Gaelic) 'lake' or 'loch'; *geal* (Scottish Gaelic) 'bright' or 'shining'. This former coal-mining town near Cowdenbeath takes its name from the small loch to the south-east of it.

Lochgilphead (Argyll & Bute) 'Head of Loch Gilp'. 'Head' with the sense of 'at the top end of'; *loch* (Scottish Gaelic) 'sea loch'; *gilb* (Scottish Gaelic) 'chisel'. The name of the loch comes from its shape. The English element in the name of the small town indicates its relatively modern growth as an administrative centre.

Lochinvar (Dumfries & Galloway) 'Loch of the height'. *Loch* (Scottish Gaelic) 'lake' or 'loch'; *an* (Scottish Gaelic) 'of the'; *bharra* (Scottish Gaelic) 'height'. The name was borrowed by Sir Walter Scott for his famous ballad 'The Young Lochinvar'.

Lochinver (Highland) 'Loch at the river mouth'. *Loch* (Scottish Gaelic) 'sea loch'; *inbhir* (Scottish Gaelic) 'river mouth'.

Loch Lomond *see* **Lomond**.

Lochmaben (Dumfries & Galloway) Mabon was a Celtic deity, associated with youth and the sun, and 'Mabon's loch' has been suggested. An alternative derivation is 'loch by the bare-topped hill'. *Loch* (Scottish Gaelic) 'loch' or 'lake'; *maol* (Scottish Gaelic) 'bare top'; *beinn* (Scottish Gaelic) 'hill'.

Lochmaddy (Western Isles) 'Loch of the dog'. *Loch* (Scottish Gaelic) 'loch' or 'lake'; *nam* (Scottish Gaelic) 'of the'; *mhadaidh* (Scottish Gaelic) 'dog'. *See also* **Portavadie**.

Lochnagar (Aberdeenshire) 'Loch of the noise or laughter'. *Loch* (Scottish Gaelic) 'loch' or 'lake'; *na* (Scottish Gaelic) 'of the'; *gàire* (Scottish Gaelic) 'noise' or 'laughter'. The mountain (3,791 feet/1,155 metres) took its name from the loch at its foot. It was also known as *Beinn nan Ciochan* (Scottish Gaelic) 'the mountain of the paps or breasts'. Prudishness may have encouraged the alternative name.

Loch Ness *see* **Ness**.

Lochore (Fife) Possibly 'brown loch'. *Loch* (Scottish Gaelic) 'lake' or 'loch'; *odhar* (Scottish Gaelic) 'brown', a reference to the peaty soil of the area. However, as the name comes from the River Ore, it may have a different and older derivation, cognate with that of the River Ayr and the English Ore and Oare (from a conjectural Pre-Celtic root-form *ora*, indicating 'flowing').

Lochty (Fife) 'Stream of the black goddess'. *Loch* here seems to be from *lòch* (Old Irish Gaelic) 'black', while *dae* (Irish Gaelic) 'goddess' is related to the Scottish Gaelic *dia*. The reference is to a 'black goddess' river spirit and is intriguingly suggestive of the nature worship of the pre-Christian Celts. There are numerous other Lochtys. *See also* **Lochy** and **Munlochy**.

Lochtyloch (West Lothian) 'Dark hill'. This locality in the neighbourhood of Bathgate stems from *lòch* (Old Irish Gaelic) 'dark' and *tulach* (Scottish Gaelic) 'hill'.

Lochwinnoch (Renfrewshire) 'Loch of St Wynnin or Finnian'. *See* **Kilwinning**.

Lochy, River and **Loch** (Highland, Argyll & Bute) 'Stream of the black goddess'. *Lòch* (Old Irish Gaelic) 'black'; *dae* (Irish Gaelic) 'goddess', related to the Scottish Gaelic *dia*. The name is not a doublet of 'loch'. It comes originally from the river in each case, after which Loch Lochy, in the Great Glen, and Glen Lochy, through which the Oban road and railway descend from Tyndrum, take their names. The River and Glen Lochay in Perthshire are of the same derivation. *See also* **Lochty** and **Munlochy**.

Lockerbie (Dumfries & Galloway) 'Loki's village'. *Loki* (Old Norse personal name); *by* (Old Danish) 'village' or 'farmstead'. It was recorded as Lokardebi in a document of 1306. In December 1988, a Pan American jumbo jet was blown up in mid-air above the town, killing all of the 259 people on board and 11 of the townspeople.

Logie (Highland and elsewhere) 'Place in the hollow'. *Lagaigh* (Scottish Gaelic) 'in the hollow'.

Logierait (Perth & Kinross) 'My-Coeddi's hollow'. *Lagaigh* (Scottish Gaelic) 'in the hollow'; *mo* (Scottish Gaelic) 'my'; *Choid* (Irish Gaelic proper name). Coeddi was a bishop of Iona who died in 712.

Lomond (Stirling, Fife, Argyll & Bute) A name with more than one possible source and a confusing history. One source is *lumon* (Brythonic) 'beacon', as in the Welsh mountain, Plynlimmon. This name suits Ben Lomond (3,194 feet/977 metres) and the twin Lomond Hills (Fife) whose prominent positions make them all eminently suitable as beacon hills. Another plausible source is *leamhan* (Scottish Gaelic) 'elm'. This almost certainly accounts for the name of the River Leven which flows out of Loch Lomond to the Firth of Clyde. There is some evidence that Loch Lomond was at one time called Loch Leven, no doubt after this river. It is documented in a text of 1535 as Levin. The Gaelic form of Loch Lomond is *Loch Laoiminn* and it may be that the similarity of the names caused the loch name to be altered from the river's name to that of the mountain which rises so commandingly above it. It is a curious fact that the Fife Lomonds also rise above a Loch Leven. Loch Lomond, broad and shallow at the south end, deep and narrow to the north, is the largest inland stretch of water in Britain.

Long, Loch (Argyll & Bute, Highland) 'Loch of ships'. *Loch* (Scottish Gaelic) 'lake' or 'loch'; *luing* (Scottish Gaelic) 'of ships'.

Longannet (Fife) 'Field of the patron saint's church'. *Lann* (Scottish Gaelic) 'field'; *annat* (Scottish Gaelic) 'patron saint's church' or 'church with relics'. It is now the site of a vast power station.

Longart (Highland) 'Camping place'. The source of the name of this forest area is of interest as it ostensibly should mean 'ship station', yet there is nowhere in the locality suitable for ships. *Long* (Irish Gaelic) 'ship' came also to mean 'dwelling' and *port* (Irish Gaelic) 'harbour' came also to mean 'encampment'. Luncarty near Perth and north of Turriff have the 'camp' meaning, as does Loch Lungard in Kintail. Camaslongart on Loch Long in Kintail preserves the 'ship-station' meaning. The topography helps clarify matters in each case.

Longforgan (Perth & Kinross) 'Field or church over the boggy place'. *Lann* (Scottish Gaelic) 'field' or 'church'; *for* (Scottish Gaelic) 'over' or 'above'; *gronn* (Scottish Gaelic, obsolete) 'marsh'. It appears as Langforgrunde in the 14th century.

Longformacus (Borders) Apparently 'church on the land of Maccus'.

Long (Brythonic form of Gaelic *lann*) 'church'; *fothir* (Brythonic) 'land' or 'meadow'; *Maccus* (Irish-Scandinavian form of personal name Magnus). *See* **Maxwell, Maxwelton.**

Longhope (Orkney) 'Long sheltered bay'. *Hop* (Old Norse) 'sheltered bay'.

Longmorn (Moray) 'Morgan's church or field'. The likeliest derivation is from *lann* (Scottish Gaelic) 'field' or 'church's field' and by extension often 'church'; and *Morgan* (Brythonic personal name) also found in Tillymorgan ('Morgan's hill') in Aberdeenshire.

Longniddry (East Lothian) 'Church of the new hamlet'. *Long* (Brythonic form of *lann*) 'church'; *nuadh* (Brythonic) 'new'; *tref* (Brythonic-Celtic) 'hamlet'. Recorded as Langnedre in 1595.

Lorn(e) (Argyll & Bute) This area of the west coast of Scotland (*Lathurna* in Scottish Gaelic) was centred on present-day Oban, together with the firth of the same name. It was named after Loarn, one of the leaders of the Irish invasion of Scotland in the late 5th century and a brother of Fergus of Ulster.

Lossie, River (Moray). This river name has been linked to the name 'Loxa' on Ptolemy's 2nd-century map from a Greek root *loxos* meaning 'crooked'. A derivation from *lus* (Scottish Gaelic) 'herbs' or 'plants' has also been suggested. The town of Lossiemouth takes its name from its position at the river mouth. The modern English 'mouth' is an indication that the town was only developed in the late 17th century, when a harbour was built here.

Loth (Highland) 'Muddy place'. *Loth* (Scottish Gaelic) 'mud'.

Lothian This area, once a Celtic kingdom, later part of the Anglian Kingdom of Bernicia, is believed to have been named after its historical founder, one Leudonus (Brythonic or Pre-Celtic personal name) of uncertain origin. Early records show Loonia *circa* 970, Lothene in 1091, Louthion *circa* 1200 and Laodinia 1245. Currently it is the name of one of the nine administrative regions of mainland Scotland, divided into four 'unitary authority' districts corresponding to the former counties of Midlothian, East Lothian, West Lothian and the City of Edinburgh.

Loudoun (East Ayrshire) 'Beacon hill'. *Lowe* (Scots from Old Norse *logr*) 'fire'; *dún* (Old English) 'hill'. An association with the Celtic god Lug has also been suggested, giving the name Lugdunon (which is cognate with Lyons Lugdunum in France).

Lovat (Highland) 'Swampy area'. The name, probably Pictish from a form *lu-vo*, 'muddy' (*see* **Loth**), was superseded by *A Mhor'oich* (Scottish Gaelic) 'seaside plain' but is retained in the title of Lord Lovat.

Lowther Hills (Borders) *see* **Lauder**.

Loyal, Ben and **Loch** (Highland) An anglicised version of the Gaelic rendering *Beinn Laoghal*. *Beinn* (Scottish Gaelic) 'mountain'; *laga* (Old Norse) 'law'; *fjall* (Old Norse) 'hill'. This would indicate a meeting-place for the discussion and ratification of laws. *Leidh* (Old Norse) 'levy' or 'mustering-place' has also been suggested. Strictly speaking, the 'Ben' is unnecessary in either case. The adjacent Loch Loyal has been named after the mountain (2,506 feet/766 metres).

Lubnaig, Loch (Stirling) 'Loch of the bend'. *Lùb* (Scottish Gaelic) 'bend', with a double Scottish Gaelic suffix, *-an*, and *-aig*, both of which indicate 'small'. Although the loch is not particularly small, it is narrow and bends. Loch Vennachar has a similar derivation from a different source.

Luce (Dumfries & Galloway) 'Place of herbs or plants'. *Lus* (Scottish Gaelic) 'herbs' or 'plants'. Herb gardens were vital for providing the elements of medicines as well as food flavourings and preservatives and were found all over the country. *See* **Luss**.

Lugar, River (East Ayrshire) 'Bright stream'. The name is conjectured from the early Celtic root-form *loucos*, 'white' with the typical Celtic termination *-ar*, indicating a river.

Luggie, River (North Lanarkshire) 'Bright stream'. The name is conjectured from the Celtic root-form *loucos*, 'white', cognate with the River Lugg in Herefordshire, England.

Lui, Ben (Stirling) 'Mountain of calves'. *Beinn* (Scottish Gaelic) 'mountain'; *laoigh* (Scottish Gaelic) 'of calves'. The reference is to the summer grazing slopes on the mountain (3,708 feet/1,134 metres).

Luib (Stirling, Highland) 'Bend'. *Lùb* (Scottish Gaelic) 'bend' or 'winding'.

Luichart, Loch (Highland) 'Place of encampment'. *Long* (Irish Gaelic) 'dwelling' or 'ship'; *phort* (Irish Gaelic) 'harbour' or 'camp ground'. Longphort is compressed into Luichart. *See* **Longart**. *Lùchairt* (Gaelic) 'palace' has also been suggested as the origin of this name but it seems much less likely.

Luing (Argyll & Bute) 'Ship island'. *Luing* (Scottish Gaelic) 'ship's'.

Lumphanan (Aberdeenshire) 'Finnan's field'. *Lann* (Scottish Gaelic) 'field' or 'enclosure'. *Fhionain* (Scottish Gaelic proper name) 'Finnan's'. The site of a property belonging to a church dedicated to St Finnan.

Lumphinnans in Fife is likely to have the same derivation as Lumphanan.

Luncarty *see* **Longart**.

Lundin Links (Fife) Perhaps 'boggy site'. A Pictish name which may be associated with *lodan* (Scottish Gaelic) 'marsh'. 'Links' is from *hlinc* (Old English) 'rising ground' or 'bank', which came to be used in Scots to describe grassy dunes by the sea and, by association, golf courses.

Lurgainn, Loch (Highland) 'Shin loch'. *Lurgan* (Scottish Gaelic) 'shin' or 'unshapely leg', probably in reference to the boomerang shape of the loch, lying in the hollow between Stac Pollaidh and Ben More Coigach.

Luss (Argyll & Bute) 'Place of herbs or plants'. *Lus* (Scottish Gaelic) 'herbs' or 'plants'. *See* **Luce**.

Lybster (Highland) 'Settlement in the lee'. *Hlie* (Old Norse) 'leeward'; *bol-stadr* (Old Norse) 'settlement'. This Caithness fishing village is set in a deep sea inlet or voe.

Lynchat (Highland) 'Wild cat's field'. *Lann* (Scottish Gaelic) 'field'; *chait* (Scottish Gaelic) 'cat's'.

Lyne Water (Fife, Borders) The two Lynes have different derivations. The Lyne in Fife is from *lleith* (Brythonic) 'moist' or 'wet', cognate with Leith. The Lyne near Peebles is *linne* (Scottish Gaelic) 'pool', 'channel' or 'waterfall'.

Lynwilg (Highland) 'Field of the bag or bulge'. *Lann* (Scottish Gaelic) 'field'; *bhuilge* (Scottish Gaelic) 'bulge' or 'bag'.

Lyon, River, Glen, Loch (Perth & Kinross) Apparently 'grinding river', from *Liobhunn*, a Scottish Gaelic place name from a Pre-Celtic root *lim*, 'file', as in the Latin *lima*. This is one of the longest glens in Scotland, reaching far west into the Grampians and meeting Strathtay at Appin of Dull.

M

Macdhui, Ben (Moray) 'Hill of the sons of Dubh or Duff'. *Beinn* (Scottish Gaelic) 'mountain'; *mac Duibh* (Scottish Gaelic) 'sons of Duff'. The MacDuffs have ancient associations with the region. This mountain in the Cairngorms (4,296 feet/1,309 metres) was believed by some to be the highest in Scotland until the superior height of Ben Nevis was established. *See* **Macduff**.

Macduff (Aberdeenshire) This fishing port was renamed in 1783 by James Duff, 2nd Earl of Fife, who redeveloped the settlement previously known as Down. Macduff, as in the surname, simply means 'son of *Dubh*; the black(-haired one)'.

Machrihanish (Argyll & Bute) 'Coastal plain of Sanas'. *Machair* (Scottish Gaelic) 'plain'. More precisely, a *machair* is the herbaceous strip lying just inland from a beach and there are many such in the West Highlands and the islands. The latter part of the name is unclear, perhaps a personal or district name. It has been linked to *sean-innse* (Scottish Gaelic) 'old haugh' or 'water-meadow', which does not seem appropriate here.

Maddiston (West Lothian) 'Mandred's place'. *Mandred* (Old English personal name); *tun* (Old English) 'settlement' or 'place'. A reference of 1366 has Mandredestone.

Maggieknockater (Aberdeenshire) 'The fuller's plain'. *Màgh* (Scottish Gaelic) 'plain'; *an* (Scottish Gaelic) 'of the'; *fhucadair* (Scottish Gaelic) 'fuller'.

Magus Muir (Fife) 'Plain with the point of land'. *Màgh* (Scottish Gaelic) 'plain'; *gasg* (Scottish Gaelic) 'tail' or 'point of land'. This accurately describes the location. *Muir* (Scots) 'moor' is a post-Gaelic addition. Archbishop Sharp was assassinated here by Covenanters in 1679.

Mains (All regions) Very often found prefixing a farm name, this indicates the main or home farm of an estate. Davidson's Mains, once a farm, is now a suburb of Edinburgh.

Mallaig (Highland) Possibly 'headland bay'. *Muli* (Old Norse) 'headland'; *aig* (Scottish Gaelic version of original Old Norse *vagr*) 'bay'. This derivation fits the topography. An alternative derivation of the first part is from *mol* (Old Norse) 'shingle'. Mallaig is the terminus of the West Highland Railway, completed to here in 1903, and the ferry-port for south Skye.

Màm 'Breast-shaped hill'. Many mountain names are prefixed by 'Màm', sometimes shown as 'Maam'. A number have been anglicised as 'Maiden Pap' from the Ord of Caithness to Dumfries.

Mamore (Highland) 'Big round hills'. *Màm* (Scottish Gaelic) 'rounded hill'; *mòr* (Scottish Gaelic) 'big'. The converse form of Mambeg (from *beag* Scottish Gaelic] 'small') is found in several places. The name has also been less probably explained as 'great plain' from *magh* (Scottish Gaelic) 'plain' and *mòr* (Scottish Gaelic) 'big'. This region, adjacent to Ben Nevis, is one of the highest parts of the country. Although its summit areas form a kind of plateau, it is a much-dissected one and hard to see as a plain.

Manuel (West Lothian) Probably 'rock of the view'. *Maen* (Brythonic) 'rock'; *gwel* (Brythonic) 'view' or 'outlook'.

Mar (Aberdeenshire) Mar together with Buchan was one of the major divisions of ancient Pictland. It appears to have been an Indo-European personal name from the Pre-Celtic period. The Gaelic form is *Marr*.

Marchmont (Edinburgh) 'Horse hill', now a residential district of Edinburgh on a ridge south of the castle. *Marc* (Scottish Gaelic) 'horse'; *monadh* (Scottish Gaelic) 'hill'.

Markinch (Fife) 'Isle or water meadow of the horse'. *Marc* (Scottish Gaelic) 'horse'; *innse* (Scottish Gaelic) 'water meadow' or 'island'. Reputedly, this place was originally built on an island in a lake that has since been drained. It was recorded as Marcinche around 1200.

Marwick (Orkney and Shetland) 'Seagull bay'. *Már* (Old Norse) 'gull'; *vik* (Old Norse) 'bay'.

Maryburgh (Highland) Earlier name of Fort William, after Queen Mary II. Maryburgh in Easter Ross is of similar date (*circa* 1690).

Maryculter (Aberdeen) 'Back land of the (church of) Mary'. *See* **Peterculter**. A Templars' church was established here and dedicated to the Virgin in 1487.

Maryhill (Glasgow) This northside suburb of Glasgow was named in 1760 after the local landowner, Mary Hill of Gairbraid.

Mauchline (East Ayrshire) 'Plain with a pool'. *Magh* (Scottish Gaelic) 'plain'; *linne* (Scottish Gaelic) 'pool'. This town, much associated with Robert Burns, lies on a fertile plain between the River Ayr and the Cessnock Water.

Maud (Aberdeenshire) 'Dog's or wolf's place'. *Madadh* (Scottish Gaelic) 'dog' or 'wolf'.

Mawcarse (Perth & Kinross) 'Plain of the carse'. *Magh* (Scottish Gaelic) 'plain'; *carse* (Scots from Old Norse *kerss*) 'low-lying river bank'.

May, Isle of (Midlothian) 'Isle of seagulls'. *Má* (Old Norse) 'seagull'; *ey* (Old Norse) 'island'. It is referred to as Maeyar in the *Orkneyinga Saga* (*circa* 1225). Scotland's first lighthouse was established here in the 15th century, or earlier, for ships entering the Firth of Forth.

Maybole (South Ayrshire) 'Maiden's house'. *Maege* (Old English) 'maiden' or 'kinswoman'; *botl* (Old English) 'house'. The oldest form known is Maybothel from the late 12th century.

Meall (Many locations) 'Humped hill'. Prefix to many mountain names, usually given to lower hills of around 3,000 feet/1,000 metres or less. In the south-west, it is often found in the form of 'Mill-' and sometimes as 'Meowl-'.

Mealfuarvounie (Highland) 'Hump of the cold mountains'. *Meall* (Scottish Gaelic) 'humped hill'; *fuar* (Scottish Gaelic) 'cold'; *mhonaidh* (Scottish Gaelic) 'of the mountain'. A distinctive mountain to the south of Inverness (2,284 feet/698 metres).

Mearns, The (Aberdeenshire, East Renfrewshire) This name has been explained as 'the stewardship'. Its Gaelic name is *An mhaoirne*, indicating an area administered by an officially appointed steward (*maor* Scottish Gaelic] 'bailiff' or 'agent'). However, the terminal *s* is not explained. The area of the Mearns covers a triangular fertile area south of Stonehaven, as far as the North Esk river, and east of the Highlands, corresponding to the eastern part of the former county of Kincardineshire. The Mearns district south of Glasgow has a river named the Earn and the most probable source here seems to be *magh* (Scottish Gaelic) 'plain', with the river name, probably a Pre-Celtic one based on the root-word *ar*, indicating 'flowing water' (*see* **Earn**).

Meggat Water (Dumfries & Galloway, Borders) 'Boggy stream'. *Mig* (Brythonic) 'swamp'.

Megginch (Perth & Kinross) Perhaps 'milk island'. *Melg* (Old Irish Gaelic) 'milk' (*see* **Castlemilk**); *innis* (Scottish Gaelic) 'water meadow' or 'island'. Earlier forms of the name include Melginch *circa* 1200.

Meig, River (Highland) 'Boggy stream'. *Mig* (Brythonic) 'swamp'.

Meigle (Perth & Kinross) 'Swampy field'. *Mig* (Brythonic) 'swamp'; *dol* (Brythonic) 'meadow'.

Meldrum (Aberdeenshire) Possibly 'mountain ridge'. *Meall* (Scottish Gaelic) 'mountain'; *druim* (Scottish Gaelic) 'ridge'. However, the 13th-century forms of the name, Melgedrom and Melkidrum, would tend to make this improbable. The meaning of the prefix is uncertain.

Melrose (Borders) 'Bare moor'. *Mailo* (Brythonic, cognate with Gaelic *maol*) 'bare'; *ros* (Brythonic, cognate with the Gaelic *ros* meaning 'wood' or 'promontory') 'moor'. It was recorded as Mailros in a document *circa* 700. The abbey here was the first (1136) Cistercian foundation in Scotland.

Melvich (Highland) 'Bay of sea-bent dunes'. *Mealbhan* (Scottish Gaelic from *melr* Old Norse] 'bent grass' or 'grassy dune') 'sea-bent'; *vik* (Old Norse) 'bay'.

Menstrie (Clackmannanshire) 'Hamlet in the plain'. *Maes* (Brythonic) 'open field' or 'plain'; *tref* (Brythonic) 'settlement' or 'hamlet'.

Menteith, Lake of (Stirling) 'Lowland of Menteith'. *Leachd* (Scottish Gaelic) 'sloping ground'. The anglicised form of this word may explain the enduring insistence on referring to this loch as Scotland's unique 'lake'. It lies within a natural basin surrounded by hills. Menteith derives as *moine* (Scottish Gaelic) 'moor' with *Teith* (Celtic river name). The Teith flows some way north of here, and neither into nor out of the lake, but documenary evidence shows its name was taken for a wide area of land around it. Early maps show Loch Monteith on the Laicht of Monteith. Records show Menetethe in 1185, Mynynteth in 1234 and Monteath in 1724.

Merchiston (Edinburgh) 'Merchion's farm'. *Merchiaun* (Brythonic proper name); *tun* (Old English) 'farmstead'. Now a district of Edinburgh. The inventor of logarithms, John Napier (1550–1617), lived here and his name is preserved in Napier University.

Merkland (Dumfries & Galloway and other regions) 'Land held for the rental of one merk'. *Merk* (Scots) 'mark', a unit of currency. A common locality name, especially in the south-west.

Merrick (Dumfries & Galloway) 'Pronged hill'. *Meurach* (Scottish Gaelic) 'pronged' or 'branched'. Merrick (2,766 feet/846 metres) is the highest point in the Galloway Forest.

Merse, The (Borders) The name of this fertile area, watered by the Tweed and its tributaries, comes from *maersc* (Old English) 'marsh', which came to mean 'low, flat land' in Scots.

Methil (Fife) Perhaps 'boundary wood'. *Maid* (Brythonic-Celtic) 'boundary'; *choille* (Scottish Gaelic) 'wood'. Alternatively, 'boggy wood' from *maoth* (Scottish Gaelic) 'bog' or, as one authority suggests, it may derive from *methl* (Old Norse) 'middle', signifying its location 'in the middle of' the two older places of Buckhaven and Leven. A record of 1250 shows Methkil.

Methven (Perth & Kinross) 'Middle stone'. *Meddfaen* (Brythonic) 'middle stone' or 'middle marker', as of a boundary. In 1306, in the early days of his kingship, Robert Bruce was defeated here by an English army.

Midmar (Aberdeenshire) 'Bog of Mar'. *Mig* (Brythonic) 'bog'; *Mar* (*see* **Mar**). The older form of the name is Migmar.

Milngavie (East Dunbartonshire) Perhaps 'windmill'. *Muilleann* (Scottish Gaelic) 'mill'; *gaoithe* (Scottish Gaelic) 'wind'. Windmills were unusual in Scotland, where water power was normally available. Alternatively, the origin of the name of this northern dormitory town for Glasgow may be derived from *meal-na-gaoithe* (Scottish Gaelic) 'hill of the wind'.

Midlothian *see* **Lothian**.

Milleur Point (Dumfries & Galloway) 'Brown point'. *Maol* (Scottish Gaelic) 'rock-brow' or 'promontory'; *odhar* (Scottish Gaelic) 'dun-coloured'.

Millport (North Ayrshire) This resort and port on the Island of Cumbrae, in the Firth of Clyde, is named after the large grain mill that stood above the harbour when the town was originally developed in the first decade of the 19th century.

Milton (All regions) 'Place of the mill'. Often an English version of the original *Baile a'Mhuileann* (Scottish Gaelic) 'place of the mill', found in anglicised form in various districts as Balavoulin.

Minch, The (Highland, Western Isles) Possibly 'great headland(s)'. *Megin* (Old Norse) 'great'; *nes* (Old Norse) 'headland'. The name of this notoriously stormy stretch of sea between the north-west mainland of Scotland and the Outer Hebrides, separated into the Minch proper and the 'Little Minch', is almost certainly Scandinavian in origin. The headland in question could either be Cape Wrath, or the Butt of Lewis, or both.

Minard (Argyll & Bute) 'Small bay'. *Minni* (Old Norse) 'small'; *fjordr* (Old Norse) 'bay' or 'loch'.

Mingary (Western Isles) Probably 'big garth'. *Mikla* (Old Norse) 'big' has become transposed to *mingil*; *gardr* (Old Norse) 'land between machair and moor' and adopted into Scottish Gaelic as *gearraidh*.

Mingulay (Western Isles) Probably 'big island'. *Mikla* (Old Norse) 'big' has become transposed to *mingil* with *ey* (Old Norse) 'island'.

Minnigaff (Dumfries & Galloway) 'Hill of the smith'. *Monadh* (Scottish Gaelic) 'hill'; *a'gobhainn* (Scottish Gaelic) 'of the smith'. *See also* **Challoch**.

Mintlaw (Aberdeenshire) 'Mint hill'. *Mint* (the same word in Old English) was always an important herb; *law* (Scots) 'hill'. The Scots name indicates an origin in the 14th century or later but the village itself is relatively modern, one of the many established in the late 18th and early 19th centuries.

Moffat (Dumfries & Galloway) Possibly the place of the 'long plain'. *Magh* (Scottish Gaelic) 'plain'; *fada* (Scottish Gaelic) 'long'. A fine statue of a Border ram in the main street testifies to the importance of sheep-rearing in the area.

Moidart (Highland) Place of the 'muddy fiord'. *Moda* (Old Norse) 'mud'; *art* (Scottish Gaelic adaptation of the Old Norse *fjordr*) 'sea loch'. This area of the West Highlands, sandwiched between Ardnamurchan to the south and Morar to the north, takes its name from the shallow and muddy sea loch that penetrates its hilly terrain.

Monadhliath (Highland) 'Grey mountains'. *Monadh* (Scottish Gaelic) 'mountain(s)'; *liath* (Scottish Gaelic) 'grey'. A mountain massif of grey mica-schist rock, lying between upper Strathspey and the Great Glen, in which the Spey, Findhorn and Dulnain rivers rise. Its greatest height is *Càrn Dearg* (Scottish Gaelic) 'red cairn' at 3,100 feet/944 metres.

Monar, Loch (Highland) Its Gaelic name, *Loch Mhonair*, means 'Loch of Monar', which has been tentatively explained as coming from a Pictish term related to the Gaelic *monadh* ('mountain') and indicating 'loch of the high ground'.

Moncrieff (Perth & Kinross) 'Wooded hill'. *Monadh* (Scottish Gaelic) 'mountain' or 'hill'; *craoibh* (Scottish Gaelic) 'of the woods'.

Moniaive (Dumfries & Galloway) Possibly 'moor of crying'. *Moine* (Scottish Gaelic) 'moor' or 'peat bog'; *eibhe* (Scottish Gaelic) 'cry' or 'death cry'.

Monifieth (Angus) 'Peat-bed of the bog'. *Moine* (Scottish Gaelic) 'moor' or 'peat bed'; *feithe* (Scottish Gaelic) 'bog'. Recorded as Munifeth in 1220. This residential town to the east of Dundee was largely developed in the 19th century on a previously worked peat moss, close to the shore.

Monklands (North Lanarkshire) 'The monks' lands'. This district, east of Glasgow and centred on the adjoining towns of Airdrie and Coatbridge, takes its name from the area's former parishes of Old and New Monkland. The name goes back to the 12th century when King Malcolm IV granted lands here to the monks of Newbattle Abbey near Dalkeith.

Montrose (Angus) 'The peat moss of the promontory'. *Moine* (Scottish Gaelic) 'moor' or 'peat bed'; *ros* (Scottish Gaelic) 'promontory'. The name accurately describes this historic east coast town's situation on a low-lying peninsula at the entrance to the tidal Montrose Basin.

The *t* in the name has been interpolated, as in another Tayside name, Montroy – *monadh* (Scottish Gaelic) 'mountain' and ruadh (Scottish Gaelic) 'red'. Records show Munros *circa*1200, Montrose in 1296, Monros in 1322 and Montross in 1480.

Monymusk (Aberdeenshire) 'Mucky peat bog'. *Moìne* (Scottish Gaelic) 'moor' or 'peat bed'; *mosach* (Scottish Gaelic) 'foul'. Despite the name, this was one of the earliest 'improved' agricultural estates in the 18th century.

Monzie (Perth & Kinross) 'Corn plain'. *Magh* (Scottish Gaelic) 'plain'; *an* (Scottish Gaelic) 'of'; *eadha* (Scottish Gaelic) 'corn'. Recorded in the 13th century as Mugheda. Moonzie in Fife has the same derivation.

Monzievaird (Perth & Kinross) Probably 'plain of the bards'. *Magh* (Scottish Gaelic) 'plain'; *bhàrd* (Scottish Gaelic) 'bards'. Bards were held in great esteem in former times and frequently given grants of land.

Morangie (Highland) Perhaps 'the big meadows'. *Mòr* (Scottish Gaelic) 'big'; *innse* (Scottish Gaelic) 'water meadows'.

Morar (Highland) 'Big water'. *Mór* (Scottish Gaelic) 'big'; *dhobhar* (Scottish Gaelic from Brythonic) 'water'. This part of the west Highlands, between Knoydart to the north and Moidart to the south, takes its name from the river that flows across the narrow isthmus between the loch and the sea. Its name was also given to the loch, which lies east-west at the centre of the area and divides it into North and South Morar. This loch is the deepest inland water in Britain at over 1,000 feet/300 metres below sea level – a depth not reached again for many miles out to sea.

Moray 'Sea settlement' from *mori*, an old Gaelic name related to the Brythonic *mor-tref*, 'sea-home'. The current administrative district and former county takes its name from the much larger ancient province of Moray, which also gave its name to the Moray Firth.

More, Ben (Many locations) 'Big mountain'. *Beinn* (Scottish Gaelic) 'mountain'; *mòr* (Scottish Gaelic) 'big'. The best-known Ben More is probably the one above Crianlarich (3,853 feet/1,174 metres); others are often identified additionally by a district name, as in Ben More Assynt and Ben More Mull.

More, Glen (Highland) 'Great glen'. *Gleann* (Scottish Gaelic) 'glen'; *mòr* (Scottish Gaelic) 'big'. It is known as The Great Glen, Glen More or Glen Albyn. This major fault valley extends 65 miles/105 kilometres across the width of Scotland from south-west to north-east. Its three lochs – Loch Ness, Loch Oich and Loch Lochy – were connected to each other and the sea in 1822 to form the Caledonian Canal.

Moriston, River and **Glen** (Highland) 'Big waterfalls'. *Mòr* (Scottish Gaelic) 'big'; *easain* (Scottish Gaelic) 'waterfalls'. Glen Moriston is well endowed with waterfalls. The 19th-century forms show Glen Morison, the *t* being a recent intrusion into the name.

Mormond (Aberdeenshire) 'Big hill'. *Mór* (Scottish Gaelic) 'big'; *monadh* (Scottish Gaelic) 'hill'. Though not specially high (768 feet/242 metres), Mormond Hill is a very prominent feature of the Buchan landscape.

Morningside (Edinburgh) Perhaps 'Morgan's seat', derived in a similar way to Longmorn. The origin of the name of this pleasant residential Edinburgh district, developed mainly in the 19th century, is not entirely clear.

Mortlach (Moray) 'Big hill'. *Mòr* (Scottish Gaelic) 'big'; *ulach* (Scottish Gaelic) 'hill'.

Morton (Dumfries & Galloway, Fife, Strathclyde) 'Farm by the moor'. *Muir* (Scots) 'moor'; *toun* (Scots from Old English *tun*) 'farm'.

Morven (Aberdeenshire, Highland) 'Big hill'. Usually taken to be a transposition of Ben More, from *mòr* (Scottish Gaelic) 'big' and *beinn* (Scottish Gaelic) 'mountain'.

Morvern (Highland) 'Sea gap'. *Mor* (Old Gaelic) 'sea'; *bhearn* (Scottish Gaelic) 'gap'. This is a triangular peninsula on the West Highland coast, lying south of Ardnamurchan and bounded by the Sound of Mull and Loch Linnhe. The 'sea gap' is possibly Loch Sunart, a long fiord that penetrates along the north of this area, virtually cutting it off.

Mossgiel (East Ayrshire) 'Plain of the smallholding'. *Maes* (Brythonic) 'plain' or 'open field'; *gafael* (Brythonic) 'holding'. This was one of several places farmed by Robert Burns.

Motherwell (North Lanarkshire) 'The Mother's well'. This former steelmaking town in the Clyde Valley to the south-east of Glasgow takes its name from an ancient well dedicated to the Virgin Mary, the site of which is today marked by a plaque in Ladywell Road.

Moulin (Perth & Kinross) 'Bare hill'. *Maolinn* (Scottish Gaelic) 'bare round hill'.

Moulinearn (Perth & Kinross) 'Mill by the alders'. *Muileann* (Scottish Gaelic) 'mill'; *fhearna* (Scottish Gaelic) 'alders'.

Mound, The (Highland) A 19th-century name from the embankment carrying the road and former Dornoch branch railway line across the head of Loch Fleet.

Mount Vernon (Glasgow) This area of Glasgow was once known as Windyedge. It is said to have been renamed by George Buchanan, one of Glasgow's 18th-century 'tobacco lords', after the Washington plantation in Virginia.

Mounth (Angus, Aberdeenshire) 'The mountain(s)'. *Monadh* (Scottish Gaelic) 'mountain'. This was the original Scots name of the mountains miscalled 'the Grampians'.

Mousa (Shetland) This island name is of uncertain derivation, though 'mossy isle' has been hazarded from *mose* (Old Norse) 'moss'.

Moy (Highland) 'The plain'. *Magh* (Scottish Gaelic) 'plain'. Loch Moy is 'the loch of the plain', at the centre of Clan MacIntosh territory.

Muck (Highland) 'Pig island'. *Muc* (Scottish Gaelic) 'pig'. The reference is usually taken to pigs being kept here rather than to any topographical feature of this small but fertile Inner Hebridean island.

Muckersie (Perth & Kinross) 'Pigs' bank'. *Muc* (Scottish Gaelic) 'pig'; *kerss* (Old Norse) 'low-lying river bank', the source of the Scots *carse*.

Muckhart (Clackmannanshire) 'Pig yard'. *Muc* (Scottish Gaelic) 'pig'; *gart* (Scottish Gaelic) 'yard' or 'enclosure'. The Yetts of Muckhart indicate the entrance to a narrow valley here, with 'Yetts' coming from *yetts* (Scots from Old English *geatan*) 'gates'.

Muckle Flugga (Shetland) 'Great cliffs'. *Micil* (Old Norse) 'great' or 'big'; *flugga* (Old Norse) 'cliffs'. This lighthouse-crowned rock is the outermost and highest of a group of sharp rocks or skerries to the north of the island of Unst. *See* **Out Stack**.

Muir of Ord (Highland) 'The moor of the rounded hill'. *Muir* (Scots version of Old English *mor*) 'moor'; *ord* (Scottish Gaelic) 'rounded hill'. The rounded hill is the western shoulder of the Black Isle and the moor is the level ground on which the village, once the site of an important cattle market, is located.

Muirkirk (East Ayrshire) 'Church on the moor'. *Muir* (Scots version of Old English *mor*) 'moor'; *kirk* (Scots from Old English *cirice*) 'church'.

Mulben (Moray) 'Bare hill'. *Maol* (Scottish Gaelic) 'bare' or 'bald'; *beinn* (Scottish Gaelic) 'mountain'.

Mull (Argyll & Bute) 'Island of the headland' suggested. *Muli* (Old Norse) 'headland'. Ptolemy's map of around AD 150 refers to the island as Maleos, sufficiently like the present name to make the suggested Old Norse derivation improbable. Other suggestions have been made, including *maol* (Scottish Gaelic) 'rocky brow' or 'bare summit' and *meuilach* (Scottish Gaelic) 'favoured one'. A Celtic source seems most likely, with *maol* or an earlier form fitting the situation for this many-caped island.

Mull of Kintyre *see* **Kintyre**.

Mullardoch, Loch (Highland) 'Loch of the bare uplands'. *Loch* (Scottish Gaelic) 'lake' or 'loch'; *maol* (Scottish Gaelic) 'bare'; *àrda-ich* (from the Scottish Gaelic *àrd* with -*ach* locative suffix) 'height'.

Munlochy (Highland) 'At the foot of the black goddess's stream'. *Bonn* (Scottish Gaelic) 'foot'; *lòch* (Old Gaelic) 'black'; *dae* (Old Gaelic, giving Scottish Gaelic *dia*) 'goddess'. *See* **Lochty**. An alternative derivation is *im Bun Locha* (Scottish Gaelic) 'at the foot of the loch'. The loch is presumably Munlochy Bay, although almost all similarly situated locations have the 'Kin-' prefix, meaning 'head'.

Murrayfield (Edinburgh) This western suburb of the city, home of Scotland's national rugby football ground, was named after an 18th-century local landowner and advocate, Archibald Murray.

Murthly (Perth & Kinross) 'Big hill'. *Mòr* (Scottish Gaelic) 'big'; *tulach* (Scottish Gaelic) 'hill'. Murthly is situated on the Highland Line, just where the hills begin.

Musselburgh (East Lothian) 'Mussel town'. *Musle* (Old English) 'mussel'; *burh* (Old English) 'town'. This ancient burgh on the Firth of Forth, immediately to the east of Edinburgh, has been famous for its mussels for over 800 years. Its name was documented in 1100 as Musleburge.

Muthil (Perth & Kinross) Perhaps 'pleasant or gentle place'. *Maothail* (Scottish Gaelic) 'soothing' or 'tender'.

N

Nairn (Highland) The name originally belonged to the river on which the town lies. It is assumed to be of Pre-Celtic origin, although its actual meaning remains obscure. It was later applied to the town at its mouth, which was formerly the county town of Nairnshire. It was also at times known as Invernairn, as Invernarran *circa* 1200, as Inernarn in 1283 and as Narne in 1583.

Naver, River, Loch, Strath (Highland) Noted on Ptolemy's map of AD 150 as Nabaros, the name derives from a Pre-Celtic root, which has been identified both as *nebh* (indicating 'water' [*see* **Nevis**]) and *nabh* (indicating 'fog' or 'cloud'), with a typical Celtic *-ar* ending (indicating a river, as with the Lugar or the English River Tamar). This long Sutherland strath, once well-populated, was 'cleared' by the landowner in 1819.

Navitie (Fife) 'Holy place'. The name of this locality just north of Ballingry, together with Navitie Hill, derives from *neimheidh* (Scottish Gaelic) 'sacred or holy place' – a term which is derived in turn from *nemeton* (Gaulish) 'a place for ritual meetings'. The sense was adopted into Christianity as 'land belonging to the church'.

Nell, Loch (Argyll & Bute) 'Loch of the swans'. *Loch* (Scottish Gaelic) 'lake' or 'loch'; *nan* (Scottish Gaelic) 'of the'; *eala* (Scottish Gaelic) 'swans'.

Ness, River and **Loch** (Highland) The name was originally that of the river (*Nis*, a Pre-Celtic river name of undetermined origin). In Adamnan's *Life of St Columba*, it is referred to as Nesa (Latin). Its meaning is unknown and it predates any likelihood of being from *nes* (Old Norse) 'cape' or 'headland'. Short, wide and prone to sudden floods, the river flows from the loch into the Moray Firth at Inverness. Loch Ness (of 'monster' fame) stretches for some 24 miles/38 kilometres down the Great Glen and is more than 600 feet/200 metres deep. It holds the largest volume of fresh water in the country. *See* **Inverness**.

Netherby (Dumfries & Galloway) 'Lower farm'. *Nedri* (Old Norse) 'lower'; *by* (Old Norse) 'farmstead'.

Nethy, River *see* **Abernethy**.

Nevis (Highland) The name of the highest mountain in the British Isles (4,406 feet/1,344 metres) is also the name of a river, glen and a sea loch. As with many other names, it was probably first that of the river at the mountain's foot (perhaps from the same Pre-Celtic root-form *nebh*, 'cloud', as has been suggested for Naver). A case has also been made for *nimheis* (Old Gaelic) 'venomous'. Many other unattested interpretations have been made, including: 'the awesome', 'the sky-high' and 'the peak in the clouds' but until the 19th-century ordnance survey, Ben Macdhui was generally considered to be higher than Ben Nevis. Loch Nevis is a long way from Ben Nevis and must have acquired its name independently – another argument for the 'water' origin.

New Abbey (Dumfries & Galloway) This small town is named after the Cistercian abbey founded here in 1273 by Devorguilla Balliol (mother of Scotland's unfortunate King John). The fact that she is buried in front of the high altar with the heart of her dead husband is probably the reason for the romantic name 'Sweetheart Abbey', now commonly given to its ruins.

New Aberdour *see* **Aberdour**.

Newbattle (Midlothian) 'New building'. The 'battle' is from *botl* (Old English) 'house' or 'dwelling' and the name dates from the foundation of the abbey in 1140.

Newburgh (Fife, Aberdeenshire) 'New town'. *Neowe* (Old English) 'new'; *burh* (Old English) 'town'. Like many such 'new' places, it is now of some antiquity, having received its *Novus burgus* charter in 1266. Newburgh on the Ythan estuary in Aberdeenshire is of similar vintage.

New Deer (Aberdeenshire) *See* **Deer** for derivation of the name. The parish of Deer was divided in two in the early 17th century but the village of New Deer dates from 1805, when it was established by James Ferguson of Pitfour.

New Galloway (Dumfries & Galloway) This small royal burgh, at the head of Loch Ken, had its charter granted to Sir John Gordon by King Charles I in 1629. Its name, first recorded as The New Town of Galloway in 1682, is probably a reference to the fact that the Gordon family already owned other properties in Galloway.

Newhaven (Edinburgh) 'New harbour'. The port, now part of the Edinburgh shore front, was founded by King James IV in 1510 to provide a harbour for his ships (as part of his development of a Scottish navy).

Newington (Edinburgh) 'New place'. The name is first found around 1720 but not in the form 'Newton', as might have been expected. The 'ing' element may have been interpolated on the model of other place names.

New Lanark *see* **Lanark**.

New Luce *see* **Luce**.

New Machar (Aberdeenshire) 'New place of (St) Machar'. The name differentiates this site from the Aberdeen parish of Old Machar.

New Pitsligo (Aberdeenshire) *see* **Pitsligo** for derivation of the name. This location dates from 1780, when it was founded by Sir William Forbes of Pitsligo.

Newport-on-Tay (Fife) This town, on the south side of the Firth of Tay and directly across from Dundee, was established as a 'new' port in medieval times. It had ferry connections until the construction of the road bridge in 1966.

New Scone *see* **Scone** for derivation of the name. This village was created in 1805, when the old village of Scone was demolished to allow for the extension of the Earl of Mansfield's park.

Newtongrange (Midlothian) This former coal-mining town south of Dalkeith was so called in contradistinction to the older grange of the nearby Newbattle Abbey, namely Prestongrange near Prestonpans.

Newtonmore (Highland) 'New town on the moor'. This village in upper Strathspey came into being towards the end of the 19th century mainly thanks to the Perth to Inverness railway and the tourist trade it brought.

Newton St Boswells *see* **St Boswells**.

Newton Stewart (Dumfries & Galloway) This 'new town' is situated on the right bank of the River Cree close to its estuary on Wigtown Bay. It was established in 1671 by William Stewart, third son of the 2nd Earl of Galloway.

Newtyle (Angus) 'New hill'. *Nuadh* (Scottish Gaelic) 'new'; *tulach* (Scottish Gaelic) 'hill'. In 1182, it was recorded as Neutyle. This Strathmore village was the terminus of one of Scotland's earliest railways, the Dundee & Newtyle, opened with horse traction in 1831.

Nick (Dumfries & Galloway) 'Pass or hill gap'. This appears to be a Scots term, found also in Middle English. Names, such as Nick of the Balloch in Carrick, suggest that it was applied when the sense of Gaelic place names was lost.

Niddrie (Edinburgh) 'New house or new farm'. *Newydd* (Brythonic) 'new'; *tref* (Brythonic) 'house' or 'farmstead'.

Nigg (Highland, Aberdeenshire) 'On the bay'. *An uig* (Scottish Gaelic adaptation of the Old Norse *vik*) 'bay'. The Ross-shire village has given the name back to Nigg Bay. The same thing has happened with the other Nigg, just south of Aberdeen. An alternative derivation is from *'n eig* (Gaelic) 'the notch' and in both cases a notch or gully in the ground can be shown.

Nithsdale (Dumfries & Galloway) 'Valley of the River Nith'. Now also the name of an administrative district centred on Dumfries and named after the River Nith. The name derives from *Nedd* (cognate with Nethy, also Neath in Wales and Nidd in England) meaning 'glistening'. (There is a Loch Nedd in Assynt, Sutherland.) The *Novios* river shown in Ptolemy's map (AD 150) is in the position of the Nith but it seems unlikely that the names are related.

Nitshill (Glasgow) 'Nut hill'. *Nit* (Scots) 'nut'.

Nochty (Aberdeenshire) 'Bare'. *Nochdaidh* (Scottish Gaelic) 'naked'. The reference is to treelessness. The Water of Nochty is one of the headstreams of the Don.

Noltland (Orkney) 'Cattle land'. *Nauta* (Old Norse) 'cattle', giving the Scots *nolt* or *nowt*.

North Berwick (East Lothian) North 'barley farmstead'. *Bere* (Old English) 'barley'; *wic* (Old English) 'farmstead'. This coastal resort on the Firth of Forth is set amidst the rich barley fields of East Lothian. However, the 'north' locative element may suggest that this name was transferred here from Berwick-Upon-Tweed, presumably at an early date, or may simply serve to differentiate it from the larger town. It was recorded as Northberwyk in 1250.

North Queensferry *see* **Queensferry.**

North Ronaldsay *see* **Ronaldsay.**

North Uist *see* **Uist.**

Noss (Shetland, Highland) 'The nose'. *Nos* (Old Norse) 'nose'. This uninhabited island, just off the far east side of Bressay, rises to a high snout in the spectacular cliffs of the Noup of Noss. Noss Head in Caithness has the same derivation.

Noup A very common name in Shetland toponymy and also found in Orkney, as in Noup Head on Westray. *Gnup* (Old Norse) 'peak'. It is also found in the form Neap, as in the North Neaps on Yell.

Novar (Highland) Possibly 'giant's house'. The Gaelic name is *Taigh an Fhuamhair*: *Taigh* (Scottish Gaelic) 'house'; *an* (Scottish Gaelic) 'of'; *fhuamhair* (Scottish Gaelic) 'giant's' or 'champion's'. There are legends of Fingal's (Finn MacCool's) exploits in the locality.

O

Oa, Mull of (Argyll & Bute) 'Bare point of the cairn'. *Haugr* (Old Norse giving the Gaelic *ho*) 'cairn'; *maol* (Scottish Gaelic) 'brow of a rock' or 'headland'.

Oakley (Fife) 'Oak field'. 'Oak' (Middle English) oak; *ley* (Scots) 'meadow'.

Oban (Argyll & Bute) 'Little bay'. *Ob* (Scottish Gaelic from Old Norse *hop*) 'bay'; *-an* (Scottish Gaelic diminutive suffix) 'little'. Indeed, its name derives from the fuller Gaelic version, *An t- Oban Latharnach*, 'the little bay of Lorn'. This West Highland port, railhead and resort lies on a small sheltered bay off the Sound of Kerrera. It is the steamer port for the southernmost of the Outer Isles, Barra and South Uist, as well as several inner Hebridean routes.

Obbe (Western Isles) 'Bay'. *Ob* (Scottish Gaelic from Old Norse *hop*) 'bay'. *See* **Leverburgh**.

Ochil Hills (Stirling, Perth & Kinross) 'High hills'. *Ocel* (Brythonic) 'high'. The earliest references are to Cind Ochil in AD 700, Sliab Nochel in 850 and Oychellis in 1461. The 'Ochils', as they are usually known, stretch some 25 miles/40 kilometres from Stirling towards Perth and rise steeply to over 2,000 feet/600 metres in places. The Battle of Sheriffmuir, in 1715, was fought on the Ochil slopes above Dunblane.

Ochiltree (East Ayrshire) 'High house'. *Ocel* (Brythonic) 'high'; *tref* (Brythonic) 'house' or 'homestead'.

Ochtertyre (Perth & Kinross) A scotticised form of Auchtertyre meaning 'upper land'. *Uachdar* (Scottish Gaelic) 'upper'; *tiridh* (Scottish Gaelic) 'land'. Auchtertyre in Wester Ross has an identical meaning.

Ogilvie (Angus) Perhaps 'high plain'. *Ocel* (Brythonic) 'high'; *fa* (Brythonic, related to Gaelic *magh*.) 'plain'.

Ogle, Glen (Stirling) This steep, landslide-prone glen may derive its name from *ocel* (Brythonic) 'high' but the Gaelic form, *Oguil*, does not correspond to this. The derivation of the name, together with that of the Angus Glen Ogil, remains uncertain.

Oich, River and **Loch** (Highland) 'Stream place'. *Abha* (Scottish Gaelic) 'stream'; *ach* (Scottish Gaelic suffix) 'place'. The loch may have originally been *Loch Abha* (as in Awe). *See* **Awe**, **Avoch**.

Old Kilpatrick (West Dunbartonshire) Old place of 'St Patrick's church'. *Cill* (Scottish Gaelic) 'church'; *Padraig* (Scottish-Irish Gaelic personal name from the Latin *patricius*) 'of noble birth'. According to one tradition, Patrick, patron saint of Ireland (AD 387–458), was born here. The village, situated on the north bank of the River Clyde, was formerly known simply as Kilpatrick until the parish was split in 1649, since when it was prefixed first by 'West' and latterly by 'Old'.

Oldmeldrum (Aberdeenshire) *see* **Meldrum**. The 'Old' was added later when the former parish was divided.

Old Scone *see* **Scone**.

Onich (Highland) 'Foamy place'. *Omhanaich* (Scottish Gaelic) 'of foam'.

Opinan (Highland) 'Place of bays'. *Obhain* (Scottish Gaelic from the Old Norse*hop*, 'sheltered bay') 'bays'; *-an* (Scottish Gaelic diminutive suffix) 'little' or 'diminutive'.

Oransay (Argyll & Bute) 'Oran's island'. There are numerous islands bearing forms of this name. *Odhrain* (St Oran) was a follower and collaborator of Columba. *See* **Oronsay**.

Orbliston (Moray) This name has resisted clear derivation. The first part has been tentatively identified with *iorbull* (Scottish Gaelic) 'peaceful'. The form suggests a proper name with *-ton* (Scots) 'town' or 'place' but no document has yet been found to back this up.

Orchy, River and **Glen** (Argyll & Bute) 'Woody stream place'. *Urcháidh* (Scottish Gaelic place name) combines the Pre-Celtic elements *ar*, indicating water, and *cet* (Brythonic *coed*), indicating 'wood'.

Orkney Possibly 'the Boar tribe's islands'. *Orc* (Pre-Celtic root mentioned in Latin texts of 320 BC) 'boar', 'pig', or 'whale'. *Uirc* (boars) were among the hieratic animals in Celtic beliefs. The name in Old Irish is *Insi-orc*, 'islands of the pigs'. The name was assimilated into Old Norse as *Orkn-eyjar*, meaning 'seal islands'. The name was recorded around 330 BC by the Greek geographer, Strabo, from Pytheas's account of his voyage around Britain, and by the Romans in the 1st century as Orcades. This latter name is still occasionally used in a literary context.

Ormiston (East Lothian) 'Orm's farm'. *Ormr* (Old Norse proper name); *tun* (Old English) 'farmstead'. Ormiston is of historical interest as the first 'model village' in Scotland, which was set up here in 1731 and bankrupted its founder, John Cockburn.

Oronsay (Argyll & Bute) 'St Oran's isle'. *Odhrain* (Irish Gaelic personal name); *ey* (Old Norse) 'island'. This small island, separated from Colonsay to the north by a narrow tidal strand, was where, traditionally, Columba first landed with Oran. Its priory was founded by John, Lord of the Isles, in 1360. *See* **Oransay**.

Orrin, River and **Glen** (Highland) 'River of the chapel'. It seems that the ancient name of the river has been replaced by that of the church of Urray, at its point of confluence with the Conon. *Oifreann* (Scottish Gaelic) 'chapel' or 'offering place'.

Orton (Moray) 'Edge of the hill'. *Oir* (Scottish Gaelic) 'edge'; *dhùin* (Scottish Gaelic) 'of the hill'.

Otter Ferry (Argyll & Bute) 'Ferry of the reef'. *Oitir* (Scottish Gaelic) 'reef'.

Out Skerries (Shetland) 'Far out islets'. *Ut* (Old Norse) 'far out' or 'farthermost'; *skjaer* (Old Norse) 'rock' or 'cliff'. This triangular shaped group of islands, some no more than rocks but with the two largest linked by a bridge and inhabited, forms the easternmost part of the Shetland archipelago. They lie 5 miles/8 kilometres out from Whalsay.

Out Stack (Shetland) 'Far out rock'. *Ut* (Old Norse) 'far out' or 'farthermost'; *stakkr* (Old Norse) 'steep-sided' and often 'conical, detached rock'. This solitary outlying rock, just under half a mile/800 metres north-east of Muckle Flugga, is the most northerly point of the British Isles.

Oxgangs (Edinburgh and other areas) This name refers to an area of land that could be ploughed by an ox in a day. Oxgangs in Midlothian, originally a field name, is now a district of south Edinburgh.

Oxnam (Borders) 'Ox farm'. *Oxenaham* (Old English) 'village of the oxen'.

Oykel, River and **Strath** (Highland) This name has been taken as related to Ochil, perhaps with reference to its high banks. *Ocel* (Brythonic) 'high'. Its connection with the site of a battle between Norsemen and Scots, *Ekkjalsbakki* (Old Norse) 'Ekkjal's bank' (*Orkneyinga Saga*) is no longer considered likely.

P

Pabay (Western Isles) 'Priest's island'. *Papa* (Old Norse) 'priest'; *ey* (Old Norse) 'island'. Also Pabbay.

Paisley (Renfrewshire) Probably 'pasture slope'. *Pasgell* (Brythonic) 'pasture'; *llethr* (Brythonic, cognate with Scottish Gaelic *leitir*) 'slope'. Recorded as Paisleth in 1158 and Paislay in 1508. It was best known for its abbey in medieval times and it became an important textile town in the 18th century.

Panmure (Angus) 'Big hollow'. *Pant* (Brythonic) 'hollow' or 'dene' (as in modern Welsh); *mawr* (Brythonic) 'big'.

Papa Stour (Shetland) 'Great priest island'. *Papa* (Old Norse) 'priest'; *ey* (Old Norse) 'island'; *storr* (Old Norse) 'great'. The 'storr' here distinguishes this island from all the other many Old Norse 'priest islands'.

Paps of Jura (Argyll & Bute) The collective term for the three breast-shaped hills of Jura, recorded by Martin Martin in 1703.

Partick (Glasgow) 'Bushy place'. *Perth* (Brythonic-Pictish) 'thicket'. Early records show Perdyec in 1136, Pertheck in 1158 and Perthik in 1362. This inner suburb of Glasgow lies on the north bank of the Clyde, which in pre-urban times was, no doubt, a bushy place. Compare **Broomielaw**.

Pathhead (Fife, Midlothian) 'Head of the steep track'. 'Path' (from the Scots *peth)* indicates a footway up a steep slope or valley, and the locations of the numerous 'path' names confirms this. It is often found as a suffix in place names such as Redpath and Cockburnspath.

Patna (East Ayrshire) The name of an Indian city, transferred to this former mining village in 1810 by the local landowner, Provost William Faulkner, who apparently had lived and made his fortune in the Indian city of Patna.

Peebles (Borders) Place of 'sheilings'. *Pebyll* (Brythonic) 'sheilings'. This market and former county town and resort on the upper Tweed river still lies in a sheep-grazing area and may have been a favoured summer pasture in the past. *See* **Galashiels**.

Pencaitland (East Lothian) Possibly 'head of the wood enclosure'. *Pen* (Brythonic) 'head' or 'top of'; *coet* (Brythonic) 'wood'; *lann* (Brythonic) 'field' or 'enclosure'. The description of a pastoral village enclosed by woods remains valid today.

Penicuik (Midlothian) 'Hill of the cuckoo'. *Pen* (Brythonic) 'head' or 'hill'; *y* (Brythonic) 'the'; *cog* (Brythonic) 'cuckoo'. This residential town lies south of Edinburgh on the lower wooded slopes of the Pentlands. Recorded as Penicok in 1250.

Penmanshiel (Borders) 'Pastureland at the head of stone'. *Pen* (Brythonic) 'head'; *maen* (Brythonic) 'stone'. Compare **Penmaenmawr** ('great head of stone') in Wales. The Scots *-shiel* termination, indicating a summer grazing place, is a later addition.

Pennan (Aberdeenshire) 'Headland water'. *Pen* (Brythonic) 'headland' or 'hill'; *an* (Brythonic) 'water' or 'stream'. The reference is to the stream which flows into the sea here over a steep cliff.

Penny This prefix generally indicates a place held on a penny rental, though it may also stem from *pen* (Brythonic) 'head'. In the north of Lewis, there are Five Penny Borve and Five Penny Ness. 'Pennyland' names in the south-west often have the prefix as 'Pin-' from the Gaelic form (*see* **Pinmore**).

Pennyghael (Argyll & Bute) 'Pennyland of the Gael'. A pennyland was an area held on a penny rental. This district of Mull was held by Gaels, as distinct from Galls or non-Gaelic strangers.

Penpont (Dumfries & Galloway) 'Head or end of the bridge'. *Pen* (Brythonic) 'head'; *pont* (Brythonic) 'bridge'. The name suggests a bridge of great antiquity.

Pentland Firth (Highland, Orkney) 'Firth of Pictland'. *Pettr* (Old Norse) 'Picts'; *land* (Old Norse) 'land'; *fjordr* (Old Norse) 'sea inlet' or 'passage'. The name of this stretch of sea between the north Caithness coast and the Orkney Islands, with its notorious tide-rips, really ought to be the Pictland Firth.

Pentland Hills (Midlothian) 'Hill land'. *Pen* (Brythonic) 'hill'; *land* (Old English) 'tract of land'. The name bears no relation to that of the Pentland Firth. The Celtic root is attested in many other local names with the 'Pen-' prefix (for example, Penicuik and Pencaitland).

Perth (Perth & Kinross) Place of the 'thicket'. *Perth* (Brythonic) 'bush' or 'thicket'. It was recorded as Perth in 1150. This ancient royal burgh, favoured by several kings of Scotland, was known for a few hundred years as St Johnstoun or St John's Toun of Perth, after the building of St John's Kirk in the 12th century. The local football club is St Johnstone.

Peterculter (Aberdeenshire) 'Corner land of St Peter'. *Cuil* (Scottish

Gaelic) 'corner'; *tir* (Scottish Gaelic) 'land'. The 'Peter' was added later to distinguish this satellite residential area of Aberdeen from the nearby village of Maryculter, hence its English form.

Peterhead (Aberdeenshire) 'St Peter's headland'. This major fishing, and one-time whaling, port was founded in 1593 and took its name from St Peter's Kirk, built here in 1132 on the headland near to the mouth of the Ugie Water.

Petty (Highland) 'Place of shares'. *Peiteach* (Scottish Gaelic from Brythonic-Pictish *pett*) 'of shares or portions'.

Pettycur (Fife) 'Portion at the high rental'. *Pett* (Brythonic-Pictish) 'portion' or 'piece of land'; *ocar* (Scottish Gaelic) 'usury' or 'extortion'.

Philiphaugh (Borders) 'Shut-in valley'. *Ful* (Old English) 'closed'; *hop* (Old English) 'hollow' or 'valley'. Recorded in the 13th century as Fulhope. It was here that Montrose's campaign on behalf of Charles I was brought to an end by defeat in 1645.

Pierowall (Orkney) 'Little bay'. *Piril* (Old Norse, giving the 'peerie' still in use today) 'small'; *vagr* (Old Norse) 'bay'.

Pinkie (East Lothian) 'Cé's height'. *Pen* (Brythonic) 'hill'; *Cé* (Brythonic proper name). A battle site, where the Scots were defeated by the English in 1547, during Henry VIII's 'rough wooing' of the child queen, Mary.

Pinmore (South Ayrshire) 'Big pennyland'. *Peighinn* (Scottish Gaelic) 'Scots penny' or 'denomination of land equal to a penny rental'; *mór* (Scottish Gaelic) 'great'.

Pinwherry (South Ayrshire) 'Pennyland of the copse'. *Peighinn* (Scottish Gaelic) 'Scots penny' or 'denomination of land equal to a penny rental'; *an fhoithre* (Scottish Gaelic) 'of the copse'. Also found as Pinwherrie.

Pirnmill (North Ayrshire) 'Tree point'. *Prenn* (Brythonic) 'tree'; *maol* (Scottish Gaelic) 'bare rock' or 'rocky brow', here in the sense of 'point'.

Pit- This prefix is common on the eastern side of the country from Fife to south-east Sutherland, more especially in Fife, Perthshire and Aberdeenshire, and found in only a handful of places elsewhere. It comes from the Brythonic-Pictish *pett*, meaning 'a portion of land' (first found in *The Book of Deer*, *circa* 1150). It has been noted that 'Pit-' names are always found on cultivable land and that in numerous instances an earlier 'Pit-' may have been replaced by the Scottish Gaelic *baile*. See also **Petty**.

Pitagowan (Perth & Kinross) 'The smith's portion'. *Pett* (Brythonic-Pictish) 'portion' or 'piece of land'; *ghobhainn* (Scottish Gaelic) 'smith's'.

Pitblado (Fife) 'Meal portion'. *Pett* (Brythonic-Pictish) 'portion' or 'piece of land'; *blatha* (Irish Gaelic) 'corn meal'.

Pitcairn (Fife) 'Portion of the cairn'. *Pett* (Brythonic-Pictish) 'portion' or 'piece of land'; *carn* (Scottish Gaelic) 'cairn'.

Pitcalzean (Highland) 'Portion of the wood'. *Pett* (Brythonic-Pictish) 'portion' or 'piece of land'; *coillean* (Scottish Gaelic) 'of the wood'. The *z* here is a misreading of *y*.

Pitcaple (Aberdeenshire) 'Horse share'. *Pett* (Brythonic-Pictish) 'portion' or 'piece of land'; *capull* Scottish Gaelic) 'horse'.

Pitfour (Angus, Highland) 'Pasture share'. *Pett* (Brythonic-Pictish) 'portion' or 'piece of land'; *phúir* (Scottish Gaelic) 'pasture'.

Pitkeathly (Perth & Kinross) 'Cathalan's land'. *Pett* (Brythonic-Pictish) 'portion' or 'piece of land'. *Cathalan* (Irish Gaelic proper name, diminutive of Cathal).

Pitlochry (Perth & Kinross) 'Piece of land by or with the stones'. *Pett* (Brythonic-Pictish) 'portion' or 'piece of land'; *cloichreach* (Scottish Gaelic) 'stones'. The 'stones' referred to here were almost certainly stepping stones across the River Tummel, by which the town is located. Nowadays, Pitlochry is an important tourist resort.

Pitmaduthy (Highland) 'MacDuff's portion'. *Pett* (Brythonic-Pictish) 'portion' or 'piece of land'; *mhic Dhuibh* (Scottish Gaelic) 'MacDuff's'.

Pitmilly (Fife) 'Portion of the mill'. *Pett* (Brythonic-Pictish) 'portion' or 'piece of land'; *muileann* (Scottish Gaelic) 'of the mill'.

Pitsligo (Aberdeenshire) 'Shelly portion'. Pett (Brythonic-Pictish) 'portion' or 'piece of land'; *sligeach* (Scottish Gaelic) 'shelly'.

Pittencrieff (Fife) 'Portion of the tree. *Pett* (Brythonic-Pictish) 'portion' or 'piece of land'; *chraoibhe* (Scottish Gaelic) 'of the trees'.

Pittendreich (Fife and other areas) 'Portion of the good aspect'. *Pett*

(Brythonic-Pictish) 'portion' or 'piece of land'; *dreach* (Scottish Gaelic) 'aspect' or 'beauty'. This is the most frequently found 'Pit-' name. Variant forms include Pittendrigh and Pendreich.

Pittenweem (Fife) 'Place of the cave'. *Pett* (Brythonic-Pictish) 'piece of land' or 'place'; *na* (Scottish Gaelic) 'of the'; *h-uamha* (Scottish Gaelic) 'cave'. This East Neuk fishing port on the Firth of Forth has a cave, near the harbour, said to be associated with St Fillan. Recorded in 1150 as Petnaweem. This area of the Fife coast has many caves. *See* **Wemyss.**

Pittodrie (Aberdeen) 'Portion by the woodland'. *Pett* (Brythonic-Pictish) 'portion' or 'piece of land'; *fhodraidh* (Scottish Gaelic) 'by the wood'. The name is now synonymous with Aberdeen FC' s ground.

Pityoulish, Loch (Highland) 'Loch at the portion of the fair station'. *Pett* (Brythonic-Pictish) 'portion' or 'piece of land'; *gheall* (Scottish Gaelic) 'fair' or 'bright'; *-ais* (Scottish Gaelic from *fas*, 'stance', indicating a drovers' stance) 'stance' or 'station'.

Plean (Stirling) 'Flat land'. *Plen* (Brythonic) 'flat land'.

Plockton (Highland) 'Town of the block'. *Ploc* (Scottish Gaelic) 'block' or 'clod'; *-ton* (Scots) 'place'. This picturesque Wester Ross village is a favourite with artists.

Pluscarden (Moray) 'Place of thickets'. *Plas* (Brythonic) 'place'; *card-den* (Brythonic) 'thicket' or 'brake'. This is the site of a 12th-century Valliscaulian abbey, which has been rebuilt and re-established in modern times.

Pollockshaws (Glasgow) 'Pool by the thicket'. *Poll* (Brythonic-Celtic) 'pool'; *-oc* (Brythonic-Celtic diminutive suffix) 'little'; *sceaga* (Old English) 'wood'.

Pollok (Glasgow) 'Little pool'. *Poll* (Brythonic) 'pool'; *-oc* (Brythonic diminutive suffix) 'little'. This south-western district of Glasgow, near the confluence of the Leven and White Cart Waters, is an area where there would have been many pools. The name also occurs in the adjoining districts of Pollokshaws and Pollokshields.

Polmont (Falkirk) 'Pool hill'. *Poll* (Scottish Gaelic) 'pool' or 'hollow'; *monadh* (Scottish Gaelic) 'hill' or 'mountain'.

Polwarth (Borders) 'Paul's fields'. *Pol* (Old English proper name, a form of Paul); *worth* (Old English) 'enclosure'. This is one of a tiny number of *-worth* location names in Scotland.

Poolewe (Highland) 'Pool of the ewe'. *Poll* (Scottish Gaelic) 'pool' or 'hollow'; *Iu* (Scottish Gaelic river name related to 'yew'). *See* **Kinlochewe**.

Port Askaig *see* **Askaig**.

Portavadie (Argyll & Bute) 'Beaching place of the dogs or foxes'. *Port* (Scottish Gaelic) 'harbour' or 'beaching place'; *mhadhaidh* (Scottish Gaelic) 'of dogs'. *See also* **Lochmaddy**.

Port Bannatyne (Argyll & Bute) This resort on the east coast of Bute takes its name from the Bannatyne family, who established their seat at the nearby Kames Castle in the 13th century.

Port Charlotte (Argyll & Bute) This coastal settlement in south-west Islay is named after Lady Charlotte, the mother of the Gaelic scholar, W F Campbell of Islay, who founded the village in 1828.

Port Ellen (Argyll & Bute) This, the main port of Islay, is situated at the south end of the island and is named after Lady Ellenor, wife of W F Campbell, who founded the small town in 1821.

Portessie (Moray) 'Port of the waterfall'. *Port* (Scottish Gaelic) 'harbour' or 'beaching place'; *easach* (Scottish Gaelic) 'waterfall' or 'steeply falling stream'.

Port Glasgow (Inverclyde) The town was developed by the municipality of Glasgow in the 1660s in order to provide a deep-water port for the city's developing Atlantic trade, and named accordingly. It was for a time the main port for Glasgow, until later dredging of the River Clyde enabled bigger ships to come up to the city.

Portgower (Highland) This coastal hamlet, south of Helmsdale, was built to house some of those evicted from the interior of Sutherland in the 19th century. It is named from the Duke of Sutherland's family name, Leveson-Gower.

Portincaple (Argyll & Bute) 'Port of the horse'. *Port* (Scottish Gaelic) 'harbour' or 'beaching place'; *nan* (Scottish Gaelic) 'of the'; *chapuill* (Scottish Gaelic) 'horse'.

Portknockie (Moray) 'Harbour by the little hill'. *Port* (Scottish Gaelic) 'harbour'; *cnoc* (Scottish Gaelic) 'rounded hill'; *-ie* (colloquial diminutive) 'little'. This small fishing port was founded in 1677.

Portlethen (Aberdeenshire) 'Port of the slope'. *Port* (Scottish Gaelic) 'harbour' or 'beaching ground'; *leathan* (Scottish Gaelic) 'slope'.

Portmahomack (Highland) 'Haven of (St) Colman'. *Port* (Scottish Gaelic) 'harbour' or 'beaching ground'; *mo* (Old Gaelic) 'my'; *Cholmáig* (Irish Gaelic) 'Colman's'. The name, borne by numerous Celtic saints, is derived from the Latin *columba*, meaning 'dove'.

Portnalong (Western Isles) 'Port of the ships'. *Port* (Scottish Gaelic) 'harbour' or 'landing ground'; *nan* (Scottish Gaelic) 'of'; *long* (Scottish Gaelic) 'ship'.

Portobello (Edinburgh) The name of this seaside district of Edinburgh comes from the name of a house built here by a sailor who had seen action at the Battle of Puerto Bello in Panama in 1739.

Portpatrick (Dumfries & Galloway) 'Harbour of St Patrick'. *Port* (Scottish Gaelic) 'harbour'; *Padraig* (Scottish Gaelic personal name from *patricius* Latin] 'nobly born') 'Patrick', patron saint of Ireland, dedicated in a chapel here. The harbour, now silted up, was once the main packet port to Ireland.

Portree (Highland) 'Harbour of the slope'. *Port* (Scottish Gaelic) 'harbour'; *ruigheadh* (Scottish Gaelic) 'of the slope'. The second element was often mistakenly thought to derive from *rí* (Scottish Gaelic) 'king', related to a royal visit here by James V in 1540. Portree is the main town of Skye.

Port Seton (East Lothian) 'Seton's harbour'. The Setons were a local landowning family who developed the harbour from the 15th century onwards to export coal from their mines and salt from their saltpans.

Portsoy (Aberdeenshire) 'Harbour of the warrior'. *Port* (Scottish Gaelic) 'harbour'; *savi* (Scottish Gaelic) 'warrior'. As in Baldragon, there is no clue as to who might be the 'warrior' in the name.

Port William (Dumfries & Galloway) This small seaport and resort, situated on Luce Bay south-west of Wigtown, takes its name from Sir William Maxwell of Monrieth, who established the town here in 1770.

Prestonpans (East Lothian) 'Priests' village by the saltpans'. *Preost* (Old English) 'priest'; *tun* (Old English) 'village'; *pans* (Scots) 'salt-pans'. The name refers to saltpanning – the extraction of salt from brine by boiling it in great iron pans – here on the Firth of Forth by monks of Newbattle Abbey from the 13th century. Recorded as Saltprestoun in 1587. Several notable battles were fought here, including Prince Charles Edward's defeat of government troops, under Sir John Cope, in 1745.

Prestwick (South Ayrshire) 'Priests' farm'. *Preost* (Old English) 'priest'; *wic* (Old English) 'farm'. This resort town on the Ayrshire coast was originally, like Prestongrange near Prestonpans, an 'outlying farm' for a religious house elsewhere. Monkton ('monks' farmstead') is also a local name. The name was recorded as Prestwic in a document of 1170. Scotland's first international airport was established here.

Q

Quanterness (Orkney) 'Bishop's point'. *Kantari* (Old Norse from English 'Canterbury') 'bishop'; *nes* (Old Norse) 'cape' or 'point'.

Quarff (Shetland) 'Shelter'. *Hvarf* (Old Norse) can mean 'shelter place' as well as 'turning' (*see* **Cape Wrath**).

Queensferry, North and **South** (Fife, Edinburgh) Both these towns, on respective sides of the Firth of Forth and lying underneath the latter-day rail and road bridges, share a name that commemorates Queen Margaret, wife of King Malcolm III of Scotland, who established a free ferry here for pilgrims on their way to St Andrews. The railway bridge here was completed in 1890, the road bridge in 1974.

Quinag (Highland) The name of this Sutherland mountain (2,651 feet/811 metres) has been compared to that of Cunningham in Ayrshire, with *cuinneag* (Scottish Gaelic) 'milk-pail' in mind (though any resemblance of shape is hard to detect). *Caoin* (Scottish Gaelic) 'fair' or 'beautiful' has also been suggested.

Quinish (Western Isles) 'Cattle-fold headland'. *Kvi* (Old Norse) 'cattle-fold'; *nes* (Old Norse) 'ness' or 'headland'.

Quiraing (Highland) 'Crooked enclosure'. *Kvi* (Old Norse) 'cattle-fold'; *rong* (Old Norse) 'crooked'. The fantastic pillar-like rock formations are the source of the name.

Quoich, River, Glen and **Loch** (Highland) Probably 'of the hollow'. *Cuach* (Scottish Gaelic genitive *cuaich*) 'hollow of a hill'. The original name was given to the river.

R

Raasay (Highland) 'Roe deer ridge island'. *Rar* (Old Norse) 'roe deer'; *ass* (Old Norse) 'ridge'; *ey* (Old Norse) 'island'. This derivation is very descriptive of this long ridge-formed island lying between Skye and the mainland, where roe deer are still found. A 16th-century source refers to Rairsay.

Rackwick (Orkney) 'Sea-wrack bay'. *Reka* (Old Norse) 'sea wrack' or 'seaweed'; *vik* (Old Norse) 'bay'.

Rafford (Aberdeenshire) 'High fort'. *Rath* (Scottish Gaelic) 'ring-fort'; *àird* (Scottish Gaelic) 'high'.

Raith (Fife) Probably 'Ring-fort'. *Rath* (Scottish Gaelic) 'ring-fort'. This name is often used as a synonym for Kirkcaldy. The local football club is Raith Rovers.

Ranfurly (Renfrewshire) 'Portion of the farthing rental'. *Rann* (Scottish Gaelic) 'part' or 'portion'; *feòirlinn* (Scottish Gaelic) 'farthing'.

Rankeilour (Fife) 'Portion by the clay stream'. *Rann* (Scottish Gaelic) 'part' or 'portion'; *cil* (Scottish Gaelic) 'red clay'; *dobhar* (Brythonic-Gaelic) 'stream'. Also found as Rankeillor.

Rannoch (Highland, Perth & Kinross) 'Bracken'. *Raineach* (Scottish Gaelic) 'bracken fern'. This name, apart from being the name of an extensive historic region of the Highlands, forms part of several places in it, including Rannoch Moor, Rannoch Forest and Loch Rannoch. The original meaning probably only applied to the area around Loch Rannoch.

Ranza, River and **Loch** (North Ayrshire) 'Rowan tree river'. *Reynis* (Old Norse) 'rowan'; *áa* (Old Norse) 'river'.

Ratagan (Highland) 'Very little fort'. *Rath* (Scottish Gaelic) 'ring-fort'; -*ag* and *an* (Scottish Gaelic double diminutive suffixes). This mountain gap, over which the Glenelg road climbs, is often known as Mam Ratagan from the hills on either side, though one is a Ben and the other a Sgùrr.

Rattray (Perth & Kinross, Aberdeenshire) 'Homestead of the ring-fort'. *Rath* (Scottish Gaelic) 'ring-fort'; *tref* (Brythonic) 'homestead'. Rattray and Blairgowrie, on opposite sides of the Ericht river, form a single urban unit in the heart of a rich farming district, famous for its berry-fields. The same name occurs in Rattray Head on the eastern coast of Buchan and Old Rattray, inland.

Reay (Highland) 'Ring-fort'. *Rath* (Scottish Gaelic) 'ring-shaped stone fort'. The area round Reay was the territory of the Clan Mackay.

Relugas (Moray) A complex name, likely to be a hybrid, with the first part perhaps *ruigh* (Scottish Gaelic) 'sheiling' and the latter part perhaps cognate with Lugar and Luggie, an early Celtic stream name.

Rendall (Orkney) 'Valley of running water'. *Renna* (Old Norse) 'flow'; *dalr* (Old Norse) 'valley'.

Renfrew (Renfrewshire) 'Point of the current'. *Rhyn* (Brythonic) 'point'; *frwd* (Brythonic) 'current'. Records show Renifry in 1128, Reinfrew in 1158 and Renfrew in 1160. This old-established former county town is located west of Glasgow at the point at which the Clyde is joined by both the White and Black Cart rivers. In 1164, Somerled, Lord of Argyll and ancestor of the Lords of the Isles, was killed here whilst on a raid. Glasgow International Airport is close by.

Renton (West Dunbartonshire, Borders) Lying in the Vale of Leven to the north of Dumbarton, the town was named in 1782 by its founder, Jean Telfer Smollett (sister of the novelist Tobias Smollett), after her daughter-in-law, Cecilia Renton. The small Borders settlement is much older: *Regna* or *Regenhild* (Old English personal name); *ing,* (Old English possessive particle); *tun* (Old English) 'farm'. Recorded as Regninton from the 11th century.

Restenneth (Angus) 'Moor of fire'. *Ros* (Brythonic-Pictish) 'moor'; *tened* (Brythonic-Pictish) 'of fire'. This was a religious centre in Pictish times and the site of a priory.

Reston (Borders) 'Rhys's place'. *Rhys* (Brythonic personal name); *tun* (Old

English) 'settlement' or 'farm'. Rhys was a princely name, likely to have stuck long after the fading of Brythonic speech from the district.

Rhiconich (Highland) 'Mossy grazings'. *Ruighe* (Scottish Gaelic) 'sheiling' or 'summer grazing'; *coinnich* (Scottish Gaelic) 'mossy'.

Rhu (Argyll & Bute) 'Cape or headland'. *Rudha* (Scottish Gaelic) 'cape'. There is a very distinct promontory jutting into the Gareloch here. *Rhu* and *Rudha* prefix many names on the west coast of Scotland. *See* **Rubha**.

Rhum *see* **Rum**.

Rhynd (Tayside) 'Point of land'. *Roinn* (Scottish Gaelic) 'tail' or 'point'. *See* **Rinns**.

Riccarton (Borders, East Ayrshire) 'Richard's place'. *Riccart* (Old English personal name); *tun* (Old English) 'settlement' or 'farm'. The name is found in various localities, sometimes as Rickarton.

Rinnes, Ben (Moray) 'Promontory hill'. *Beinn* (Scottish Gaelic) 'mountain'; *roinn* (Scottish Gaelic) 'promontory'. The name of this humped inland hill (2,755 feet/842 metres) does not seem to correspond well with other 'Rinns' names. *See* **Rinns of Galloway**.

Rinns of Galloway (Dumfries & Galloway) 'Promontories'. *Roinn* (Scottish Gaelic) 'point' or 'promontory'. The term is often found applied to any similar piece of topography, not only coastal but in connection with inland lochs and rivers.

Rinns of Islay (Argyll & Bute) Whilst it is possible that this place name is from the same derivation as the Rinns of Galloway, it has also been taken to be from *rann* (Scottish Gaelic) 'division'.

Risk (Dumfries & Galloway) 'Marsh or bog'. *Riasg* (Scottish Gaelic) 'morass'. One of the many words used to define boggy terrain. It is also found in other regions and cognate forms include Reisk and Ruskie, which, along with Ruskich, are from the related *riasgach* (Scottish Gaelic) 'boggy place'.

Robroyston (Glasgow) 'Robert's place'. Noted as Roberstoun in the 16th century. Popular speech has interpolated the 'roy' but this area of Glasgow has nothing to do with Rob Roy MacGregor.

Rockall (Western Isles) 'Bare island in the stormy sea'. *Rok* (Old Norse) 'stormy sea'; *kollr* (Old Norse) 'bald head'. This derivation aptly describes this uninhabited and remote isolated rock that rises to only 63 feet/19 metres above sea level and lies some 186 miles/300 kilometres west of St Kilda. It wasformally annexed to Scotland in 1972.

Rodil (Western Isles) Perhaps 'roe deer valley'. *Rá* (Old Norse) 'roe'; *dalr* (Old Norse) 'valley'. (Raadil might be expected, *see* **Raasay**.) The old church of St Clement here has some fine carvings.

Rogart (Highland) 'Red enclosure'. *Raudr* (Old Norse) 'red' or 'reddish'; *gardr* (Old Norse) 'enclosure' or 'garth'.

Rogie, Falls of (Highland) 'Deep cleft'. *Ro* (Scottish Gaelic prefix of intensity); *agaidh* (Scottish Gaelic) 'cleft' or 'narrow pass'. There are waterfalls on the River Blackwater here.

Rohallion (Perth & Kinross) 'Ring-fort of the Caledonians'. *Ràth* (Scottish Gaelic) 'ring-fort'; *chaileainn* (Scottish Gaelic) 'of the Caledonians'. The name was presumably bestowed by the eastward-migrating Scots, encountering settlements of the Picts. *See* **Dunkeld**.

Romanno (Borders) 'Fort of the monk'. *Rath* (Scottish Gaelic) 'ring-fort'; *manaich* (Scottish Gaelic) 'of the monk'. In 1677, two gypsy tribes, the Faas and the Shaws, fought a pitched battle at Romanno Bridge.

Rona (Highland) 'Rough rocky island'. *Hraun* (Old Norse) 'rough' or 'rocky'; *ey* (Old Norse) 'island'. The island is closely identified with the hermit, St Ronan. His name comes from *rónan* (Scottish Gaelic) 'little seal' and there has been occasional confusion between the two derivations. It is a small, uninhabited island lying to the north of Raasay, with a terrain of mainly exposed ancient Lewisian gneiss bedrock. It is sometimes referred to as South Rona to distinguish it from North Rona, a small, isolated, rocky islet in the Atlantic Ocean, 45 miles/72 kilometres north-west of Cape Wrath.

Ronaldsay, North (Orkney) Apparently 'Ringan's isle'. *Ringan* (Old Norse personal name, a form of Ninian); *ey* (Old Norse) 'island'. This island, the most northerly and one of the smallest in the Orkney archipelago, is the farthest from South Ronaldsay, with which it appears to share, but only by coincidence, a basic name element.

Ronaldsay, South (Orkney) 'Rognvaldr's isle'. *Rognvaldr* (Old Norse personal name equivalent to the Scottish Gaelic *Raghnall* and the Scots *Ronald*); *ey* (Old Norse) 'island'. South Ronaldsay is connected to Burray, which is in turn joined on to the Orkney mainland by the Churchill Barrier, a causeway built as a World War II defence to close off entrances to Scapa Flow.

Rosehearty (Aberdeenshire) 'The point or wood of Abhartach'. *Abhartach* (Old Gaelic personal name); *ros* (Scottish Gaelic prefix) 'point' or 'wood'. The coastal position of this fishing port might suggest the former sense here.

Rosemarkie (Highland) 'Promontory of the horse'. *Ros* (Scottish Gaelic) 'point' or 'promontory'; *marc* (Scottish Gaelic) 'horse' or 'steed'. This Black Isle village was the site of an important Celtic monastery. It lies to the north of the long promontory known as Chanonry Point, which juts into the Moray Firth. The town south of Chanonry Point is Fortrose and just inland is Drummarkie, 'ridge of the horse'.

Roslin (Midlothian) 'Holly moor'. *Ros* (Brythonic) 'moor'; *celyn* (Brythonic) 'holly'. This former mining village lies on the north bank of the North Esk river, close to the 14th-century Rosslyn Castle and its famous collegiate chapel of 1446. The name was recorded as Roskelyn in 1240.

Rosneath (Argyll & Bute) 'Point of the sanctuary'. *Ros* (Scottish Gaelic) 'point' or 'promontory'; *neimhidh* (Scottish Gaelic) 'of the holy place'. An older spelling is Roseneath. *See* **Navitie**.

Ross (Highland, Argyll & Bute, Dumfries & Galloway) This ancient territorial name referred only to the eastern side, which became 'Easter Ross' when the county of Ross was formed. Earlier forms of this name are found both in Brythonic and in Scottish Gaelic. The Brythonic *ros* or *rhos* means 'moor' and the Scottish Gaelic *ros* can mean both 'promontory' and 'wood'. The name of this Highland district and former county is generally taken to mean 'promontory' because of its eastern peninsulas. However, the alternative meaning of 'wood' might be equally appropriate here. The locations of the Ross of Mull and the several Ross names on the western tip of Kirkcudbright Bay also suggest the 'promontory' meaning.

Rosque, Loch (Highland) 'Loch of the crossing or pass'. *Loch* (Scottish Gaelic) 'lake' or 'loch'; *chroisg* (Scottish Gaelic) 'crossing'. The loch lies where two routes from the west converge on Achnasheen.

Rosyth (Fife) Possibly a hybrid name, combining *ros* (Scottish Gaelic) 'promontory' with *hide* (Old English) 'landing place'. 'Headland of the arrows' from *saighead* (Scottish Gaelic) 'arrow' has also been suggested. This town on the Forth, close to Dunfermline, is an important naval dockyard.

Rothes (Moray) 'Ring-fort'. *Rath* (Scottish Gaelic) 'ring-fort'. This small town, situated south-east of Elgin, is the site of a 13th-century castle, probably located on the site of an earlier fortification.

Rothesay (Argyll & Bute) 'Rotha's isle'. *Rotha* (Old Norse personal name); *ey* (Old Norse) 'island'. The name originally referred to Rothesay Castle, which is still surrounded by a moat, and was extended to the town. Rothesay is the chief town of Bute.

Rothiemurchus (Highland) 'Muirgus's fort'. *Rath* (Scottish Gaelic) 'ring-fort', later developing the sense of 'fortified house'; *Muirgus* (Old Gaelic personal name). The Rothiemurchus Forest still has many stands of the native Scots Pine. This was the territory of the Clan Grant.

Rousay (Orkney) 'Hrolfr's island'. *Hrolfr* (Old Norse personal name, an adaptation of the Old German *Hrodulf*) 'renown-wolf'; *ey* (Old Norse) 'island'. The name of the island was documented in 1260 as Hrolfsey.

Rowardennan (Stirling) 'Eunan's high promontory'. *Rudha* (Scottish Gaelic) 'cape' or 'promontory'; *àird* (Scottish Gaelic) 'height'; *Eonain* (Scottish Gaelic proper name) 'of Eunan'.

Roxburgh (Borders) 'Hroc's fortified dwelling'. *Hroc* (Old English personal name) 'rook'; *burh* (Old English) 'fortified dwelling' or 'castle'. Recorded as Rokisburc in 1127. This once important royal burgh is now a mere village with a mound to show the site of its former castle, the scene of James II's accidental death during the siege of 1460.

Roy, River and **Glen** (Highland) 'Red river'. *Ruaidh* (Scottish Gaelic) 'red'. Glen Roy's distinctive terraces, the 'parallel roads', were believed to be the work of giants until 19th-century geologists showed they were caused by glacial lakes.

Rubha 'Point of land or headland'. The conventional Scottish Gaelic term for a promontory, also found in the older form *Rudha*. It is found most frequently on the west coast of the mainland and on the inner isles, from Arran northwards, but it is rare on the north and east coasts.

Rubislaw (Aberdeen) 'Rubie's Hill'. *Rubie* (Scots diminutive of

Reuben); *law* (Scots) 'hill'. This district of Aberdeen is the site of great granite quarries.

Ruchil (Perth & Kinross, Glasgow) The Perthshire Ruchil is 'red flood'. *Ruadh* (Scottish Gaelic) 'red'; *thuil* (Scottish Gaelic) 'flooding stream'. The Glasgow district name is 'red wood' with its second part being *choille* (Scottish Gaelic) 'wood'. It is sometimes found as Ruchill.

Rudha *see* **Rubha.**

Rum (Highand) Perhaps 'spacious (island)'. *Rùm* (Scottish Gaelic) 'room' or 'space'. A Pre-Celtic origin has also been suggested for the name. The *h* in the alternative spelling, 'Rhum', was inserted early in the 20th century by its owner, Sir George Bullough, a Lancashire textile magnate. It was recorded as Ruim in 677.

Rutherford (Borders) 'Ford of the horned cattle'. *Hrythera* (Old English) 'horned cattle'; 'ford' as in modern English.

Rutherglen (South Lanarkshire) Place in the 'red valley'. *Ruadh* (Scottish Gaelic) 'red'; *gleann* (Scottish Gaelic) 'glen' or 'valley'. This industrial town is situated south-east of Glasgow in the Clyde Valley where reddish coloured soils are to be found.

Ruthven (Highland, Perth & Kinross) 'Red river'. *Ruadh* (Scottish Gaelic) 'red'; *abhainn* (Scottish Gaelic) 'river'. The stream at Ruthven, Inverness-shire, is said to be reddish-coloured from mineral ore.

Ruthwell (Dumfries & Galloway) 'Well of the cross'. *Rode* (Old English) 'cross', 'rood' or 'well'. The cross, one of the finest carved Celtic crosses, is still to be seen here.

Ryan, Loch (Dumfries & Galloway) Possibly 'of the chief'. *Rigon* (Brythonic) 'chief', cognate with the Welsh *rhion*. This south-western sea loch is noted on Ptolemy's map of AD 150 as Rerigonios Kolpos.

S

Saddell (Argyll & Bute) Referred to as Sagadul in old texts, perhaps 'a place for sawing timber', from *sag* (Old Norse) 'saw' and *dalr* (Old

Norse) 'valley' or 'dale'. Saddell Abbey was traditionally founded in 1160 by Somerled, Lord of Argyll.

St Abb's Head (Borders) Named after Aebba, the first prioress of Coldingham, and sister of the 7th-century King Oswald of Northumbria. Many capes on the eastern coast are named 'Head' from the Scots *heid* (from Old Norse *hofud*) or, as more likely here, from the Old English *heafod*.

St Andrews (Fife) This historic town and international headquarters of golf is named after its now-ruined cathedral, dedicated to Scotland's patron saint. Prior to its elevation as a Christian cult centre, which happened under the influence of a Pictish king during the 9th century, it was *Mucros*, 'wood or point of the pigs'. According to legend it was St Regulus, or Rule, who brought the relics of St Andrew here from Greece, and the town became known in Gaelic as *Baile Reuil*, 'town of Rule'. It was the ecclesiastical capital of Scotland until the Reformation. The country's first university was founded here by Bishop Wardlaw in 1411.

St Boswells (Borders) Named after St Boisil, the 7th-century abbot of Melrose and friend of St Cuthbert. The '-wells' is from the Norman French *-vil* or *-ville*, 'town'. Nearby is Newtown St Boswells, the administrative headquarters for the Borders region.

St Cyrus (Angus) 'Place dedicated to St Cyricus'. Formerly known as Eglesgreig (from the Gaelic *Eaglais Girig*, 'Girig's church'). The church here was dedicated to St Cyricus by Girig, a ninth-century king of the Scots and Picts.

St Fillans (Perth & Kinross) 'Place dedicated to St Fillan'. *Faolán* (Irish Gaelic proper name, literally 'little wolf') was the name of sixteen saints. The most important of these in Scotland was this one. He succeeded St Mund as abbot in the monastery of the Holy Loch and died in AD 777. The decorated hook end, or *coigreach*, of his crozier is still preserved as one of the country's most ancient and venerable relics.

St Kilda (Western Isles) This remote group of steep Atlantic islands, lying 35 miles/56 kilometres north-west of North Uist, appears to have got its English name as the result of a misunderstanding. No saint of the name Kilda is known. The name Skildar (from

Old Norse *skildir*, 'shields', more suitable for describing low-lying rather than peaked islands) is found in a document of 1540 but it appears to have been describing some islands closer to shore. A 16th-century mapmaker's mistake transferred the name to the remoter archipelago. The suggested source of the name (*kelda* [Old Norse] 'well') is based on the Gaelic name of the landing place on Hirta, *Tobar Childa*, which in the post-Norse era may have been misunderstood as 'Kilda's well', although it simply means 'well' in both Old Norse and Gaelic. The Gaelic name of the island group was and is *Hirt*, applied in English only to the main island as Hirta. The islands, inhabited for centuries despite their remoteness, were finally evacuated in 1930.

St Margaret's Hope (Orkney) 'St Margaret's bay'. *Hop* (Old Norse) 'bay' or 'hollow place', named after St Margaret, wife of Malcolm III, who was canonised in 1251.

St Monans (Fife) Once believed to be named after St Ninian, this East Neuk harbour town is now thought to bear the name of St Monan, the 6th-century Bishop of Clonfert in Ireland, to whom its handsome 13th-century Auld Kirk is dedicated. This place name was formerly spelt as St Monance.

St Ninian's Isle (Shetland) The missionary activities of St Ninian of Whithorn along the east coast have left traces in local names all the way to this, the most northerly one.

St Rollox (Glasgow) 'St Roche'. A chapel to St Roche was set up here in 1502. In the 19th and early 20th centuries this district was at the centre of Glasgow's railway engineering industry.

St Vigeans (Angus) Perhaps a form of St Féchín, an Irish saint whose death is recorded in the mid-7th century.

Salen (Argyll & Bute) 'Inlet'. *An* (Scottish Gaelic) 'the'; *sailein* (Scottish Gaelic) 'little inlet of the sea'.

Saline (Fife) 'Salt pit'. In 1613, the name is recorded as Sawling.

Saltcoats (North Ayrshire) Place of the 'salt huts'. *Salt* refers to the process of saline extraction by boiling it out in great iron pans (*see* **Prestonpans**); *cots* (Scots) 'cottages' or 'huts'. The name of this town and resort on the Firth of Clyde derives from the salt-works established here in the 16th century by James V.

Sanday (Orkney) 'Sand island'. *Sand* (Old Norse) 'sand'; *ey* (Old Norse) 'island'.

Sanquhar (Dumfries & Galloway) Place of the 'old fort'. *Sean* (Scottish Gaelic) 'old'; *caer* (Brythonic) 'fort'. An ancient earthwork known as the 'Sean Caer' is on a hillock just north of the town. Recorded as Sanchar in 1150.

Sauchieburn (West Lothian) 'Burn by the willows'. *Saileach* (Scottish Gaelic) 'willow'; *burn* (Scots) 'stream'. Here, in 1488, James IV and his rebel army fought his father, James III, who was assassinated in a house nearby.

Saughton (Edinburgh) 'Place by the willows'. *Saileach* (Scottish Gaelic) 'willow'; *tun* (Old English) 'settlement'.

Scalloway (Shetland) 'Bay of the huts'. *Skali* (Old Norse) 'huts'; *vagr* (Old Norse) 'bay'. This port and former main settlement of Shetland lies 6 miles/10 kilometres west of Lerwick. It derives its name from the temporary huts or booths erected in the bay here by the Viking people attending the annual 'Lawting', or open assembly, at nearby Tingwall. Scalloway remained Shetland's capital until the early 1600s.

Scalpay (Western Isles, Orkney) 'Ship isle' in the Western Isles from *skálp* (Old Norse) 'skiff' and 'ship' with *ey* (Old Norse) 'island'. 'Ship isthmus' in Orkney from a different interpretation of the suffix as *eidh* (Old Norse) 'isthmus'.

Scapa Flow (Orkney) Probably 'sea flood bay of the boat isthmus'. *Skálp* (Old Norse) 'boat'; *eidh* (Old Norse) 'isthmus'; *floa* (Old Norse) 'flood'. This vast, almost circular bay, is surrounded by a chain of islands, which are separated by narrow channels, some of which have been blocked by the 'Churchill barrier' causeways of World War II. It was used as a major naval base in both World Wars.

Scarba (Argyll & Bute) 'Cormorant island'. *Skarfr* (Old Norse) 'cormorant'; *ey* (Old Norse) 'island'.

Scarinish (Argyll & Bute) 'Seagull point'. *Skári* (Old Norse) 'young seagull'; *nes* (Old Norse) 'point' or 'headland'. In the north of Scotland, 'scorrie' is still used to refer to seagulls.

Scarp (Western Isles) 'Cliff island'. *Skarpr* (Old Norse) 'steep-faced'.

Scavaig, River and **Loch** (Highland) The derivation of the first part of this Skye name is unclear, though it has been linked to *ska*, an Old Norse root meaning 'scrape'. The suffix is *vik* (Old Norse) 'bay'. It may be an old river name with *-vaig* back-formed on to it.

Schiehallion (Perth & Kinross) The name of this conspicuous and isolated mountain (3,554 feet/1,087 metres) may be related to *sith* (Scottish Gaelic) both 'fairy' and 'hill' and *chailleainn* (Scottish Gaelic) 'of the Caledonians', with the notion of it being a 'fairy hill'. An alternative suggestion is 'maiden's pap' from *sine* (Scottish Gaelic) 'breast' and *chailean* (Scottish Gaelic) 'girl's'.

Sciennes (Edinburgh) The name refers to the former monastery of St Catherine of Siena in this part of Edinburgh, once outside the walls. It was recorded in the 16th century as Shenis.

Scone (Perth & Kinross) 'Mound'. *Sgonn* (Scottish Gaelic) 'mound' or 'lump'. The reference here is to the Mote Hill, an ancient ritual site of the Scottish kings. The *Lia Fail* or 'Stone of Destiny' of the Scots, brought here some time in the 9th century after the Norsemen over-ran Iona, became the crowning-place of the Scottish kings. Recorded as Sgoinde in 1020. In the early 19th century, the site of this village became Old Scone to distinguish it from the re-situated New Scone immediately to the east.

Scoraig (Highland) 'Bay of the gully'. *Sguvr* (Old Norse) 'rift' or 'gully'; *aig* (Scottish Gaelic form of Old Norse *vik*) 'bay'.

Scotland 'Land of the Scots'. The original Scots (*Scoti* in Latin) were Gaelic-speaking immigrants from northern Ireland who in the 5th and 6th centuries settled in the south-west of what was then Caledonia or Pictavia, the Latin names for northern Scotland. By the mid-9th century, these names had been replaced by Scotia. 'Scot' was legendarily supposed to derive from Scota, daughter of an Egyptian pharaoh, but the actual derivation is obscure. Scotland, with its Anglian suffix *-land*, is probably a name awarded from outside by the Anglian-speaking population of Northumbria and Lothian.

Scotscalder (Highland) 'Calder of the Scots'. Nearby to Scotscalder there was a Norn Calder. Both were noted in 1538 and originally they both demarcated land held by those of Scots and Norse extraction in this once-Norse region on the border of Sutherland and Caithness. *See* **Calder**.

Scotstarvit (Fife) A hybrid name signifying 'Scot's bull place'. *Tarbh* (Scottish Gaelic) 'bull'; *ait* (Scottish Gaelic suffix indicating place). The *Scot-* prefix may indicate an owner's name or perhaps goes back to the encroachment of Scots speech into this once-Gaelic-speaking region in the 13th and 14th centuries. Just south of Cupar there is a spread of 'bull' names on each side of Tarvit Hill.

Scourie (Highland) 'Place of the wood'. *Skógr* (Old Norse) 'wood'.

Scrabster (Highland) 'Skari's farmstead'. *Skari* (Old Norse nickname from *skári*, 'seagull'); *bólstadr* (Old Norse) 'farmstead'. In the *Orkneyinga Saga* (*circa* 1225) it is noted as Ská-ra-bólstadr. It is the ferry-port for Orkney, with frequent sailings to Stromness.

Seaforth, Loch (Western Isles) 'Loch of the sea firth'. *Saer* (Old Norse) 'salt lake'; *fjordr* (Old Norse) 'firth' or 'fjord'. This apparently tautological name is explained by the semi-landlocked part of the loch, a common feature on the west coast of Lewis.

Seil (Argyll & Bute) 'Seal Island'. *Seil* (Old Norse) 'seal'.

Selkirk (Borders) 'Church by the hall'. *Sele* (Old English) 'hall' or 'manor house'; *cirice* (Old English) 'church', becoming Scots *kirk*. This woollen-manufacturing town on the Yarrow Water was recorded as Selechirche in 1124.

Sgùrr Alasdair (Highland) 'Alexander's peak'. *Sgùrr* (Scottish Gaelic) 'high, pointed hill'; *Alasdair* (Scottish Gaelic) 'Alexander'. The Skye peak (3,309 feet/1,011 metres) is named after the 19th-century Gaelic scholar, Alexander Nicholson, who was its first recorded climber in 1873. Previously it was *Sgùrr nan Gillean* ('the lad's peak').

Shandon (Argyll & Bute) 'Old fort'. *Sean* (Scottish Gaelic) 'old'; *dùn* (Scottish Gaelic) 'fort'.

Shandwick (Highland) 'Sand bay'. *Sand* (Old Norse) 'sand'; *vik* (Old Norse) 'bay'. There is a fine sandy bay here on the Moray Firth, overlooked by the 'Shandwick Stone' – a finely carved standing stone of Pictish origin.

Shanter (South Ayrshire) 'Old land' (probably as opposed to 'new land' that has been taken into cultivation from the moors). *Sean* (Scottish Gaelic) 'old'; *tir* (Scottish Gaelic) 'land'. This Ayrshire name has been made famous by Robert Burns's poem, 'Tam o' Shanter'.

Shapinsay (Orkney) 'Hjalpand's island'. *Hjalpand* (Old Norse proper name); *ey* (Old Norse) 'island'. Noted in the *Orkneyinga Saga* (1225) as Hjalpandisay.

Shawbost (Western Isles) 'sea-lake-farm'. *Sjá* (Old Norse) 'lake partly open to the sea'; *bolstadr* (Old Norse) 'farmstead'.

Shawfield (Glasgow) 'Wood field'. *Shaw* (Scots from Old English *ceaga*, 'thicket') 'wood'.

Shee, Glen (Perth & Kinross) 'Fairy glen or glen of peace'. *Gleann* (Scottish Gaelic) 'valley' or 'glen'; *sith* (Scottish Gaelic) 'fairy' or 'spirit' or 'peace'.

Shetland Perhaps 'hilt land'. The Old Norse name was 'Hjaltland'. *Hjalt* (Old Norse) 'hilt of a sword' or 'dagger'; *land* (Old Norse) 'land'. The reference could be to the long, narrow outline of the archipelago as appreciated by the early Viking navigators. While the first *l* was dropped, the initial *Hj* was mutated to *Sh* and in some areas by the Gaelic mutation to *Z*, giving the alternative spelling of Zetland. The derivation is a conjectural one. The Norse form is still preserved in the diminutive 'Sheltie', referring to the Shetland breed of pony.

Shettleston (Glasgow) Originally 'the vill or villa of Seadna's daughter'. *Villa* (Latinised form of Scottish Gaelic *baile*) 'place'; *inghine* (Scottish Gaelic) 'of a daughter'; *Seadna* (Scottish Gaelic proper name). By the late 12th century, it was written as Schedinestun and later as Schedilstoune.

Shiant Isles (Argyll & Bute) 'Holy islands'. *Na-Eileanan* (Scottish Gaelic) 'the islands'; *sianta* (Scottish Gaelic) 'holy'. These islands were inhabited by religious hermits.

Shiel, River, Loch and **Glen** (Highland) Probably 'flowing water', from a Pictish word stemming from the continental Celtic root-form *sal* ('flowing'). The Gaelic *seileach* ('willow' stems) is from the same source. The Battle of Glenshiel in Kintail marked the end of the 1719 Jacobite Rising. *Sgùrr na' Spainnteach* ('Spaniards' Peak') commemorates the Spanish troops who fought on the Jacobite side. Loch Shiel is in Moidart, well to the south.

Shieldaig (Highland) 'Herring bay'. *Sild* (Old Norse) 'herring' or 'sild'; *aig* (Gaelic form of Old Norse *vik*) 'bay'. Its Gaelic form is *Sìldeag*. Compare **Whiting Bay**.

Shin, River and **Loch** (Highland) Derived from a Pre-Celtic root-word *sinn*, indicative of flowing water. Recorded in 1610 as Shyne. The Shin is a notably fast-flowing river, famous for its falls and its salmon leaps.

Shira, River and **Glen** (Stirling) 'Lasting river'. *Siorabh* (Scottish Gaelic) 'lasting river', indicating a stream that flows all year. This glen above Loch Fyne was the sanctuary of Rob Roy MacGregor's family during his time as an outlaw.

Shiskine (North Ayrshire) 'Marshy place'. *Sescenn* (Scottish Gaelic) 'marsh'.

Shotts (North Lanarkshire) Place of 'steep slopes'. *Sceots* (Scottish Gaelic) 'steep slopes'. This former mining town lies on a high undulating plateau that forms part of the watershed between the Forth and Clyde river basins.

Shuna (Argyll & Bute) Probably 'sighting place'. *Sjón* (Old Norse) sight. The Isle of Shona has the same probable derivation.

Sidlaw Hills (Perth & Kinross) Perhaps 'pasture hills'. *Saetr* (Old Norse) 'shieling' or 'hill pasture'; *hlaw* (Old English) 'hill'. 'Hills of seats' has also been suggested, from *suidhe* (Scottish Gaelic) 'seat', which is often used in association with the name of a holy man. In either case, 'Hills' is a linguistically unnecessary addition.

Sinclairtown (Fife) This suburb of Kirkcaldy is named after the Sinclair family who lived in the nearby Dysart House.

Skara Brae (Orkney) 'Bank by the shore'. *Skari* (Old Norse) 'shore'; *brae* (Scots) 'bank'. This describes the situation at Skaill Bay (Old Norse *skali*, 'shieling') of this remarkable Neolithic village (3100–2450 BC). It was preserved by the high bank of sand behind the shore which covered it until its excavation in 1850.

Skene, Loch (Aberdeenshire, Dumfries & Galloway) Perhaps 'Loch of bushes'. *Loch* (Scottish Gaelic) 'lake'; *sgeachan* (Scottish Gaelic) 'of bushes' or 'of hawthorns'. The Aberdeenshire loch is known as Loch of Skene. Loch Skene, source of the 'Grey Mare's tail', is also found as Skeen.

Skelbo (Highland) 'Shelly farm'. *Skel* (Old Norse) 'shell'; *bol* (Old Norse) 'farm'.

Skelmorlie (North Ayrshire) 'Scealdamer's meadow'. *Scealdamer* (Old English proper name); *ley* (Scots) 'meadow'.

Skerryvore (Western Isles) 'Great skerry'. *Skjaer* (Old Norse) 'sharp rock', giving *sgeir* (Scottish Gaelic) 'reef'; *mhòr* (Scottish Gaelic) 'big'. Its lighthouse, built by Alan Stevenson in 1844, was refurbished after a fire in 1959.

Skibo (Highland) Possibly 'barn place or granary'. *Sgiobal* (Scottish Gaelic) 'granary'. However, with Norse Embo and Skelbo close by, 'Skithi's farm' has also been suggested. *Skithi* (Old Norse personal name); *bol* (Old Norse) 'farm'.

Skipness (Argyll & Bute) 'Ships' headland'. *Skipa* (Old Norse) 'ship'; *nes* (Old Norse) 'headland'. The castle here, controlling the northern entrance to Kilbrannan Sound, was a strategic point in medieval times.

Skye (Highland) Perhaps 'winged isle'. *Sgiathach* (Scottish Gaelic) 'winged'. The reference appears to be to the shape of the island, with its many peninsulas. It is noted as *Scia* in Adamnan's *Life of St Columba*. It is the largest of the islands of the Inner Hebrides and since 1992 has been joined to the mainland by a bridge at Kyle of Lochalsh.

Slamannan (Clackmannanshire) 'Hill of Mannan'. *Manau* was the Brythonic name of the area at the head of the Firth of Forth, cognate with the Isle of Man. The prefix is *sliabh* (Scottish Gaelic) 'hill' but was originally *mynnyd* (Brythonic) 'hill'. *See* **Clackmannan**.

Slapin, Loch (Highland) The derivation of this Skye sea loch may be from *slappi* (Old Norse) 'lump-fish'. If this is so, the attenuated 'fjord' or 'bay' ending found in other Norse Skye loch names, as in Snizort or Scavaig, has gone completely.

Sleat (Highland) 'Slope'. *Sliabh* (Scottish Gaelic, plural *sleibhte*) 'slope' or 'dry moor'. This district of Skye, the territory of the Macdonalds, has sometimes been derived from an archaic Gaelic word *sletta*, meaning 'plain', but it is not in any way like a plain.

Sligachan (Highland) 'Shelly place'. *Sligeach* (Scottish Gaelic) 'abounding in shells'; *-an* (Scottish Gaelic diminutive termination).

Smoo Cave (Highland) 'The hiding place'. *Smuga* (Old Norse) 'hiding place'. The name of a vast sea cavern eaten into the cliffs near Durness in north-west Sutherland.

Snizort, Loch (Highland) This name may come from *sneisfjordr* (Old

Norse) 'split firth' but *sneasfjordr* (Old Norse) 'snow firth' has also been suggested. The form of the inner loch, divided by the Aird river, supports the former explanation.

Soay (Western Isles) 'Sheep island'. *Sautha* (Old Norse) 'sheep'; *ey* (Old Norse) 'island'. The name of Soay in the St Kilda group is preserved in the Soay breed of sheep but there are numerous other Soays.

Solway Firth (Dumfries & Galloway) 'Firth of the muddy ford'. *Sol* (Old Norse) 'mud'; *vath* (Old Norse) 'ford'; *fjordr* (Old Norse) 'fiord', 'firth' or 'estuary'. It was recorded as Sulewad in a document of 1229. The shallow Solway, stretching far in between Cumbria and Galloway, helped to 'isolate' Galloway from the south.

Sorbie (Dumfries & Galloway) 'Bog settlement'. *Saur* (Old Norse) 'bog' or 'marsh'; *by* (Old Norse) 'settlement'.

South Queensferry *see* **Queensferry, North** and **South**.

South Ronaldsay *see* **Ronaldsay, South**.

South Uist *see* **Uist, North** and **South**.

Soutra (Borders) 'Homestead with the wide view'. *Sulw* (Brythonic) 'broad view'; *tref* (Brythonic) 'homestead'. The older form is Soltre.

Spean, River and **Glen** *see* **Spey**.

Spey, River and **Strath** (Highland, Moray) The derivation of the name of Scotland's swiftest river is not clear. 'Hawthorn river' has been suggested, from a conjectured word *spiathan* (Old Scottish Gaelic) 'thorn', cognate with *yspyddad* (Brythonic) 'hawthorn'. A link with the Pre-Celtic root-form *squeas* meaning 'vomit' or 'gush' has also been suggested. With the *-an* (Scottish Gaelic) diminutive ending, the Spean, which rises close to the Spey, is seen as a diminutive form of the same name

Spinningdale (Highland) Perhaps 'speckled dale'. It is noted as Spanigidill in the mid-15th century. An origin has been suggested in *spong* (Old Norse) 'spangle' or 'speckle' with *dalr* (Old Norse) 'valley' or 'dale'.

Spittal (Moray, Highland) 'Refuge'. *Spideal* (Scottish Gaelic) 'refuge' or 'hospital'. Spittals tend to be on remote hill passes, like the Spittal of Glen Shee. *See* **Dalnaspidal**.

Spynie (Moray) 'Hawthorn place' from a conjectured *spiathan*

(Old Scottish Gaelic) 'thorn', cognate with *yspyddad* (Brythonic) 'hawthorn'. *See also* **Spey**. Spynie was the site of a cathedral before the headquarters of the See of Moray was moved a little way south to Elgin in 1224. Spynie Palace remained the Bishop's residence.

Stack Polly (Highland) 'Mountain of the River Pollaidh'. *Stac* (Scottish Gaelic) 'steep rock'; *pollaidh* (Scottish Gaelic) 'pools' or 'holes', designating the river that flows to the north side of the mountain (2,009 feet/614 metres) in the Inverpolly Nature Reserve.

Staffa (Argyll & Bute) 'Pillar island'. *Stafr* (Old Norse) 'staff', 'rod' or 'pillar'; *ey* (Old Norse) 'island'. This clearly describes the famous vertical columns of basaltic rock found on this small uninhabited island to the west of Mull.

Stake, Hill of (North Ayrshire, Renfrewshire) Perhaps from *stac* (Scottish Gaelic) 'steep rock' or *stakkr* (Old Norse) 'steep'. At 1,712 feet/521 metres, this is the highest point in the Clyde Muirshiel Regional Park.

Stanley (Perth & Kinross) The name was given around 1700 in honour of Lady Amelia Stanley, who became Marchioness of Atholl.

Start Point (Orkney) The name of this headland on Sanday is derived from *stertr* (Old Norse) 'tail'. Start Point in South Devon, at the other end of the British Isles, is from the cognate Old English *steort*.

Stenhousemuir (Falkirk) 'Moorland by the stone house'. *Stan* (Old English) 'stone'; *hus* (Old English) 'house'; *mor* (Old English) 'moor'. The meaning in this order rather than the other way round ('of the stone house on the moor') is clearly the case, as the final element was added only in the 17th century. It was recorded in 1200 as Stan House and in 1601 as Stenhous.

Stenness (Orkney) 'Headland of stones'. *Stein* (Old Norse) 'stone'; *nes* (Old Norse) 'headland'. The reference is probably to the standing stones on this site, already ancient when the Norsemen reached Orkney.

Stepps (North Lanarkshire) 'Wooden road'. *Stap*, *stepp* (Scots) 'stave'. The reference is to a roadway made with wooden staves laid parallel, sometimes called a 'corduroy road'.

Stewartry (Dumfries & Galloway) The contemporary name of the administrative district set up in 1975 records the former judicial stewardship by the Earls of Douglas over the 'Stewartry', or Stewardship, of Kirkcudbright. *See* **Mearns, The**.

Stirling Possibly 'land enclosure by the stream'. *Sruth* (Scottish Gaelic) 'stream'; *lann* (Scottish Gaelic) 'land enclosure'. This fits the site, enclosed in a loop of the River Forth, but remains a conjecture. It was recorded as Strivlin in 1124, Estriuelin *circa* 1250, Striviling in 1445 and Sterling in 1470. Stirling Castle was for centuries Scotland's principal stronghold, secure on its precipitous rock and strategically placed in the narrow centre of the country. The fight for it was the immediate cause of the Battle of Bannockburn (1314). It is now the centre of a unitary authority.

Stobinian (Stirling) The original name of this distinctive mountain (3,827 feet/1,165 metres) appears to have been *Am Binnein*, 'the peak'. *Stob*, which also means 'peak', was a later addition, perhaps because of numerous other 'Stob-' mountains in the vicinity. Despite the flat-looking form of the summit, it seems unlikely to stem from *innean* (Scottish Gaelic) 'anvil'.

Stobo (Borders) 'Hollow of stumps'. *Stub* (Old English) 'stump'; *how* (Old English) 'hollow'. The name is noted in the 12th century as Stoboc.

Stonehaven (Aberdeenshire) Possibly 'stony landing place'. *Stan* (Old English) 'stone'; *hyth* (Old English) 'landing place'. Recorded in documents as Stanehyve in 1587 and Steanhyve in 1629, which would suggest that the above derivation is more probable than the alternative *steinn* (Old Norse) 'stone' and *hofn* (Old Norse) 'harbour'. This east coast fishing port, former county town of Kincardineshire, is also the market centre for a large landward area.

Stormont (Perth & Kinross) 'Moor of the stepping-stones'. *Stair* (Scottish Gaelic) 'stepping-stones'; *monadh* (Scottish Gaelic) 'mountain' or 'moor'. Older forms include Starmonth in 1374. The name of this Perthshire district between the Tay and the Ardle-Ericht strath is also found as Stormonth.

Stornoway (Western Isles) 'Steering bay'. *Stjorn* (Old Norse) 'rudder' or 'steering'; *vagr* (Old Norse) 'bay'. The exact sense of this description remains uncertain. Recorded as Steornaway in 1549, now the main port and town of Lewis and administrative headquarters of the Western Isles authority.

Stow (Borders) 'Place'. *Stow* (Old English) 'place' or 'town'. It is unusual to find it on its own with no other defining word.

Stracathro (Angus) 'Strath of the fort'. *Srath* (Scottish Gaelic) 'broad valley'; *cathrach* (Scottish Gaelic) 'of the fort'.

Strachan (Aberdeenshire) 'River valley'. *Srath* (Scottish Gaelic) 'broad valley'; *eithin* (Old Gaelic) 'of the river'. The pronunciation was 'Strawn' but nowadays it is often pronounced as it is spelt.

Strachur (Argyll & Bute) 'Twisting valley'. *Srath* (Scottish Gaelic) 'broad valley'; *cor* (Scottish Gaelic) 'twist' or 'bend'.

Stranraer (Dumfries & Galloway) Place of the 'fat peninsula'. *Sron* (Scottish Gaelic) 'nose' or 'peninsula'; *reamhar* (Scottish Gaelic) 'fat' or 'thick'. This description appears to be a reference to the location at the foot of the thicker of the two arms of the Rinns of Galloway. Stranraer is the railhead and main ferry port for Northern Ireland.

Strath is from *srath,* which has slightly different meanings in Irish and Scottish Gaelic. The Irish sense, of level land by a lake shore, is rarely found in Scotland (*see* **Gartney**). The normal sense in Scotland is that of a wide valley between hills, with a level or gently sloping floor and traversed by a river. Normally the valley is named after the river. *See* **Glen**.

Strathallan *see* **Allan**.

Strathaven [Pronounced locally as Stray-ven] (South Lanarkshire) 'Wide valley of the Avon'. *Srath* (Scottish Gaelic) 'wide valley'; *ab-hainn* (Scottish Gaelic) 'river'. The river flowing through this small town south of Hamilton is the Avon Water. *See* **Avon**.

Strathbungo (Glasgow) 'Mungo's strath'. *Srath* (Scottish Gaelic) 'wide valley'; *Mhungo* (Scottish Gaelic nickname) 'Mungo's'. It was the nickname of St Kentigern and meant 'dear one'.

Strathclyde (Renfrewshire, South Lanarkshire) 'Wide valley of the cleansing stream'. *Srath* (Scottish Gaelic) 'wide valley'; *Cloid* (Brythonic Celtic river name) 'cleansing one'. Properly the Clyde Valley, it was the largest local authority area in Britain from 1975 to

1994. It encompassed the whole of the River Clyde basin and also large parts of the western Highlands up to the north of the former county of Argyll, together with the closer islands of the Hebrides. *See* **Clyde**.

Strathconon *see* **Conon**.

Strathdon *see* **Don**.

Strathearn *see* **Earn**.

Strathfarrar *see* **Farrar**.

Strathkinness (Fife) 'Strath of the water-head'. *Srath* (Scottish Gaelic) 'wide valley'; *cinn* (Scottish Gaelic) 'at the head of'; *eas* (Scottish Gaelic) 'water' or 'waterfall'.

Strathmiglo (Fife) 'Strath of the bog-loch'. *Srath* (Scottish Gaelic) 'wide valley'; *mig* (Brythonic) 'bog'; *loch* (Scottish Gaelic) 'lake' or 'loch'.

Strathmore (Perth & Kinross, Angus) 'Great wide valley'. *Srath* (Scottish Gaelic) 'wide valley'; *mór* (Scottish Gaelic) 'big' or 'great'. This wide and fertile valley lies between the southern edge of the Mounth and the Sidlaw Hills.

Strathpeffer (Highland) 'Wide valley of the shining stream'. *Srath* (Scottish Gaelic) 'wide valley'; *pevr* (Brythonic) 'radiant one'. Set above the valley of the Peffery Burn, west of Dingwall, the town was developed in the 19th century as a spa resort, drawing on the chalybeate springs that rise here.

Strathtay *see* **Tay**.

Strathy (Highland) 'Of the strath'. *Srath* (Scottish Gaelic) 'wide valley', with *-ach* (Scottish Gaelic ending denoting place).

Strathyre (Stirling) Probably derived, like Strachur, as 'twisty strath'. *See* **Strachur**.

Strawfrank (South Lanarkshire) 'Valley of the French'. *Srath* (Scottish Gaelic) 'wide valley'; *frangaich* (Scottish Gaelic) 'of the French'. A reference to incoming landholders in medieval times.

Striven, Loch (Argyll & Bute) 'Loch of the point'. *Loch* (Scottish Gaelic) 'lake' or 'loch'; *sroighean* (Scottish Gaelic) 'of the nose or point', referring to the promontory between it and the Kyles of Bute.

Strome Ferry (Highland) 'Ferry of the channel'. *Straumr* (Old Norse) 'current' or 'stream'. The ferry has been superseded by a road to the south side of Loch Carron.

Stromness (Orkney) 'The headland of the current'. *Straumr* (Old Norse) 'sea current'; *nes* (Old Norse) 'headland'. This describes the most notable aspects of the situation of this fishing port and second town of Orkney. The headland at the end of the settlement rounds on to the Sound of Hoy with its many conflicting currents. Records show it as Straumness in 1150. An earlier alternative name was Hamnavoe, meaning 'harbour on the bay'.

Stronachlachar (Stirling) 'The mason's point'. *Srón* (Scottish Gaelic) 'point' or 'nose'; *a'* (Scottish Gaelic) 'of'; *chlachair* (Scottish Gaelic) 'the mason's'.

Strone (Stirling, Highland) 'Nose or point'. *Srón* (Scottish Gaelic) 'nose'. A descriptive name for a headland or crag. 'Stron-' or 'Sron-' are often found as prefixes in other names. The spelling 'Stroan' is often found in the south-west.

Stronlairig (Stirling) 'Point of the beaten path'. *Srón* (Scottish Gaelic) 'point' or 'nose'; *lairig* (Scottish Gaelic) 'pass' or 'beaten path'.

Strontian (Highland) 'Promontory of the beacon'. *Srón* (Scottish Gaelic) 'promontory'; *teine* (Scottish Gaelic) 'beacon'. The mineral strontium, first discovered near here in 1790, is named after this Loch Sunart village.

Sullom Voe (Shetland) 'The gannets' fiord'. *Sulan* (Old Norse giving the Scots *solan*) 'gannets'; *agr* (Old Norse) 'bay' or 'sea inlet'. This deep sheltered inlet has housed a major North Sea oil terminal since the 1970s.

Struan (Perth & Kinross, Highland) This place name has two forms, both connected with streams. Struan in Atholl is from *sruthán* (Scottish Gaelic) 'current place' or 'stream place'. Struan in Skye is from *an sruthán* (Scottish Gaelic) 'the little stream'.

Struy (Highland, Perth & Kinross) 'Stream place'. *Sruth* (Scottish Gaelic) 'stream', with -*ach* suffix denoting place. *Sruthaigh* is its locative form. At Struy in Inverness-shire the Rivers Glass and Farrar meet and there are rivers or large streams at the other locations (usually spelt as 'Struie').

Suie (Stirling, Highland) 'Seat'. *Suidhe* (Scottish Gaelic) 'seat' or 'resting-place', often with the sense of having been a holy person's seat. This is an often-found name in hilly districts.

Suilven (Highland) Perhaps 'sun mountain'. *Sul* (Old Scottish Gaelic) 'sun'; *bheinn* (Scottish Gaelic) 'mountain'. However, the Gaelic name of Suilven is *Beinn Buidhe* (Scottish Gaelic) 'yellow'. The derivation of the first part of the name from *súlr* (Old Norse) 'pillar' has also been suggested, as it suits the shape of the mountain (2,399 feet/733 metres) as seen from the sea.

Sumburgh (Shetland) Probably 'Sweyn's stronghold'. *Sweyn* (Old Norse personal name); *borgar* (Old Norse) 'fort' or 'stronghold'. The name of this southern headland of Shetland, and of the busy airport nearby, was recorded as Swynbrocht in 1506.

Summer Isles (Highland) These now uninhabited islands off the coast of Coigach, Wester Ross, are so called because they were used by crofters for summer grazing. The Gaelic is *Na h-Eileanan Samhraidh*, translated directly into English.

Sunart, Loch (Highland) 'Sweyn's fjord'. *Sweyn* (Old Norse personal name); *fjordr* (Old Norse) 'sea inlet' or 'firth'.

Sutherland (Highland) 'Southern territory'. *Suthr* (Old Norse) 'south'; *land* (Old Norse) 'territory'. This present-day administrative district and former county was named by Norsemen coming from further north.

Sutors of Cromarty (Highland) The two headlands of the Cromarty Firth are known in Gaelic as *na Sùdraìchean*, 'the tanners', and the combination of sound and meaning has produced the Scots *Sutors*, 'cobblers'.

Swanbister (Orkney) 'Sweyn's farm'. *Sweyn* (Old Norse proper name); *bolstadr* (Old Norse) 'farmstead'.

Swanton (Borders) 'Suen's place'. *Suen* (Old English proper name); *tun* (Old English) 'settlement' or 'place'.

Symbister (Shetland) The full meaning of the name of this fishing port and main settlement on the island of Whalsay remains obscure. The first part may be a Norse personal name. The second element is *bolstadr* (Old Norse) 'farmstead', a common suffix in Northern Isles place names.

Symington (South Ayrshire) 'Simon's farm'. *Symon* (Old English personal name); *tun* (Old English) 'farmstead'. As well as the Symington in the Clyde Valley, there is another further west, near Troon.

T

Tain (Highland) 'Water'. This old royal burgh, once a pilgrimage place to St Duthac's shrine, stands at the mouth of a small river, the Tain Water. Once thought to be Norse, the name is now ascribed to a Pre-Celtic root-form indicating 'river' or 'water'. It is recorded as: Tene in 1227, Tayne in 1375 and Thane in 1483.

Taing This very common name along the Orkney and Shetland coasts is from the Old Norse *thang*, indicating 'a low headland'.

Talisker (Highland) 'Sloping Rock'. *T-hallr* (Old Norse) 'sloping'; *skjaer* (Old Norse) 'rock'.

Talla (Borders) 'The brow'. *Talg* (Brythonic) 'front' or 'brow'.

Tanera (Highland) 'Harbour isle'. *T-h-fnar* (Old Norse) 'harbour'; *ey* (Old Norse) 'isle'. There are two Taneras in the Summer Isles, differentiated in Gaelic as *Mór*, 'big' and *Beag*, 'small'.

Tankerness (Orkney) 'Tancred's cape'. *Tancred* (Old Norse and Norman personal name); *nes* (Old Norse) 'headland' or 'cape'.

Tantallon (East Lothian) 'High-fronted fort'. *Din* (Brythonic) 'fort'; *talgan* (Brythonic) 'of the high front' or 'of the high brow'.

Taransay (Western Isles) 'Isle of (St) Taran'. *Taran* (Pictish personal name); *ey* (Old Norse) 'island'.

Tarbat Ness (Highland) 'Cape of the isthmus'. *Tairbeart* (Scottish Gaelic) 'isthmus' or 'portage point'; *nes* (Old Norse) 'cape' or 'headland'.

Tarbert (Argyll & Bute, Western Isles) 'Place of the isthmus'. *Tairbeart* (Scottish Gaelic) 'isthmus' or 'portage point'. The ancient practice of portage – the dragging of boats and contents from sea to sea across narrow necks of land – is commemorated in the many places of this name or a similar form, such as Tarbat and Tarbet.

Tarff (Highland, Perth & Kinross, Dumfries & Galloway) 'Bull stream or bull place'. *Tarbh* (Scottish Gaelic) 'bull'. This frequently found place name is also found as Tarves and Tarvie. It is a reminder both of the commercial and mythological importance of the bull in the Celtic world. *See* **Scotstarvit**.

Tarland (Aberdeenshire) 'Bull's enclosure'. *Tarbh* (Scottish Gaelic) 'bull'; *lann* (Scottish Gaelic) 'field' or 'enclosure'.

Tarradale (Highland) 'Bull's dale'. *Tarfr* (Old Norse) 'bull'; *dalr* (Old Norse) 'dale'.

Tarskavaig (Highland) Suggested as 'cod bay'. *Thorskr* (Old Norse) 'cod'; *vaig* (from Old Norse *vik*) 'bay'. An alternative derivation is from *tar* (Scottish Gaelic prefix) 'across from', and the name may mean 'across from Scavaig'. This sense may have been 'grafted' onto the Norse name after the decline of Norse speech in Skye. *See* **Scavaig**.

Tay, River, Strath and **Loch** (Perth & Kinross) Scotland's longest river was noted by Tacitus as *Taus* and by Ptolemy, around AD 150, as *Tava*. It flows 120 miles/192 kilometres mainly eastwards through Loch Tay and on into the North Sea by way of the Firth of Tay. The name may derive from a Brythonic root *tau*, or *teu*, meaning 'silent one' or 'strong one' – aspects of the river's controlling deity – or simply 'flowing' (*see also* **Teith**). The Tay has the greatest volume of water of any river on the British mainland.

Tayinloan (Argyll & Bute) 'House in the meadow'. *Taigh* (Scottish Gaelic) 'house'; *an* (Scottish Gaelic) 'of the'; *lón* (Scottish Gaelic) 'meadow'.

Taymouth (Perth & Kinross) This town is situated where the river flows out of Loch Tay, not at the estuary of the Tay, thus the name refers to the mouth of the loch rather than that of the river.

Taynuilt (Argyll & Bute) 'House by the stream'. *Taigh* (Scottish Gaelic) 'house', *an* (Scottish Gaelic) 'of the'; *-uillt* (Scottish Gaelic) 'of the stream'.

Tayport (Fife) This town lies on the southern side of the Firth of Tay, opposite Broughty Ferry, with which it had long-serving ferry links prior to the rail and road bridges being built nearby. The current name dates only from 1888. Before then, this port was successively called: Scotscraig, South Ferry, Portincraig, Ferryport-on-Craig and South Craig. All these names refer either to the crag on which the town is situated or to its ferry across the Tay.

Tayvallich (Argyll & Bute) 'House in the pass'. *Taigh* (Scottish Gaelic) 'house'; *bhealaich* (Scottish Gaelic) 'of the hill pass'.

Teith, River (Stirling) Another ancient river name whose origin is unclear but which is presumed to stem from the same Pre-Celtic, or possibly non-Indo-European, root element *tau*, meaning 'flowing' or 'melting', as the Tay and Teviot rivers. *See* **Menteith**.

Templand (Aberdeenshire, Dumfries & Galloway) 'Temple-land', indicating land once belonging to the Knights Templar. The origin of the place name Temple (Lothian and elsewhere) is the same.

Tentsmuir (Fife) 'Moor of the fort'. *Dinas* (Brythonic) 'fort'; *muir* (Scots) 'moor'. Tentsmuir is now largely forested.

Teviot, River (Borders) As with so many river names, its origin goes far back into unrecorded history. It has been linked to a Pre-Celtic root-form *tau*, 'flowing' or 'melting'. It appears to be cognate with Welsh and Cornish river names like Teifi and Tavy.

Threipland (Aberdeenshire) 'Debateable land'. *Threap* (Middle English and Scots) 'scold' or 'dispute'; *lann* (Scottish Gaelic) 'land'. A tract of ground at one time under disputed ownership.

Throsk (Stirling) 'House on the river'. *Tref* (Brythonic) 'dwelling'; *usc* (Brythonic, related to Gaelic *uisge*) 'river' or 'water'. The situation of Throsk is right by the River Forth, south of Stirling.

Thurso (Highland) 'Bull's river'. *Thjor-s* (Old Norse) 'bull's'; *aa* (Old Norse) 'river'. It was recorded as Thorsa in a document of 1152 and this still accords with local pronunciation. This market town on the north Caithness coast takes the name of the salmon river on whose estuary it stands.

Tibbermore (Perth & Kinross) 'Big well' or 'Mary's well'. *Tobar* (Scottish Gaelic) 'well'; with either *mór* (Scottish Gaelic) 'great' or *Mhoire* (Scottish Gaelic) 'Mary's'. Also found as Tippermuir.

Tighnabruaich (Argyll & Bute) 'House of the bank'. *Taigh* (Scottish Gaelic) 'house'; *na* (Scottish Gaelic) 'of the'; *bruaich* (Scottish Gaelic) 'bank'. Originally a solitary house stood here, on the high ground overlooking the western arm of the Kyles of Bute.

Tillicoultry (Clackmannanshire) 'Hillock in the back land'. *Tulach* (Scottish Gaelic) 'hillock'; *cul* (Scottish Gaelic) 'back'; *tir* (Scottish Gaelic) 'land'. This former coal-mining town lies at the base of the Ochil Hills.

Tillienaught (Aberdeenshire) 'Bare hill'. *Tulach* (Scottish Gaelic) 'hill slope'; *nochd* (Scottish Gaelic) 'bare'.

Tilt, River and **Glen** (Perth & Kinross) The Gaelic name is *Abhainn Teilte*, with *Abhainn* meaning 'river'. The derivation of *Teilte* is unclear but it may be from a Old Gaelic personal name.

Timsgarry (Western Isles) 'Tumi's garth'. *Tuma* (Old Norse proper name) 'Thomas's'; *gardr* (Old Norse) 'enclosure'.

Tinto (South Lanarkshire) 'Beacon hill'. *Teine* (Scottish Gaelic) 'fire' or 'beacon'; *ach* (Scottish Gaelic suffix denoting place). It was known as Tintock into the 19th century. Tinto (2,320 feet/709 metres) is a landmark visible for many miles.

Tiree (Argyll & Bute) Possibly 'land of corn'. *Tir* (Scottish Gaelic) 'land'; *eadha* (Scottish Gaelic) 'corn'. This low-lying, fertile island was renowned for its high production of grain crops. However, the Old Irish personal name *Ith* has also been suggested as the source of the latter part, giving 'Ith's land'.

Tobermory (Argyll & Bute) Place of 'Mary's well'. *Tobar* (Scottish Gaelic) 'well'; *Moire* (Scottish Gaelic) 'Mary'. The main town on the Island of Mull, developed in the 18th century by the British Fisheries Society, is named after a well dedicated to the Virgin Mary, still to be found nearby in an old ruined chapel.

Tolsta (Western Isles) Perhaps 'Toli's stead' or 'hollow stead'. *Tolu* (Old Norse proper name); *stadr* (Old Norse) 'farmstead'. If 'hollow', it would be by a *t* to *h* mutation of the first letter giving *hol* (Old Norse) 'low' or 'hollow'.

Tomatin (Highland) 'Juniper hill'. *Tom* (Scottish Gaelic) 'hill' or 'knoll'; *aitionn* (Scottish Gaelic) 'juniper'.

Tomdhu (Highland) 'Black hill'. *Tom* (Scottish Gaelic) 'hill'; *dubh* (Scottish Gaelic) 'black'. Tomdow (Grampian) is of the same origin.

Tomintoul (Moray) 'Little hill of the barn'. *Tom* (Scottish Gaelic) 'hill'; *an t-sabhail* (Scottish Gaelic) 'of the barn'.

Tomnahurich (Highland) 'Little hill of the yew wood'. *Tom* (Scottish Gaelic) 'hill' or 'knoll'; *na* (Scottish Gaelic) 'of the'; *Iubhraich* (Scottish Gaelic) 'yew wood'. This hill outside Inverness, now a cemetery, is reputed to have been the site of the fort of the Pictish king.

Tong (Western Isles, Highland) 'Tongue or spit of land'. *Tunga* (Old

Norse) 'tongue (of land)'. Tongue in Sutherland, Toung in Orkney and Shetland and Teangue in Skye all share the same derivation.

Tongue *see* **Tong**.

Tore (Highland) 'Bleaching place'. The name of this village in the centre of the Black Isle has sometimes been construed as the Gaelic *torr*, meaning 'hill', but the Gaelic name is *An Todhar*, meaning 'of the bleaching place'. *See* **Balintore**.

Torlundy (Highland) 'Mound of the boggy place'. *Torr* (Scottish Gaelic) 'mound'; *lud* (Brythonic-Pictish giving Scottish Gaelic *lodan*) 'muddy' or 'boggy'.

Torness (East Lothian, Highland, Shetland) On the mainland, 'mound of the headland'. *Torr* (Scottish Gaelic) 'mound' or 'hill'; *nes* (Old Norse) 'headland'. Torness in the Highlands may also be *Torr nan eas* (Scottish Gaelic) 'of the stream' or 'of the waterfall'. The Lothian site, east of Edinburgh, is now dominated by a nuclear power station. Tor Ness in Shetland may have a similar derivation to Thurso.

Torphichen (Aberdeenshire, Midlothian) 'Hill of magpies'. *Torr* (Scottish Gaelic) 'mound' or 'hill'; *phigheainn* (Scottish Gaelic) 'magpies'. Torfichen Hill in the Moorfoots has the same derivation.

Torphin (Edinburgh) 'White mount'. *Torr* (Scottish Gaelic) 'mound' or 'hill'; *fionn* (Scottish Gaelic) 'white' or 'fair'.

Torridon (Highland) The name of this region of rugged mountains remains unexplained. The first part may well be *torr* (Scottish Gaelic) 'hill(s)'. However, a meaning based on the Irish Gaelic verb *tairbhert*, 'transfer' (related to Tarbert) has also been suggested, on the supposition that Glen Torridon was a portage route from the head of Upper Loch Torridon to Loch Maree.

Torrisdale (Highland) 'Thor's dale'. *Thoris* (Old Norse, genitive form of the personal name *Thorir*); *dalr* (Old Norse) 'valley'. Thorir derives from Thor, the Norse thunder god.

Torry (Aberdeen) 'Hilly place'. *Torr* (Scottish Gaelic) 'hill'; *aidh* (Scottish Gaelic suffix denoting place).

Touch Hills *see* **Tough**.

Tough (Aberdeenshire) 'Hills or hilly place'. *Tulach* (Scottish Gaelic) 'hill' or 'ridge'. The Touch Hills to the south of Flanders Moss have the same derivation.

Town Yetholm *see* **Yetholm.**

Tradeston (Glasgow) This Glasgow district was developed around 1790 by the Glasgow Trades House, a guild of merchants.

Tranent (East Lothian) Apparently 'village by the valley'. *Tref* (Brythonic) 'settlement'; *nant* (Brythonic) 'valley'. This former coal-mining town sits on a ridge of rising ground above the valley of the River Esk. Recorded as Traunent in 1147.

Traprain (East Lothian) 'Homestead of the tree'. *Tref* (Brythonic) 'homestead'; *pren* (Brythonic) 'tree'. Traprain Law has the addition of *law* (Scots) 'hill'. Trabrown, also in Lothian, has the same origin.

Traquair (Borders) 'Homestead on the River Quair'. *Tref* (Brythonic) 'homestead'; the river name has been derived from *vedra* (Brythonic) 'clear one' and it is cognate with Weir. Older forms of Traquair include Treverquyrd in 1124.

Trool, Loch and **Glen** (Dumfries & Galloway) 'Loch of the stream'. *Loch* (Scottish Gaelic) 'lake' or 'loch'; *an t-* (Scottish Gaelic) 'of the'; *sruthail* (Scottish Gaelic) 'stream'.

Troon (South Ayrshire) 'Headland'. *Trwyn* (Brythonic) 'headland' or 'point'. Alternatively, this name has been derived by some as *an t-sron* (Scottish Gaelic) 'nose' or 'point'. Either way, the name is apt. Recorded as le Trune in 1464.

Trossachs, The (Stirling) Apparently 'the cross-hills', from *trawsfynnydd* (Welsh) 'cross-hill', rendered into the Gaelic form in modern times as *Na Trosaichean*. *Tros* (Old Welsh) signifies 'across'. The name applies to the picturesque countryside of transverse wooded ridges and lochs between Loch Achray and Loch Katrine, with Aberfoyle as its main centre.

Trotternish (Highland) 'Thrond's headland'. *Throndar* (Old Norse personal name); *nes* (Old Norse) 'headland'. Recorded as Tronternesse in the mid 16th century. With Minginish and Vaternish, it forms one of the three main divisions of the island of Skye.

Truim, River and **Glen** (Highland) 'Of the elder trees'. *Trom* (Scottish Gaelic) 'elder tree'. Glen Tromie has a similar derivation.

Tullibardine (Perth & Kinross) 'Hill of warning'. *Tulach* (Scottish Gaelic) 'hill slope'; *bàrdainn* (Scottish Gaelic) 'warning'. The reference is to a signal beacon.

Tullibody (Clackmannanshire) 'Hill of the hut'. *Tulach* (Scottish Gaelic) 'hill slope'; *bothaich* (Scottish Gaelic) 'of the hut'. Now an industrial and residential village to the west of Alloa.

Tulloch (Highland, Perth & Kinross) 'Hill slope'. *Tulach* (Scottish Gaelic) 'hill slope' or 'eminence'. This is a frequent local and farm name and an often-disguised element in many other names. *See* **Tillicoultry**.

Tullochgorum (Angus) 'Greenish hill'. *Tulach* (Scottish Gaelic) 'hill slope'; *gorm* (Scottish Gaelic) 'blue-green'.

Tullybelton (Perth & Kinross) 'Beltane hill'. *Tulach* (Scottish Gaelic) 'hill slope' or 'eminence'; *Bealtainn* (Scottish Gaelic) 'Beltane', the Celtic May feast, when fires were lit on conspicuous hilltops.

Tullymet (Perth & Kinross) 'Fertile hill'. *Tulach* (Scottish Gaelic) 'hill slope'; *meith* (Scottish Gaelic) 'fertile'.

Tullynessle (Aberdeenshire) 'Hill of spells'. *Tulach* (Scottish Gaelic) 'hill'; *an* (Scottish Gaelic) 'of'; *eoisle* (Scottish Gaelic) 'charm' or 'spell'. This seems to be an alternative version of Esslemont, in the same region.

Tummel, River, Strath and **Loch** (Highland) 'Dark river'. *Teimheil* (Old Scottish Gaelic) 'dark'. Like many other river names, it may be older than this suggests, from a Pre-Celtic form that contains the same meaning and the same root element.

Turnberry (South Ayrshire) The ending has been taken as *borgar* (Old Norse) 'fort' but the first part has yet to be satisfactorily explained. Now the site of a luxury hotel and golfing resort, it was established originally by the Glasgow & South-Western Railway.

Turnhouse (Edinburgh) The name is found at Turnhouse Hill in the Pentlands, west of Penicuik, and at the site of Edinburgh Airport. A possible derivation is 'hill of the spectre'. *Torr* (Scottish Gaelic) 'hill'; *na* (Scottish Gaelic) 'of'; *fhuathais* (Scottish Gaelic) 'spectre'.

Turret, River and **Glen** (Highland, Perth & Kinross) 'Little dry stream'. *Tur* (Scottish Gaelic) 'dry'; *that*, a suffix indicating small. The reference is to a stream that dries out in summer.

Turriff (Aberdeenshire) Possibly 'hill of anguish'. *Torr* (Scottish Gaelic) 'hill'; *bruid* (Scottish Gaelic) 'anguish' or 'a stab'. This is a name in which the second element may have changed and, as such, its exact derivation remains uncertain. Records show Turbruad in the *Book of Deer* (*circa* 1000), Turrech in 1300 and Turreff in 1500.

Tuskerbuster [Pronunciation approximates to Tusherbost] (Orkney) 'Peat-cutter's farm'. *Torf* (Old Norse) 'peat'; *skeri* (Old Norse) 'cutter'; *bolstadr* (Old Norse) 'farmstead'.

Twatt (Orkney) 'Clearing or settlement'. *Thveit* (Old Norse) 'clearing' or 'meadow', cognate with English 'thwaite'.

Tweed (Borders) Another river name of uncertain derivation. It may stem from the same root as Tay and Tyne, in being derived from the Brythonic root-form *tau* or *teu*, indicating 'strong', 'silent', or 'flowing'. This in turn has been linked to the Sanskrit *tavas*, meaning 'surging' or 'powerful'. The name was recorded in an early text of around AD 700 as Tuuide. This famous salmon river, which rises at Tweed Well north of Moffat and flows eastwards across Tweedsmuir to enter the North Sea at Berwick-on-Tweed, marks for part of its course the Border between England and Scotland. Its name was transferred to the woollen cloth made in the area by a London clerk's misreading of the Scots *tweel*, 'twill' (first noted in 1847).

Tyndrum (Argyll & Bute) 'House on the ridge'. *Taigh* (Scottish Gaelic) 'house'; *an* (Scottish Gaelic) 'on the; *druim* (Scottish Gaelic) 'ridge'.

Tyne, River (East Lothian) This river name remains of obscure origin, probably from a Pre-Celtic root and cognate with Tain and Tay.

Tyninghame (East Lothian) 'Village of the dwellers by the Tyne'. *Tyn* (*see* **Tyne**); *inga* (Old English) 'of the people'; *ham* (Old English) 'settlement' or 'village'.

U

Uamh, Loch nan (Highland) 'Loch of the cave'. *Loch* (Scottish Gaelic) 'lake' or 'loch'; *nan* (Scottish Gaelic) 'of'; *uamh* (Scottish Gaelic) 'cave'. This was where Prince Charles Edward Stewart's vessel dropped anchor in July 1745 and from where he was rescued in August 1746. A cairn marks the spot.

Uddingston (South Lanarkshire) 'Oda's people's farmstead'. *Oda* (Old English personal name); *inga* (Old English) 'of the people'; *tun* (Old English) 'farmstead'. Curiously, an early form of 1296 is recorded as Odistoun, just 'Oda's farmstead'.

Udny (Aberdeenshire) 'Streams'. *Alltan* (Scottish Gaelic) 'streams'; *-ait* (Scottish Gaelic suffix denoting place).

Ugie, River (Aberdeenshire) 'Stream of nooks and corners'. *Ugeach* (Scottish Gaelic) 'nook' or 'hollow'. The South Ugie Water, especially, is a very twisty stream.

Uig (Highland, Argyll & Bute, Western Isles) 'Bay'. A Gaelic form of *vik* (Old Norse) 'bay'. The Skye village on Loch Snizort is the island's main port for onward ferry crossings to the Western Isles.

Uist, North and **South** (Western Isles) 'An abode'. *I-vist* (Old Norse) 'in-dwelling'. The latter is the literal meaning traditionally ascribed to the basic name of these two Outer Hebridean islands, separated by the intervening Benbecula. It was recorded in 1282 as Iuist and in the 14th century as Ywest. The meaning of the name appears to correspond with that of Lewis.

Ullapool (Highland) 'Olaf's settlement'. *Olaf* (Old Norse personal name); *bol* (Old Norse mutated form of *bol-stadr*) 'settlement'. The name of this west Highland fishing and ferry port, developed in 1788 by the British Fisheries Society to encourage the herring industry, was earlier recorded in 1610 as Ullabill.

Ulva (Argyll & Bute) 'Ulf's island'. *Ulfa* (Old Norse proper name or nickname) 'Wolf'; *ey* (Old Norse) 'island'.

Unapool (Highland) 'Uni's farm'. *Uni* (Old Norse proper name); *bol* (Old Norse) 'farm'.

Unst (Shetland) 'Eagles' nest'. *Orn* (Old Norse) eagle; *nyst* (Old Norse) 'nest'. This, the most northerly of Shetland's main islands, is still the home of many rare birds. Its name was recorded in a document of around 1200 as Ornyst.

Urie (Aberdeenshire) Perhaps 'place of the yews' from *Iubharach* (Scottish Gaelic) 'of yews', though a derivation from *uar* (Scottish Gaelic) 'landslip' or 'water-spout' may also be possible, with the often-found river name suffix -*aidh*. A further suggestion is *uidhre*, genitive of *odhar*, meaning 'drab' or 'grey-coloured'.

Urquhart (Highland) 'Woodside'. *Air* (Scottish Gaelic) 'on' or 'upon'; *cardden* (Brythonic) 'thicket' or 'wood'. A parish and district to the west of Loch Ness.

Urr, River (Dumfries & Galloway) Another river name from remote antiquity, ascribed to a Pre-Celtic origin.

Urray (Highland) 'Remade fort'. *Air* (Scottish Gaelic) 'on'; *rath* (Scottish Gaelic) 'ring-fort'. A fortification set up on top of an earlier one. The church here gave its name to the River Orrin.

Uyea (Shetland) Two islands bear this name, a small one off Yell and a larger off Unst. It comes from *öyja* (Old Norse) 'island'.

V

Vatersay (Western Isles) Perhaps 'glove island'. *Vottr-s* (Old Norse) 'glove's'; *ey* (Old Norse) 'island', though the significance is not clear. A small island to the south of Barra and linked to it by a causeway.

Venue, Ben (Stirling) 'Little mountain'. *Beinn* (Scottish Gaelic) 'mountain'; *mheanbh* (Scottish Gaelic) 'small'. The name of this mountain (2,386 feet/730 metres) is given perhaps by comparison with its loftier neighbour, Ben Lomond.

Vennachar, Loch (Stirling) 'Horned loch'. 'Loch of the fair valley' has been put forward. *Loch* (Scottish Gaelic) 'lake or 'loch'; *bhana* (Scottish Gaelic) 'fair'; *choire* (Scottish Gaelic) 'mountain hollow' or 'corrie'. However, an older form of the name is Banquhar, *circa* 1375, and the Gaelic form is *Bheannchair*, making it cognate with Banchory, from *beannchar* (Scottish Gaelic) 'horn-shaped' (incorporating the elements *beann*, 'horn' and *cor*, 'situation' or 'setting'). The loch's gently curving shape is the source of the name. *See* **Banchory**.

Voe (Shetland) 'Bay'. *Vagr* (Old Norse) 'bay', normally a long indented inlet, as often found in Shetland. Several Shetland mainland settlements at the head of voes take this name or have it as an element.

Voil, Loch (Stirling) Perhaps 'lively'. *Beò* (Scottish Gaelic) 'life'.

Vorlich, Ben (Argyll & Bute, Perth & Kinross) 'Mountain of the sea-bag'. *Beinn* (Scottish Gaelic) 'mountain'; *muir* (Scottish Gaelic) 'sea'; *bolc* (Scottish Gaelic) 'bag'. The reference to a bag-like bay in the adjacent loch has been accepted in the case of Ben Vorlich (Loch Lomond – 3,088 feet/944 metres) but disputed in that of Ben Vorlich (Loch Earn – 3,231 feet/988 metres), which has also been linked to a hypothetical Old Gaelic proper name, *Murlag*.

Vrackie, Ben (Perth & Kinross) 'Speckled mountain'. *Beinn* (Scottish Gaelic) 'mountain'; *bhreachaidh* (Scottish Gaelic) 'speckled'. This mountain (2,760 feet/844 metres) dominates the northern view from Pitlochry. Ben Bhraggie, above Golspie in Sutherland, has the same derivation.

W Y Z

Walkerburn (Borders) 'Waulker's stream'. *Waulker* (Scots from Old English *walcere*) 'fuller of cloth'; *burna* (Old English) 'stream'. This small town on the River Tweed developed around a woollen mill in 1854 but the name suggests cloth-working from a much earlier date.

Walls (Orkney, Shetland) 'Bays'. *Vágar* (Old Norse) 'bays'.

Wallyford (Midlothian) *Wally* in Scots means 'beautiful' or 'fine' and this place name may be a descriptive one, effectively meaning 'good ford'.

Wamphray (Dumfries & Galloway) Perhaps 'cave of the offerings'. *Uamh* (Scottish Gaelic) 'cave'; *aifrionn* (Scottish Gaelic) 'place of offerings' or 'chapel'.

Wanlockhead (Dumfries & Galloway) Place of the 'white flat stone'.

Gwyn (Brythonic) 'white'; *llech* (Brythonic) 'flat stone'. The third element, 'head', was added at a much later date. Set 1,380 feet/425 metres up in the Lowther Hills (the highest village in Scotland), it has been involved in mineral extraction, especially gold and silver, since at least Roman times.

Ward Hill (Orkney, Shetland) 'Sentry hill'. *Vardr* (Old Norse) 'watch' or 'guard'. Ward Hill on Hoy (1,577 feet/480 metres) is the highest point in Orkney. There are numerous Ward Hills, particularly in Shetland, which are sometimes spelt as Vord.

Wardlaw (Highland) 'Sentry hill'. The meaning is the same as that of Ward Hill but the derivation is from the cognate Old English *weard*, meaning 'guard' or 'watch' and Old English *hlaew*, meaning 'hill'.

Waterloo A number of locations, like those east of Wishaw and adjoining Bankfoot in Perthshire and on the Isle of Skye, have this name in commemoration of the Battle of Waterloo in 1815.

Waternish (Highland) 'Water headland'. *Vatn* (Old Norse) 'water'; *nes* (Old Norse) 'headland'. With Minginish and Trotternish, one of the three main divisions of the island of Skye.

Watten (Highland) 'Water or lake'. *Vatn* (Old Norse) 'water'. The locality, west of Wick, takes its name from the loch, now inevitably known as Loch Watten.

Wauchope (Dumfries & Galloway) 'Den of strangers'. *Walc* (Old English) 'stranger' or 'foreigner'; *hop* (Old English) 'hollow place'.

Weem (Perth & Kinross) 'Cave'. *Uamh* (Scottish Gaelic) 'cave'.

Wemyss (Fife, Inverclyde) 'Caves'. *Uamh-s* (Scottish Gaelic) 'caves'. In the case of both East Wemyss and West Wemyss on the Firth of Forth and Wemyss Bay on the Firth of Clyde, there are many coastal caves to be found in their raised-beach cliff locations.

Western Isles This name, given official recognition as the 'Island Authority' in 1975, is a long-standing alternative term for the Outer Hebrides – the archipelago of 200-plus islands that stretches for 130 miles/200 kilometres in a crescent off the north-west mainland of Scotland, from Lewis to Barra Head.

Wester Ross *see* **Ross**.

West Lothian *see* **Lothian**.

Westray (Orkney) 'West island'. *Vestr* (Old Norse) 'west'; *ey* (Old Norse) 'island'. Although this island is not the most westerly of the group, apparently it was so to the Vikings on account of the fact that their compass cardinal points were set at a 45 degree difference from the current bearings.

Whalsay (Shetland) 'Whale's island'. *Hval-s* (Old Norse) 'whale's'; *ey* (Old Norse) 'island'. The meaning here may relate to the whale-like shape of the island but more likely to the presence of whales or the practice of hunting them. It was recorded in the mid-13th century as Hvalsey.

Whitburn (Lothian) 'White stream'. *Hwit* (Old English) 'white'; *burna* (Old English) 'stream'.

Whiten Head (Highland) 'White cape'. *Hvítr* (Old Norse) 'white'; *hofud* (Old Norse) 'head'. The reference may be to breaking waves on this exposed north-western headland.

Whithorn (Dumfries & Galloway) 'White house'. *Hwit* (Old English) 'white'; *erne* (Old English) 'house'. Called *Candida Casa* (Latin for 'white house') from its foundation in 397 by St Ninian, this was a leading religious centre for many centuries.

Whiting Bay (North Ayrshire) The name 'bay of the whitings' appears to be quite literal. Compare Shieldaig and Laxford.

Wick (Highland) 'Bay'. *Vik* (Old Norse) 'bay'. The fishing port and former county town of Caithness takes its name from the narrow bay on which it stands. It was recorded as Vik in 1140.

Wigtown (Dumfries & Galloway) 'Wicga's farm'. *Wicga* (Old English personal name); *tun* (Old English) 'farm'. This derivation is the same as for Wigton (Cumbria) across the Solway Firth. Recorded as Wyggeton in 1283.

Winchburgh (West Lothian) 'Winca's fort'. *Winca* (Old English proper name); *burh* (Old English) 'fortified place'.

Windygates (Fife) 'Windy gap'. *Geat* (Old English) 'gate' became the Scots *yett*, also with the meaning of 'hill pass' or 'gap', as in Yetts of Muckhart. Although some documents refer to Windeyetts, the *g-* form has been preserved here. There is a Windy Yet on the Cunningham Moors in Ayrshire

Wishaw (North Lanarkshire) Probably 'Willow wood'. *Withig* (Old

English) 'willow'; *sceaga* (Old English giving Scots *shaw*) 'wood'. Such a description of this industrial town, south-east of Motherwell, is still evident in the wooded banks of the South Calder Water, on which it stands.

Wormit (Fife) 'Wormwood'. *Wormit* is the Scots word for 'wormwood' and here presumably refers to a plantation of trees.

Wrath, Cape (Highland) 'Turning point'. Cape (English from Latin *caput*, 'head', via Old French *cap*) 'promontory' or 'headland'; *hverfa* (Old Norse) 'to turn'. This is Scotland's only headland to bear the designation of 'Cape'. It was the point around which Viking seamen changed course on the route between Scandinavia and western Scotland.

Wyvis, Ben (Highland) 'Majestic mountain'. *Beinn* (Scottish Gaelic) 'mountain'; *uais* (Scottish Gaelic) 'noble' or 'majestic', a shortened form of *uasal*, 'proud'. *Fhuathais* (Scottish Gaelic) 'of the bogle or goblin' has also been suggested for this mountain (3,433 feet/1,050 metres).

Yarrow, River (Borders) 'Rough river'. *Garbh* (Scottish Gaelic) 'rough'. This secluded river, flowing from St Mary's Loch, has been a subject for numerous poets.

Yell (Shetland) 'Barren' place. *Geldr* (Old Norse) 'barren'. This old Viking name remains descriptive of Shetland's second largest island, lying between Mainland and Unst. In the *Orkneyinga Saga* (*circa* 1225) the name was recorded as Ala and in later documents as Jala, Jella and Yella.

Yester (East Lothian) 'House or dwelling'. *Ystre* (Brythonic) 'dwelling'.

Yetholm (Borders) 'Village of the pass'. *Geat* (Old English, becomes Scots *yett*) 'gate' or 'gap'; *ham* (Old English) 'village'. This ancient 'gateway' settlement is split into Kirk Yetholm and Town Yetholm, on opposite banks of the Bowmont Water. *Holmr* (Old Norse) 'island', including 'river island', would seem to be the source of the suffix but early records show the *ham* form (Gatha'n *circa* 800, Jetham in 1233 and Kirkyethame *circa* 1420).

Yetts of Muckhart *see* **Muckhart**.